The Making of the Presidential Candidates 2012

The Making of the Presidential Candidates 2012

Edited by
William G. Mayer
and
Jonathan Bernstein

ROWMAN & LITTLEFIELD PUBLISHERS, INC.
Lanham • Boulder • New York • Toronto • Plymouth, UK

Published by Rowman & Littlefield Publishers, Inc.
A wholly owned subsidiary of The Rowman & Littlefield Publishing Group, Inc.
4501 Forbes Boulevard, Suite 200, Lanham, Maryland 20706
http://www.rowmanlittlefield.com

Estover Road, Plymouth PL6 7PY, United Kingdom

British Library Cataloguing in Publication Information Available

Library of Congress Cataloging-in-Publication Data

The making of the presidential candidates 2012 / edited by William G. Mayer and Jonathan Bernstein.
p. cm.
Includes bibliographical references and index.
ISBN 978-1-4422-1169-8 (cloth : alk. paper) — ISBN 978-1-4422-1170-4 (pbk. : alk. paper) — ISBN 978-1-4422-1171-1 (electronic)
1. Presidents—United States—Election—2012. 2. Presidential candidates—United States—History—21st century. I. Mayer, William G., 1956– II. Bernstein, Jonathan, 1963–
JK5262012.M35 2012
324.973'0932—dc23 2011032012

™ The paper used in this publication meets the minimum requirements of American National Standard for Information Sciences—Permanence of Paper for Printed Library Materials, ANSI/NISO Z39.48-1992.

Printed in the United States of America

To Our Children

Natalie and Thomas Logan Mayer
Rachel and Miriam Bernstein
Ross and Ryan Adkins
Katie, Daniel, and Elizabeth Busch
John, Andrea, and Kara Dukakis
Matthew Cornfield
Ava Brogi Lichter

Contents

Preface		ix
Chapter 1	Why Are Presidential Nomination Races So Difficult to Forecast? *Wayne P. Steger, Andrew J. Dowdle, and Randall E. Adkins*	1
Chapter 2	Financing Presidential Nominations in the Post-Public Funding Era *Anthony Corrado*	23
Chapter 3	Political Movements, Presidential Nominations, and the Tea Party *Andrew E. Busch*	59
Chapter 4	The Experience of Running for President *Michael S. Dukakis*	93
Chapter 5	More: Digital Media and the Densification of Presidential Campaign Discourse *Michael Cornfield*	107
Chapter 6	How Television Covers the Presidential Nomination Process *Stephen J. Farnsworth and S. Robert Lichter*	133

Chapter 7 Theory Meets Practice: The Presidential Selection Process in the First Federal Election, 1788–89 159
William G. Mayer

Appendix By the Numbers: A Statistical Guide to the Presidential Nomination Process 203
Alan J. Silverleib and William G. Mayer

Index 227

About the Contributors 239

Preface

This is the fifth in a quadrennial series of books about the presidential nomination process. Like its predecessors, it was put together with two objectives in mind: to present a broad overview of the presidential nomination process through a detailed examination of some of its most significant components; and to showcase some of the most interesting work now being done on the politics of presidential selection. We are particularly pleased that this book includes Michael Dukakis's essay on his experiences running for president in 1988.

The authors would like to express their gratitude to the people at Rowman & Littlefield, especially Jon Sisk, Darcy Evans, and Melissa McNitt, for dealing so expeditiously with a manuscript that was submitted far later than it should have been. Our thanks also to Niels Aaboe, who is no longer with R&L but was responsible for all of the early arrangements concerning this book.

Besides an early association with the late great Nelson Polsby, the editors of this book have both been blessed with extraordinary families, whose love and support has made our work both dramatically easier and infinitely more rewarding. With all due respect to Bill, Jonathan's favorite collaborators are his wife Jessica and his daughters Rachel and Miriam. Bill feels similarly about his wife, Amy Logan, and his children Natalie and Thomas.

Chapter 1

Why Are Presidential Nomination Races So Difficult to Forecast?

Wayne P. Steger, Andrew J. Dowdle, and Randall E. Adkins

The campaign for the 2012 Republican nomination is in full stride. Journalists, pundits, and bloggers offer analyses and speculations about which candidate will be the Republican nominee to face off against Barack Obama in the 2012 general election. But predicting the winner of the nomination campaign is more than a political spectator sport with entertainment value. Forecasting the winner tells us something about our understanding of the politics and processes of leadership selection in the United States. Forecast models are valuable diagnostic tools. Election forecasts generate an expectation for an outcome using theoretical arguments and empirical measures. If the outcome differs from the prediction, then the theory and/or the measures are wrong.

Above all, the accuracy or failure of a nomination forecast informs us about the locus of power in presidential nominations. To the extent that presidential nominations can be forecast with data from before the caucuses and primaries, we can infer that the critical period of the campaign occurs prior to rather than during the primaries. In that case, the caucuses and primaries would merely confirm the results of the campaign that occurs before the primaries. If predictions using data from prior to the delegate selection season are inaccurate, while predictions incorporating the results of caucuses and primaries are closer to the mark, then the caucuses and primaries would appear to have an independent influence on the nomination. In this scenario, caucus and primary voters could be said to have relatively greater power or influence on the selection of the presidential nominees.

Beyond this macro-level picture, nomination forecasts inform us about which elements of a campaign are critical in presidential nominations. For example, Mayer demonstrated that a candidate's standing in preprimary national opinion polls is a powerful predictor of which candidate will win the nomination.[1] Similarly, Adkins and Dowdle found that cash reserves rather than total funds raised are an important predictor of a campaign's success in presidential nominations.[2] Steger and Cohen et al. found that elite endorsements of candidates play about as influential a role as mass partisan preferences.[3] In short, nomination forecasts are more than just speculations about who will win or lose a campaign. The task of predicting a winner is a tool that can be used to understand presidential nominations.

ELECTION FORECASTING: AN INTRODUCTION

All forecasting models are premised on the idea that we can predict the outcome of an event using information from a time period prior to that event. Economic forecasts, to take the best known example, take data about current economic conditions—new housing starts, factory inventories, changes in the money supply—and, if they work, use those data to predict what the economy will look like three, six, or twelve months in the future.

Election forecasting, at least as a scholarly endeavor, began in the late 1970s and early 1980s, when a number of political scientists and economists argued that certain factors could be used to predict how elections (presidential and congressional) would turn out months before the votes were actually cast. In the 1990s, the same logic and set of statistical methods was extended to presidential nomination races. Consider, for example, the first column of data in Table 1.1. For at least a year before the first delegates are selected, national pollsters frequently ask ordinary Americans which party they belong to and then, depending on the answer, ask them which candidate they would be most likely to support for their party's next presidential nomination. In Table 1.1, we report the results from 1992, 2000, and 2008 of the last survey that the Gallup Poll took before the start of the delegate selection season—that is to say, the last poll before the Iowa caucuses. [The results for all years since 1980 are presented in the Appendix to this book.] In the first four races shown here—the Democratic and Republican races of 1992 and 2000—the candidate leading in the last national poll went on to win the nomination. In 2008, by contrast, the final preseason poll was less helpful. The poll leaders were Rudy Giuliani and Hillary Clinton, but the nominations went to John McCain and Barack Obama.

The second column of data in Table 1.1 shows another variable that might plausibly be used to forecast presidential nomination races: how much money each candidate had raised in the year before the election year (e.g., in the 2008 race, how much the candidates had raised in 2007). At first glance, these data seem to predict the winner in five of the six races shown in this table. As we will see, however, almost all scholars have found this to be a spurious

Table 1.1. Two Possible Predictors of the Presidential Nomination Race: National Poll Results and Total Fund-Raising at the End of the Invisible Primary

Nomination Race	*Candidate (winner in bold)*	*Support in the National Polls (percent)*	*Candidate (winner in bold)*	*Total Net Receipts*
1992 Republican	**George H.W. Bush**	84	**Bush**	$10,092,532
	Patrick Buchanan	11	Buchanan	707,106
	David Duke	4	Duke	8,764
1992 Democratic	**Bill Clinton**	42	**Clinton**	$3,304,020
	Jerry Brown	16	Tsongas	2,629,892
	Bob Kerrey	10	Harkin	2,182,070
	Paul Tsongas	9	Kerrey	1,945,313
	Tom Harkin	9	Brown	1,034,474
2000 Republican	**George W. Bush**	63	**Bush**	$67,630,541
	John McCain	19	Forbes	34,150,997
	Steve Forbes	6	McCain	15,532,082
	Gary Bauer	2	Bauer	8,761,166
	Alan Keyes	1	Keyes	4,483,505
	Orrin Hatch	1	Hatch	2,285,829
2000 Democratic	**Al Gore**	60	**Gore**	$27,847,335
	Bill Bradley	27	Bradley	27,465,950
2008 Republican	Rudy Giuliani	27	Romney	$90,075,401
	Mike Huckabee	16	Giuliani	56,062,084
	John McCain	14	**McCain**	39,873,514
	Mitt Romney	14	Paul	28,028,877
	Fred Thompson	14	Thompson	21,389,395
	Ron Paul	3	Huckabee	8,917,191
2008 Democratic	Hillary Clinton	27	**Obama**	$99,560,365
	Barack Obama	45	Clinton	98,698,196
	John Edwards	15	Edwards	41,280,440
	Joseph Biden	3	Richardson	22,792,073
	Bill Richardson	2	Biden	10,194,238
	Dennis Kucinich	2	Kucinich	3,855,686

Source: All poll data are taken from the Gallup Poll; fund-raising results are taken from the campaign finance reports filed by the candidates, available at fec.gov.

Table 1.2. A Simple Model for Forecasting Presidential Primary Vote Shares

Variables	*Regression Coefficients*	*Standard Error*
National poll standings	1.05	0.11
Total funds raised	–0.02	0.06
Constant	1.75	2.57
R^2	.78	
Adjusted R^2	.77	
N	53	

relationship. It works because popular candidates also tend to be successful fund-raisers; but once a candidate's standing in the polls is taken into account, the fund-raising totals add nothing to the accuracy of our forecasts.

Can we be more precise about the effect of these or any other variables on the outcome of a contested nomination race? The final step in election forecasting is to take the sort of data shown in Table 1.1 and enter them into a regression equation, a statistical technique that enables us to generate a numerical prediction about the vote that each candidate will receive in all of his or her party's presidential primaries. An example is shown in Table 1.2. In general, according to this equation, every additional percentage point of support a candidate received in the national preprimary polls translated into 1.05 percentage points in the total primary vote. By contrast, as already noted, once poll standings are held constant, preseason fund-raising has no effect on the primary vote.

General elections forecasts are based on factors known to affect the two-party popular vote, such as the incumbent president's popularity, measures of economic conditions, and the relative strengths of the political parties.[4] Such indicators are not much use in forecasting presidential nominations, however, since these factors affect voters' choices *between* the political parties rather than among candidates of the same party. The next section discusses presidential primary vote forecasts, with special attention to those factors that have been found to be significant predictors of nomination outcomes. The latter part of the chapter analyzes why presidential nominations are difficult to forecast and why nomination forecasts generally have more error than general election forecasts.

PRESIDENTIAL NOMINATION FORECASTING: A REVIEW

Forecasts of the presidential primary vote implicitly assume that the critical period in the presidential nomination process occurs before the primaries.[5] Only candidates who emerge from the preprimary campaign—often called the "invisible" primary—as viable options for primary voters have a realistic chance of winning the nomination. If the preprimary competition for resources and support affects candidates' ability to compete for and win votes during the primaries, then models accounting for these effects should predict and at least partially explain the presidential primary vote. Comparing the results of preprimary forecasts with the actual results of the primaries gives us an important assessment of the relative impact of the preprimary and primary periods on the outcome. The specific variables used in presidential nomination forecasts inform us about the relative weight of these factors in determining which candidates will be viable options for voters in primaries. In general, the front-runner going into the primaries is the candidate who gained his or her position as the favorite by obtaining campaign funds, the support of party insiders, media coverage, and the support of rank-and-file partisans as expressed in national opinion polls.[6]

Presidential primary forecasts typically begin with the 1980 election. Presidential nominations prior to 1972 were largely determined by party organizations, which selected national convention delegates through party-run caucuses and state conventions. Most states did not hold presidential primaries, and many that did have primaries did not actually use the presidential preference vote to select or bind the delegates.[7] In the early 1970s, however, the rules of the presidential nomination process were radically rewritten, resulting in a sharp increase in the number of presidential primaries.[8] The presidential nomination campaigns of 1972 and 1976 were highly volatile affairs, as candidates, party insiders, campaign activists, and the media all adjusted to the new rules of the game.[9] These nominations were decided during the primaries and heavily influenced by candidate decisions to contest or avoid certain caucuses and primaries, patterns of candidate spending, mass media coverage, and campaign momentum during the primaries.[10]

Forecasting models became possible only after the nominating process stabilized and the preprimary campaign became relatively more important to determining the outcome.[11] Campaign momentum during the caucus and primary period appeared to decline in its potency, becoming more of a factor for the candidate who emerged as the main challenger to the nominee rather than as a determinant of the nominee.[12] The result was that, from 1980 to 2000, presidential nominations appeared to have become reasonably predictable, as can be seen in the success of various forecasting models in predicting the eventual nominee. Table 1.3 presents the predicted finish of the eventual nominees in open presidential nominations from 1980 to 2008 from four different primary vote forecasts. As can be seen, primary vote forecasts were generally correct from 1980 to 2000, but were usually wrong in 2004 and 2008. These last two nominations will be discussed in more detail later. For now, we will focus on how these forecasts were obtained and what they tell us about nominations.

Table 1.3. Predicted Order of Finish of the Eventual Nominee in Open Nomination Races, 1980–2008

		Model Author(s) and Principal Variables Used			
Year and Party	*Nominee*	*Mayer: National Poll Standings and Total Funds Raised*	*Adkins and Dowdle: National Poll Standings and Cash on Hand*	*Steger: Elite Endorsements and Party Interaction*	*Steger: Elite Endorsements, Competitiveness,*
1980 Republican	Ronald Reagan	1st	1st	1st	1st
1984 Democratic	Walter Mondale	1st	1st	1st	1st
1988 Democratic	Michael Dukakis	2nd	1st	1st	1st
1988 Republican	George H.W. Bush	1st	1st	1st	1st
1992 Democratic	Bill Clinton	1st	1st	1st	1st
1996 Republican	Bob Dole	1st	1st	1st	1st
2000 Democratic	Al Gore	1st	1st	1st	1st
2000 Republican	George W. Bush	1st	1st	1st	1st
2004 Democratic	John Kerry	4th	6th	4th	4th
2008 Democratic	Barack Obama	2nd	2nd	2nd	2nd
2008 Republican	John McCain	4th	4th	4th	3rd

Source: Wayne P. Steger, "How Did the Primary Vote Forecasts Fare in 2008?" *Presidential Studies Quarterly* 39 (March 2009): 141–54.

Note: Models were estimated using the aggregate vote through all primaries held before the eventual nominee Steger predicted the vote across all primaries. Using the votes from all primaries inflates the vote shares of advocacy candidates who remain in the race for symbolic reasons as well as the votes shares of the eventual nominee, since most other candidates drop out once the race has been clinched.

In the first primary vote forecasting model, Mayer predicted the presidential primary vote in contested nominations using candidates' funds raised and standing in the last national Gallup poll before the Iowa caucuses.[13] Mayer found that candidates' support in national polls of the rank-and-file membership of the political parties was a powerful predictor of the aggregate primary vote in contested presidential nominations from 1980 to 2000. Preference polls contained a wide variety of information about the candidates as it had been perceived and synthesized by the public. The idea was that candidates' personal and policy appeals were reflected in the national polls of party identifiers and leaners—the people most likely to vote in presidential primaries.

A forecasting model by Adkins and Dowdle affirmed the importance of mass partisan support before the primaries, but also showed that the total amount of money raised—the variable Mayer had used—is not as important as how much money the candidates still have on hand when the primaries begin.[14] Candidates who raise large sums of money demonstrate their support among campaign contributors of a political party. However, candidates who spend most of that money before the primaries usually do so because they lack support among the rank-and-file membership of the party. Candidates who raise money and *do not* have to spend it are in the strongest position to compete for votes during the primaries. These candidates have the money on hand to take advantage of momentum if they get it or beat back a rival if they do not do well in the early primaries.

Using different models, Steger and Cohen et al. found that endorsements by party and elected officials were a significant predictor of the presidential primary vote.[15] Endorsements by party elites reflect an insiders' game as opposed to the influence of the mass electorate. Elite endorsements of candidates serve as a cue to attentive publics about which candidates are both viable and desirable. Such cues may be important when voters cannot use party labels to differentiate candidates and when prospective voters have little information about candidates' policy positions.[16] Steger also found that more liberal Democratic and more conservative Republican candidates received relatively larger shares of the primary vote than would otherwise be expected given their mass partisan support, cash reserves, and endorsements.[17]

Finally, Steger, Dowdle, and Adkins found that the effects of these variables differed between the two major parties.[18] The candidates' cash reserves, they concluded, significantly affected the Democratic primary vote but preprimary poll standings did not; and that the candidates' poll standings predicted the Republican primary vote but cash reserves did not. Steger subsequently found that these differences owed more to the competitiveness of the race than to inherent differences in the nature of the two parties' nomination contests.[19] Nomination campaigns can be competitive for either political party. The critical factor here seemed to be the relative strength of the candidates who decided to enter the race.[20] Party activists, donors, and elites tend to coalesce around certain candidates more readily than others. Uncertainty about which candidates will enter the race tends to freeze the race, as happened in 1992 when New York Governor Mario Cuomo left the Democratic Party hanging until November of 1991, when he finally announced that he would not be seeking the presidency. In that year, few party elites endorsed candidates, campaign contributions lagged the levels typical of other years, and no candidate emerged as particularly strong in preprimary national Gallup polls. In a year with considerable uncertainty about who will run and the relative strengths of the candidates, political party elites and activists tend to take a wait-and-see approach. Such nominations are hard to predict before the primaries and primary voters play a greater role in selecting the eventual nominee. The 2012 Republican nomination race is shaping up to be just such a race.

As noted above, recent nomination campaigns have not been well predicted by the existing forecasting models (see Table 1.3). As we will argue in more detail later, forecasting the presidential primary vote is difficult in part because the primary vote is distributed across time, with the results of early caucuses and primaries affecting the vote in subsequent primaries. Candidates who gain momentum by beating expectations for the vote share in early caucuses and primaries receive a surge in media coverage, fund-raising, and support in subsequent primaries, while others drop out as they fall behind in convention delegate tallies or run out of money.[21] The errors in the pre-Iowa forecasting models are greatest for candidates who gained the most momentum (e.g., Gary Hart in 1984, John McCain in 2000, John Kerry in 2004, and Barack Obama and John McCain in 2008) and for those who lost the most momentum (e.g., John Glenn in 1984 or Howard Dean in 2004).

To account for the impact of campaign momentum from the earliest caucuses and primaries, Adkins and Dowdle developed a "momentum model" that used their original model plus candidate vote shares from the Iowa caucuses and the New Hampshire primary to predict candidates' vote shares in the remaining primaries.[22] Including "momentum" variables that reflect the results of the Iowa and New Hampshire contests helps correct for over- and under-predictions resulting from the gains or losses of momentum due to these events. These models do not, however, account for momentum gained in subsequent caucuses or primaries. Combining the data from before the Iowa caucuses with the results of Iowa and New Hampshire considerably improves the predictive accuracy of the models, as can be seen by comparing Table 1.3 with Table 1.4. Note that these models still predicted Hillary Clinton to be the Democratic nominee in 2008. Clinton did win the most primary votes, though only if one includes the votes from the Michigan and Florida primaries. (Because these two primaries were held in violation of the Democratic Party's national scheduling rules, Obama's name was not listed on the ballot in Michigan and he did not campaign actively in Florida.) So the models were arguably correct in this respect. The models did

Table 1.4. Predicted Order of Finish of the Eventual Nominee in Open Nomination Races Using "Momentum Models," 1980–2008

		Model Author(s) and Principal Variables Used		
Year and Party	*Nominee*	*Adkins and Dowdle: National Poll Standings and Cash on Hand*	*Steger: Elite Endorsements and Party Interaction*	*Steger: Elite Endorsements, Competitiveness, and Ideology*
1980 Republican	Ronald Reagan	1st	1st	1st
1984 Democratic	Walter Mondale	1st	1st	1st
1988 Democratic	Michael Dukakis	1st	1st	1st
1988 Republican	George H.W. Bush	1st	1st	1st
1992 Democratic	Bill Clinton	2nd	1st	1st
1996 Republican	Bob Dole	1st	1st	1st
2000 Democratic	Al Gore	1st	1st	1st
2000 Republican	George W. Bush	1st	1st	1st
2004 Democratic	John Kerry	1st	1st	1st
2008 Democratic	Barack Obama	2nd	2nd	2nd
2008 Republican	John McCain	1st	1st	1st

Source: Wayne P. Steger, "How Did the Primary Vote Forecasts Fare in 2008?" *Presidential Studies Quarterly* 39 (March 2009): 141–54.

Note: Models were estimated using the aggregate vote through all primaries held before the eventual nominee won enough delegates to clinch the nomination. The original forecasts by Mayer, Adkins and Dowdle, and Steger predicted the vote across all primaries. Using the votes from all primaries inflates the vote shares of advocacy candidates who remain in the race for symbolic reasons as well as the vote share of the eventual nominee, since most other candidates drop out once the race has been clinched.

not, however, forecast the candidates' vote shares for states that held caucuses. Barack Obama won these states by an average margin of three to one over Clinton, which greatly contributed to his success in winning the nomination.

We now turn to a more detailed examination of the challenges that make forecasting nominations more difficult than forecasting general elections.

THE CHALLENGES OF PRESIDENTIAL NOMINATION FORECASTING

As Table 1.3 indicates, none of the preprimary forecasting models was particularly good at predicting the winner in recent nomination campaigns. Forecasting presidential nominations is more challenging than forecasting general elections for a number of reasons. Difficulties arise due to the choices presented to voters in primaries and caucuses as opposed to the choices presented to voters in general elections. The structure and process of the presidential nomination system also make predicting winners more difficult. Other complications are due to recent changes in the nominating system, which only a few years ago seemed to be relatively stable and more predictable. A final array of obstacles is the uncertain nature of the candidate field, which tends to affect the ability of political party elites and party identifiers to coalesce behind a front-runner.

THE CHALLENGES OF VOTER CHOICE

The factors driving individual voters to choose one candidate over others influence the outcome of an election. The best predictor of the vote choice in general elections is which of the two major parties an individual feels more closely aligned with. Even most voters who classify themselves as independents tend to lean more towards one of the two major parties and tend to vote accordingly.[23] While the study of individual-level voting and the study of aggregate election results differ in many ways, votes ultimately determine electoral outcomes. The popular vote in presidential elections has become closer in recent decades because voters have become more equally divided in their loyalties to the Democratic and Republican parties.

In addition to party identification, the state of the economy also plays a role in explaining voter choice in presidential elections. A strong economy helps the party holding the White House, a weak economy helps the challenger. The debate among general election forecasters is only over the relative importance of various economic indicators and how best to measure economic effects on the election.[24] Are voters driven more by past performance or concerns about the future? Are voters more concerned about its influence on them directly (i.e., pocketbook voting) or more focused on the overall shape of the economy (i.e., sociotropic voting)? Is unemployment, inflation, personal income, or macroeconomic growth the best variable to use? Whichever is chosen, all these indicators help or hurt one of the two major-party presidential nominees at the expense of the other. This information is available months before the November general election and is "generic," or generally applicable to whoever is nominated by either party. For example, the economic downturn that began in late 2007 would have helped whoever was the Democratic nominee and would have disadvantaged any Republican candidate in the general election.

Predicting presidential nomination outcomes is more difficult because forecasting models cannot rely on these same factors. Primary voters have no "easy" decision rule like party identification to help them decide who to vote for, since all candidates belong to the same party. Likewise, it is more difficult to assign blame or give credit for a strong economy to any one candidate. While the state of the economy probably would have hurt any Republican presidential candidate in the 2008 general election, it is difficult to say which Republican candidate was hurt (or helped) most during the primaries. The effects of economic performance and the president's popularity have well-known and predictable effects on the general election vote. The effects of such variables on primary voting are less studied, but in most cases, they do not appear to have any systematic effect on the selection of the two political parties' nominees.

The demographic characteristics of voters are also less useful as predictors of vote choice in nomination races. In general elections, many subgroups within the population tend to identify disproportionately with one political party. For example, African-Americans generally support Democratic candidates in general elections, whereas more affluent, white evangelical Christians who regularly attend church tend to vote Republican. This makes these socio-economic and demographic characteristics useful in explaining vote choices in general elections. By contrast, it is a very different task to try to predict whether African-American voters will prefer one Democratic presidential candidate over another Democratic candidate and by what sort of margin; or how much white evangelical Christians will prefer one Republican presidential contender over another.

Moreover, the turnout of various constituency groups in one party's primaries can change across nomination races as the party coalitions evolve. Ronald Reagan's success in the 1980 Republican presidential nomination illustrates the point nicely. Starting at least four years before the 1980 elections, Reagan had sought to appeal to and mobilize white evangelical Christians as a voting group in Republican nominations. Greater turnout of these voters in Republican primaries helped Reagan gain the nomination and changed the Republican Party coalition in profound ways. Similarly, forecasts of the Democratic primary vote have been made more challenging by different levels of voter turnout among southern whites. Southern white presidential candidates used to have an advantage in Democratic primaries that no longer exists.[25] To the extent that these factors—immeasurable before the primaries—affect the vote in caucuses and primaries, nomination forecasts will have error in their predictions.

THE CHALLENGES OF THE MODERN NOMINATING STRUCTURE AND PROCESS

It is important to understand how unique presidential nominations are when compared to almost every other U.S. electoral contest. There is much greater uncertainty and volatility in presidential nominations, which stems from two major sources. First, the primary calendar is sequential, with voting in multiple caucuses and primaries spread out over months rather than on a single day. Second, while most delegates to the national nominating conventions are selected in primaries, many are selected in caucuses and a few are still selected by state party conventions. Whichever mode is used, each state uses a different set of rules with different implications for which candidate is likely to win. Each challenge will be discussed in turn.

Since the primary vote is distributed across time, early caucuses and primaries can affect the vote in subsequent primaries. Nomination forecasts are generally based on the relative standing of the candidates before the primaries as a predictor of their vote shares in the primaries. Some candidates fare much better in the early primaries and caucuses than they were expected to. Candidates who do so often gain momentum and thus receive greater support in subsequent primaries. Others withdraw as they fall behind in the delegate count or run out of campaign funds.[26] Forecast models based on information from the time period *before* the primaries cannot account for the effects of positive or negative momentum *during* the caucuses and primaries, resulting in under- and over-predictions of vote shares for candidates who beat or lag expectations. This is perhaps the greatest source of error in preprimary nomination forecasts, which is why "momentum forecasts," which take into account the results from Iowa and New Hampshire, are more accurate.

To further complicate matters, the nature of momentum is itself variable and hard to quantify, which makes its impact difficult to predict. Even before the McGovern-Fraser reforms elevated the decision-making power of primaries and caucuses over that of party conventions, the reelection campaigns of Harry Truman in 1952 and Lyndon Johnson in 1968 foundered after poor showings in the New Hampshire primary. Johnson's demise, in particular, demonstrates the subjective nature of momentum, as his victory as a write-in candidate in New Hampshire was dismissed as a poor showing because he "only" beat Senator Eugene McCarthy of Minnesota by 7 percentage points.

Conversely, in a scene made famous by the novel and movie "Primary Colors," many observers believe that Bill Clinton's scandal-ridden campaign was saved by a second-place finish in the 1992 New Hampshire primary.

During the 1970s, strong finishes in early contests were enough to propel little-known candidates such as George McGovern in 1972 and Jimmy Carter in 1976 to the Democratic presidential nomination. The Iowa caucuses and the New Hampshire primary became the "kingmakers" of presidential nominations. By the late 1980s, however, a series of front-runners emerged who were able to survive poor finishes in Iowa and/or New Hampshire and still become their party's nominee. In 1984 Walter Mondale lost the New Hampshire primary, and in 1988 both George H.W. Bush and Michael Dukakis lost the Iowa caucuses. Similar losses by Bill Clinton in 1992 (Iowa and New Hampshire), Robert Dole in 1996 (New Hampshire), and George W. Bush in 2000 (New Hampshire) suggested that momentum had a minimal impact on who would win the nomination, though it probably did have an effect on whether a race was close or not. As a result, forecasts made before the formal voting began correctly predicted the nominee, and there was reason to believe that presumptive nominees emerged as early as nine months before the Iowa caucuses.[27]

Momentum returned to prominent view during the presidential nomination contests of 2004 and 2008. Every model forecasting the primary vote underestimated the vote share of John Kerry in 2004 by at least 44 percent, McCain's share of the vote in 2008 by at least 20 percent, and Obama's share of the primary vote by at least 15 percent.[28] John Kerry used victories in Iowa and New Hampshire to emerge from the middle of the pack in preprimary preference polls and capture the 2004 Democratic nomination. In 2008 a victory in the Iowa caucuses was not enough for Republican Mike Huckabee to win his party's nomination, but a victory in Iowa was an important step in propelling Barack Obama to become his party's standard-bearer. Similarly, John McCain used a victory in New Hampshire to salvage his flagging campaign.

The effects of momentum, like other factors affecting the campaign, would be easier to account for in predictive models if scholars better understood precisely how it works to alter voters' initial preferences. Are voters in later contests simply "jumping on the bandwagon" of a promising candidate? Are they using the information gained from these early campaigns to make rational decisions about the respective viability (i.e., the likelihood of a particular candidate winning the nomination) of their top preferences and then reordering their choices so that they are not "wasting" their vote on a candidate who is unlikely to win the nomination?[29] Are they engaging in a quasi-rational strategy of paying more attention to candidates who perform well in early contests and, as a result, finding previously unknown information that leads them to support the new front-runner?[30] Are they using these results to determine which candidates are more electable (i.e., likely to win the general election)? Or, are they engaged in "wishful thinking," and thus ignoring the possibility that the person who seems destined to be their party's nominee may be likely to lead the party to defeat in the general election?[31] Understanding the effects of momentum during the primaries is also complicated by a continuously changing primary calendar. While front-loading is not new, it has clearly increased, as more states attempt to move their primaries and caucuses earlier into the election year. By changing the flow of the calendar, front-loading can alter the relative weight of early momentum and resources raised during the preprimary period, both of which factor heavily into many forecasting models.

Another complicating factor in nomination forecasting is that delegates to the national nominating conventions are selected via caucuses, conventions, and primaries that use a different set of rules in every state. In comparison, the process of selecting presidential electors is relatively homogeneous. Every state except Nebraska and Maine allow voters to participate in a single, winner-take-all election. Both types of contests rely on intermediaries (i.e., "delegates" and "electors") to execute the will of the voters, but presidential nomination contests are much less uniform. Today, most states utilize presidential primaries to select delegates. While the process is similar in many ways to general election balloting, there are important differences. Most importantly, many states hold closed primaries that limit participation to individuals who are already registered with a particular party. Though the distinction between closed and open primaries may seem trivial, some candidates perform markedly better in one format than the other. For example, John McCain's strong showing in the early Republican contests in 2000 may be due in part to a quirk in scheduling, in which most of the initial contests occurred in states holding the party's few open primaries. McCain, who polled well at that time among independents and Democrats, tended to win in these early, open primaries in states such as New Hampshire and Michigan. In March, by contrast, most of the primaries were closed. George W. Bush, who polled more strongly among Republicans, quickly clinched the Republican nomination.[32] Other state parties rely primarily on caucuses and a series of district and state conventions to select their national convention delegates. Unlike a simple trip to the polling booth, these events typically require extended participation and often require individuals to indicate publicly their choice of candidate, which is likely to cause some individuals to alter their behavior.[33] The time and public nature of the commitment tend to lessen the number of individuals who participate in caucuses and cause certain biases in caucus outcomes, such as stronger showings by ideologically extreme candidates.[34] Caucuses proved to be critical in the 2008 Democratic nomination race. While Hillary Clinton narrowly edged Barack Obama in the overall primary vote (if one counts the votes from the Michigan and Florida primaries), Obama beat Clinton by almost a three-to-one margin in the caucus states. These states gave Obama a critical advantage in the delegate count and largely account for his success in gaining the Democratic nomination.

THE CHALLENGES OF CAMPAIGNING.

Changes in the foundational and strategic elements of campaigning also make forecasting presidential nominations more challenging. The foundational elements of campaigning refer to the basic formula for constructing a winning campaign, such as fielding the best possible candidate, raising a substantial amount of money, and building an effective campaign organization.[35] By the strategic elements of the campaign, we mean the day-to-day choices that candidates and their campaigns make in order to achieve a competitive advantage.

While the foundational elements of campaigning have generally remained fairly constant during the modern nominating era (i.e., since 1976), some important rules have changed. One of the most significant such changes was the passage of the Bipartisan Campaign Reform Act of 2002 (BCRA), also known as the McCain-Feingold bill because its principal sponsors in the Senate were John McCain and Russ Feingold. This legislation raised the $1,000 limit on individual contributions that had been in place for almost three decades to $2000 and then indexed it to inflation. The result is an environment in which it is often claimed that serious candidates for the presidential nomination need to raise at least $100 million before the primaries begin. This fund-raising escalation means that most serious presidential aspirants no longer participate in the federal matching-funds program, which had previously provided a stable structure in which all participating campaigns agreed to abide by voluntary spending limits, both for total expenditures and for spending within each state.[36] The abandonment of these voluntary strictures likely increases the variation in resources across campaigns, especially in the key early caucuses and primaries.

When candidates are equal in resources and ideological positions, the strategic elements of the campaign—the day-to-day choices that candidates and their campaigns make to achieve a competitive advantage—create new challenges for nomination forecasting. For example, the rise of the Internet has caused considerable change in presidential nomination campaigns, in ways that make forecasting vote shares more difficult. Part of this change is due to the Internet's effect on how candidates raise money, especially on the time needed to raise money. Traditionally, raising money was an elite, time-intensive enterprise. Candidates sought to build national fund-raising networks among people who were known contributors to political party candidates. Presidential hopefuls had to spend years developing their own networks, identifying potential contributors and cultivating proven donors. Candidates spent considerable time, for example, attending fund-raising dinners and other such events at which they would meet and greet large donors, pose for pictures, and so forth. Presidential aspirants also worked with other elites—such as elected or party officials—so these people would sponsor events for the candidate. These pyramid-style networks required substantial investments in time and resources to develop and milk.

The Internet dramatically decentralized fund-raising, reducing both the costs and the time needed to raise money. Through the Internet and, more recently, phone apps that allow users to push a button to contribute money, candidates in the right circumstances—for example, a candidate who has just run better than expected in Iowa or New Hampshire—can appeal to and raise funds from tens of thousands of small donors almost instantaneously.

In conjunction with momentum, the Internet made possible "viral" candidacies like those of Howard Dean in 2004 and, most notably, Barack Obama in 2008. One study found that in January 2008, Obama's campaign raised 87 percent of its money online. Further, raising these funds required virtually no time from the candidate and minimal commitment of organizational resources. As the study's author noted, "In February, Obama didn't attend one single fund-raiser and still managed to raise $55 million online."[37] The Internet has also greatly reduced the costs of organization and campaigning at the grassroots level. Candidates can appeal to party activists in virtually every corner of the country to solicit volunteers. At the same time, activists who are interested in a candidate can easily go online and "friend" a candidate, volunteer to canvass, or help with the final Get-Out-The-Vote (GOTV) drive on Election Day. All of these technological changes are likely to be even more evident as campaign professionals better understand how to embrace the various new forms of social media. This creates a remarkable potential for sudden changes in candidates' fortunes, since money can now be raised in hours or days—lessening the value of funds held in reserve and magnifying the potential for momentum. The effects of the Internet appear to have played a critical role in the triumphs of John Kerry in 2004 and especially Barak Obama in 2008.

One final factor that complicates the strategic elements of a nomination campaign is the nature and size of the candidate field. General election forecasts try to predict the vote shares of the two major-party candidates (third-party and independent candidates are almost always excluded from such predictions). Nomination forecasts, by contrast, are required to predict the vote shares of multiple candidates. There is also less public awareness of the candidates in nomination campaigns, so substantial shifts in candidate preferences can occur when new information becomes available or when public attention shifts from one candidate to another.[38] In the 2008 Republican presidential nomination campaign, Rudy Giuliani, Mike Huckabee, and John McCain all led the national Gallup polls at one point or another during the first two weeks of January.

The size of the nomination field is often influenced by the decisions of a relatively small number of strong contenders about whether to enter the race or not. Incumbent presidents running for a second term have the greatest record of success in securing their party's nomination. They often run unopposed and typically attract no more than one serious (or even symbolic) challenger. Similarly, since 1952, no sitting vice-president who has sought his party's nomination has been defeated. This may have helped contribute to a Democratic field of only two candidates in 2000: Vice-President Al Gore and former Senator Bill Bradley. By contrast, an open nomination contest, without an incumbent president, has drawn an average of seven serious contenders in the post-reform era. On the other hand, the specter of a popular presidential nominee from the other party can discourage many prospective candidates from seeking their party's nomination. In 1991, a number of high-profile Democrats decided not to run for the 1992 nomination. While a number of factors may have influenced these decisions, one reason was George H. W. Bush's extraordinarily high approval ratings in the immediate aftermath of the 1991 Persian Gulf War.

Uncertainty about who is running has powerful effects on presidential nomination campaigns. Party elites, activists, and aligned groups are limited in their ability to coordinate with each other and come to a consensus as to which candidate the "party establishment" should support. Potential campaign contributors do not know whether they are wasting their money on a long shot or not. The news media do not know which candidates to focus on. Party identifiers do not know who they should pay attention to, much less support. In March of 2011, for example, none of the potential candidates had the support of more than 18% of Republican Party identifiers.[39] These conditions make it highly likely that the nomination will be competitive, with no candidate emerging as a strong front-runner going into the Iowa caucuses and New Hampshire primary.

THE VALUE OF NOMINATION FORECASTING

Both major political parties have developed a process for selecting presidential nominees in which the key decisions apparently rest in the hands of ordinary voters. In practice, however, jockeying for position in the presidential nomination process begins more than a year before the start of the primary season. If presidential nominees can be forecast prior to the primary season, then caucuses and primaries perhaps play only a more limited, confirmatory role. In other words, caucuses and primaries merely ratify the results of the campaign that occurred before the primary season started. This is a tremendously important question, because knowing whether nominations are determined mostly before or mostly during the primaries makes a difference in our understanding of where power resides in presidential nominations.

In order to field the best possible nominee, both major political parties have developed a process that tests similar characteristics. First, candidates must be able to raise sufficient financial support to communicate their message to the voters. Those that cannot are quickly winnowed from the race. Second, candidates must be able to organize a campaign staff that functions both effectively and efficiently. Those that cannot will be plagued with setbacks, unable to secure the nomination. Third, the candidates and their messages must resonate with voters. Those that cannot gain traction in the polls either withdraw to prevent embarrassment or remain in the race in order to use the campaign as a platform for discussing their policy views. Models that forecast the primary vote further our understanding of the presidential campaign's foundational elements.

While these foundational elements may add an element of predictability to nomination races, presidential candidates will frequently break with tradition and seek out innovations that will provide them with a competitive advantage. Races that are more difficult to forecast are those in which a campaign's strategic elements were more important in determining the winner. The question here is not whether a campaign's strategic elements matter. The question here is *when* a campaign's strategic elements matter. Sometimes a campaign's strategic elements are highly important. At other times, they are not.

In 1796, George Washington chose to return to his estate at Mt. Vernon and not seek reelection to the presidency. From that point on, nominating presidential candidates became a very high stakes enterprise. The nomination of a presidential candidate shapes the image, policy direction, and unity of each major political party heading into the general election in the fall. In electoral politics there is no single decision made in which the stakes are higher, which makes its study valuable to students of leadership selection. In many respects, political parties have developed a nomination process that looks an awful lot like governing. Successful candidates must navigate a difficult course that includes building the support of those in society with means, managing a large bureaucracy, and earning the approval of the public.

NOTES

1. William G. Mayer, "Forecasting Presidential Nominations or, My Model Worked Just Fine, Thank You," *PS: Political Science and Politics* 36 (2003): 153–157.

2. Randall E. Adkins and Andrew J. Dowdle, "Break Out the Mint Juleps in New Hampshire? Is New Hampshire the 'Primary' Culprit Limiting Presidential Nomination Forecasts?" *American Politics Quarterly* 28 (2000): 251–269; and Randall E. Adkins and Andrew J. Dowdle, "How Important are Iowa and New Hampshire to Winning Post-Reform Presidential Nominations?" *Political Research Quarterly* 54 (2001): 431–44.

3. Wayne P. Steger, "Who Wins Nominations and Why? An Updated Forecast of the Presidential Primary Vote," *Political Research Quarterly* 60 (2007): 91–99; Marty Cohen, David Karol, Hans Noel, and John Zaller. "Polls or Pols: The Real Driving Force Behind Presidential Nominations," *Brooking Review* 3 (2003): 36–39; and Marty Cohen, David Karol, Hans Noel, and John Zaller, "The Invisible Primary in Presidential Nominations, 1980–2004," in *The Making of the Presidential Candidates*, ed. William G. Mayer (Lanham, MD: Rowman & Littlefield, 2008), 1–38.

4. See, for example, Thomas M. Holbrooke, "Incumbency, National Conditions, and the 2008 Presidential Election," *PS: Political Science and Politics* 41 (2008): 709–712; Robert S. Erickson and Christopher Wlezien, "Leading Economic Indicators, the Polls, and the Presidential Vote," *PS: Political Science and Politics* 41 (2008): 703–707; Michael S. Lewis-Beck, "The Job of the President and the Jobs Model Forecast," *PS: Political Science and Politics* 41 (2008): 687–690; and James E. Campbell, "The Trial Heat Forecast of the 2008 Presidential Vote," *PS: Political Science and Politics* 41 (2008): 697–701.

5. See, for example, William G. Mayer, "Forecasting Presidential Nominations," in *In Pursuit of the White House: How We Choose Our Presidential Nominees*, ed. William G. Mayer (Chatham, NJ: Chatham House, 1996), 44–71; Adkins and Dowdle.,"Break Out the Mint Juleps"; Wayne P. Steger, "Do Primary Voters Draw from a Stacked Deck? Presidential Nominations in an Era of Candidate-Centered Campaigns," *Presidential Studies Quarterly* 30 (2000): 727–753; and Cohen et al., "Polls or Pols."

6. See, for example, Steger, "Do Primary Voters Draw from a Stacked Deck?"; Marty Cohen, David Karol, Hans Noel, and John Zaller, *The Party Decides: Presidential Nominations Before and After Reform* (Chicago, IL: University of Chicago Press, 2008); Audrey A. Haynes, Paul-Henri Gurian, Michael H. Crespin, and Christopher Zorn, "The Calculus of Concession: Media Coverage and the Dynamics of Winnowing in Presidential Nominations," *American Politics Research* 32 (2004): 310–337; Adkins and Dowdle, "Break Out the Mint Juleps"; Randall E. Adkins and Andrew J. Dowdle, "Continuity and Change in the Presidential Money Primary," *American Review of Politics 28* (2008): 319–341; Mayer, "Forecasting Presidential Nominations"; Mayer, "Forecasting Presidential Nominations or, My Model Worked Just Fine, Thank You;" and William G. Mayer. "Handicapping the 2008 Nomination Races: An Early Winter Prospectus," *The Forum* (2008).

7. See for example, V. O. Key, Jr., *Politics, Parties, and Pressure Groups,* 5th ed. (New York: Thomas Y. Crowell, 1964).

8. James W. Ceaser, *Reforming the Reforms: A Critical Analysis of the Presidential Selection Process* (Cambridge, MA: Ballinger Publishing, 1982); and Nelson W. Polsby, *Consequences of Party Reform* (New York: Oxford University Press, 1983).

9. Ryan J. Barilleaux and Randall E. Adkins, "The Nomination: Process and Patterns," in *The Elections of 1992*, ed. Michael Nelson (Washington, DC: Congressional Quarterly, 1993).

10. See, for example, William R. Keech and Donald R. Mathews, *The Party's Choice* (Washington, DC: Brookings Institution, 1976); Joel H. Goldstein, "The Influence of Money in the Prenomination Stage of the Presidential Selection Process: The Case of the 1976 Election," *Presidential Studies Quarterly* 8 (1978): 164–179; Thomas E. Patterson, *The Mass Media Election* (New York: Praeger, 1980); Barbara Norrander, "Party, Ideology, and the Lure of Victory: Iowa Activists in the 1980 Prenomination Campaign," *Western Political Quarterly* 35 (1986): 527–38; John H. Aldrich, *Before the Convention: Strategies and Choices in Presidential Nominations* (Chicago, IL: University of Chicago, 1980); and Larry M. Bartels, *Presidential Primaries and the Dynamics of Public Choice* (Princeton, NJ: Princeton University Press, 1988).

11. Steger, "Do Primary Voters Draw from a Stacked Deck?"

12. Barbara Norrander, "Nomination Choices: Caucus and Primary Outcomes, 1976–88," *American Journal of Political Science* 37 (1993): 343–364.

13. Mayer, "Forecasting Presidential Nominations"; Mayer, "Forecasting Presidential Nominations or, My Model Worked Just Fine, Thank You." Mayer's forecast model included the Democratic nomination race of 1980 and the Republican race of1992, in which incumbent presidents Jimmy Carter and George H. W. Bush were challenged for renomination. The other forecasts are limited to open nominations — i.e., those without an incumbent president.

14. Randall E. Adkins and Andrew J. Dowdle, "Overcoming Pitfalls in Forecasting Presidential Nominations," *Presidential Studies Quarterly* 35 (2005): 646–60.

15. Wayne P. Steger, "Who Wins Nominations and Why?"; Cohen et al., "Polls or Pols"; and Cohen et al., *The Party Decides.*

16. Kathleen Hall Jamieson, Richard Johnston, and Michael G. Hagen, "The 2000 Nominating Campaign: Endorsements, Attacks, and Debates," Research Report, Annenberg Public Policy Center, University of Pennsylvania, 2000.

17. Wayne P. Steger, "How Did the Primary Vote Forecasts Fare in 2008?" *Presidential Studies Quarterly* 39 (2009): 141–154.

18. Wayne P. Steger, Andrew J. Dowdle, and Randall E. Adkins, "The New Hampshire Effect in Presidential Nominations," *Political Research Quarterly* 57 (2004): 375–90.

19. Wayne P. Steger, "Forecasting the Presidential Primary Vote: Viability, Ideology, and Momentum," *International Journal of Forecasting* 24 (2008): 193–208.

20. Randall E. Adkins, Andrew J. Dowdle, and Wayne P. Steger, "Progressive Ambition, Opportunism, and the Presidency, 1972–2008," paper presented at the annual meeting of the American Political Science Association, Philadelphia, PA, September, 2006; Wayne P. Steger, Andrew J. Dowdle, and Randall E. Adkins, "Competition, Viability, and Choice in Presidential Nominations," paper presented at the annual meeting of the Midwest Political Science Association, Chicago, IL, April, 2010.

21. Bartels, *Presidential Primaries*; Barbara Norrander, "The Attrition Game: Initial Resources, Initial Contests, and the Exit of Candidates during the U.S. Presidential Primary Season," *British Journal of Political Science* 36 (2006): 487–507.

22. Adkins and Dowdle, "How Important are Iowa and New Hampshire"; Steger, Dowdle, and Adkin, "The New Hampshire Effect."

23. Ruy A. Teixeira, *The Disappearing American Voter* (Washington, DC: Brookings Institution, 1992).

24. See, for example, Erickson and Wlezien, "Leading Economic Indicators"; Lewis-Beck, "The Job of the President."

25. Steger, Dowdle, and Adkins, "The New Hampshire Effect."

26. Bartels, *Presidential Primaries*; and Norrander, "Attrition Game."

27. Adkins and Dowdle, "Overcoming Pitfalls."

28. Steger, "How Did the Primary Vote Forecasts Fare in 2008?"

29. Bartels, *Presidential Primaries*; Walter J. Stone, Ronald B. Rapoport, and Lonna Rae Atkeson, "A Simulation Model of Presidential Nomination Choice," *American Journal of Political Science* 39 (1995): 135–161.

30. Samuel L. Popkin, *The Reasoning Voter: Communication and Persuasion in Presidential Campaigns*, 2nd ed. (Chicago, IL: University of Chicago Press, 1994).

31. For contrasting views, see Alan I. Abramowitz, "Viability, Electability, and Candidate Choice in a Presidential Primary Election: A Test of Competing Models," *Journal of Politics* 51 (1989): 977–992; and Kevin J. McMahon, David M. Rankin, Donald W. Beachler, and John Kenneth White, *Winning the White House 2004: Region by Region, Vote by Vote* (New York: Palgrave Macmillan, 2005).

32. Phillip Paolino and Daron R. Shaw, "Lifting the Hood on the Straight-Talk Express: Examining the McCain Phenomenon," *American Politics Research* 29 (2001): 483–506. For other explanations, see Randall E. Adkins and Andrew J. Dowdle, "Bumps in the Road to the White House: How Influential Were Campaign Resources to Nominating George W. Bush?" *Journal of Political Marketing* 3 (2004): 1–27; and James W. Ceaser and Andrew E. Busch, *The Perfect Tie* (Lanham, MD: Rowman & Littlefield, 2000).

33. Christian R. Grose and Carrie A. Russell, "The Social Costs of Voting in Public: A Field Experiment of Voter Turnout in the 2008 Iowa Caucus," unpublished manuscript, 2008.

34. Norrander, "Nomination Choices."

35. Randall E. Adkins, "Presidential Campaigns and Elections," in *New Directions in the American Presidency*, ed. Lori Cox Han (New York: Routledge Press, 2010), 33–53.

36. Adkins and Dowdle, "Continuity and Change."

37. Ryan Peddycord, "How Obama Raised 87% of his Funds through Social Networking," available at http://www.resourcenation.com/blog/how-obama-used-social-networking-to-set-fund-raising-records/ (accessed March 12, 2011).

38. For example, see Bartels, *Presidential Primaries*; and Popkin, *Reasoning Voter*.

39. Ronald Brownstein, "Along for the Ride," *National Journal*, March 10, 2011.

Chapter 2

Financing Presidential Nominations in the Post-Public Funding Era

Anthony Corrado

The 2008 race for the White House was the most expensive presidential campaign in American history. Candidates seeking the 2008 party nominations raised more than $1.2 billion, nearly double the amount raised by candidates during the 2004 primaries and almost four times the sum achieved in 2000.[1] This steep rise was primarily due to the extraordinary fund-raising strength of Barack Obama, who raised an unprecedented $400 million in his winning campaign for the Democratic presidential nomination. Obama was so successful raising money that he refused public funding not only in the primaries, but also in the general election, thereby becoming the first presidential candidate since the creation of the public funding program in 1974 to run for the Oval Office without accepting public funds. By Election Day, he had raised a total of $745 million from private contributions, which was more than the combined total of private and public monies received by then-President George W. Bush and his Democratic challenger, John Kerry, in the entire 2004 election.[2]

While Obama's fund-raising was unparalleled, his tactics were emblematic of the changes taking place in the financing of presidential campaigns. The 2008 election was not the first in which candidates competing for the presidential nominations refused public financing. But it was the first in which most of the candidates were expected to reject public funding and its attendant spending limits from the start—and did. As a result, candidates in both parties engaged in a frenzied chase for campaign dollars, trying to raise as much money as possible in hopes of gaining a strategic advantage over their opponents. These efforts were spurred by the structure of competition, since both parties featured highly competitive contests with well-established candidates, and were facilitated by new communications technologies, which allowed candidates to solicit funds in innovative and interactive ways.

The financial activity in 2008 thus affirmed what many observers had noted after the 2004 election, that presidential campaign finance had entered a new era, a post-public funding era, defined by an emphasis on private fund-raising and the irrelevance of public funding as a means of campaign finance. This chapter examines the financing of the 2008 nomination contests in an effort to define the characteristics of this new fund-raising environment and determine how the 2008 experience will influence financial strategies in 2012.

A CHANGING FUND-RAISING ENVIRONMENT

Presidential candidates always face intense pressure to raise money. A presidential campaign is an expensive endeavor and those who hope to be competitive typically have to raise substantial sums just to contest the early contests in Iowa and New Hampshire. Because fund-raising totals are one of the few measures available to assess the relative prospects of candidates before the voting begins, those who hope to be ranked among the front-runners in the months before the initial contests usually have to raise tens of millions of dollars in the year before the election year. No matter how well-known a candidate may be, this is a daunting task.

In 2008 the demand for campaign money, especially early in the election cycle, was especially acute. Some political observers estimated that a candidate who hoped to be financially competitive would need to raise as much as $100 million by the end of 2007.[3] To put this figure in some perspective, in the 2004 election cycle Howard Dean and John Kerry, the leaders in the fund-raising race among Democrats, had respectively raised $41 million and $25 million by the end of 2003, while President George Bush, running unopposed for reelection, had raised $132 million.[4] As political scientist Michael Malbin noted, a candidate would have to raise, on average, more than $10,000 "every single hour, every single day, including weekends and holidays, for an entire year" to reach $100 million.[5] What was most surprising was that the leading candidates almost did just that.

The heightened fund-raising expectations posited in advance of the election and the unprecedented sums eventually attained during the race reflected the developments taking place in the broader environment of campaign finance. Some of these developments were a continuation of financial patterns that had emerged in previous elections. Others resulted from the particular political dynamics of the 2008 race or changes in law and communications technology that occurred after the 2004 campaign. Whatever the case, these changes formed the context of the financial activity in 2008 and determined the central features of campaign fund-raising in the new era of private financing.

THE DEMISE OF PUBLIC FUNDING

The rules governing presidential campaign finance were established in 1974 when Congress responded to financial abuses in the 1972 election and the Watergate scandal by adopting the Federal Election Campaign Act (FECA). The FECA imposed a limit of $1,000 per election ($1,000 in a primary and $1,000 in a general election) on the amount an individual could contribute to a presidential candidate, and $5,000 per election on the amount a political action committee (PAC) could give. In 2002 Congress adopted the Bipartisan Campaign Reform Act (BCRA), which did not change the PAC limit but did increase the amount an individual could give to $2,000 per election, with annual adjustments for inflation. Accordingly, in 2008 the individual contribution limit was $2,300 per election. The FECA also required candidates to report any contributions or expenditures of $200 or more to the Federal Election Commission (FEC), which is the agency responsible for implementing and administering the law.

The hallmark of the FECA was a voluntary program of public funding in presidential elections that made public funds available to qualified candidates during each stage of the selection process. During the prenomination period, a candidate could receive matching public funds on a dollar-for-dollar basis on the first $250 contributed by an individual donor. To be eligible, a candidate must raise $5,000 in contributions of $250 or less in twenty states and agree to abide by state-by-state and aggregate spending limits that are set forth in the law. A candidate who accepts public funds must also agree to limit personal contributions to his or her own campaign to $50,000.[6]

From 1976 to 1996, every major-party nominee and almost every major-party challenger accepted public matching funds. During this period, presidential aspirants raised on average about a third of their campaign funds in public money.[7] But, as David Magleby and William Mayer have noted, by the time of the 1996 election, the system was under strain.[8] Changes in the presidential selection process, most notably the increased "front-loading" of the schedule of party caucuses and primaries, intensified the financial demands of the selection process. Candidates, particularly front-runners for the nomination, found it increasingly difficult to finance the extensive campaigns needed to win the nomination, yet remain within the spending limits. With a growing number of state contests scheduled early in the election year, candidates needed to raise and spend more money early in the process, which meant that the prospective nominee began to reach the spending cap earlier in the election year. Winners commonly clinched the nomination, that is, had enough delegates to be certain of a convention victory, by early April or late March of the election year. A prospective nominee thus faced what can be called a "bridge period" after securing the nomination, consisting of the months between the effective end of the primaries and the convention. During this period, a candidate who emerged from a competitive primary race often was no longer able to spend significant amounts of money due to the spending limit. Republican Robert Dole had to confront this strategic problem in 1996 when he won the party nomination by early April, but had little room left to spend money under the expenditure cap. He was then outspent throughout the summer by President Bill Clinton, who was unopposed for the Democratic nomination and had millions of dollars left to spend during the bridge period. The 1996 experience thus highlighted the strategic vulnerability that could arise from the spending limits.[9]

In 2000 George W. Bush sought to avoid the problem encountered by Dole in 1996 by forgoing matching funds and the accompanying spending limits.[10] By doing so, he was able to raise $94 million for his nomination campaign and became the first major-party candidate in the public funding era to win the presidential nomination without public funds. He was also able to outspend his eventual Democratic opponent, Al Gore, who accepted matching funds, by a margin of two to one, and exploited this financial advantage during the summer months leading up to the nominating convention, when Gore was essentially prohibited from spending additional sums due to the spending limits.[11]

In 2004 President Bush, who was running unopposed in a bid for reelection, again opted out of public funding, which placed pressure on his prospective opponents in the Democratic Party to follow suit. Whether any of the Democratic challengers would do so was an unknown early in the nomination contest because no Democrat had previously eschewed public funds. But in November 2003 Howard Dean, who led the Democratic field in fund-raising and was successfully raising millions of dollars through the Internet, announced that he would forgo matching funds.[12] Soon thereafter, John Kerry also decided not to take public money. Kerry, however, needed campaign cash at the time and his decision reflected his desire to spend more than $50,000 of his own money on his campaign, which would not have been permitted under the public funding rules. Kerry loaned more than $6 million to his campaign, and won the Iowa caucuses and the New Hampshire primary, which launched his successful bid for the nomination.[13] Consequently, in 2004 both party nominees, Bush and Kerry, were free to spend as much as they could raise prior to the party conventions. In total, Bush raised $269 million in primary funds, while Kerry raised $235 million.[14] In other words, each of these aspirants raised about five times more than the $50 million in prenomination funding that would have been allowed under the public funding expenditure limits.

The 2004 election thus signaled the collapse of the public matching program. The experience of the 2000 and 2004 elections had demonstrated that the basic trade-off at the core of the program—public subsidies in exchange for the agreement to abide by spending limits—was no longer a strategically attractive option for most leading candidates. Matching funds typically constituted a minor portion of a candidate's resources, and this potential benefit no longer outweighed the risks inherent in this approach. Given the rising expenditures in presidential campaigns, the spending cap could not accommodate the financial demands candidates had to confront. Any candidate who accepted public money was likely to be outspent by an opponent who refused such funding and was certain to face a severe financial disparity during the period between the end of the primary race and the national convention. Front-running candidates in particular could raise and spend much more than the amount permitted by the spending limit, and thereby gain a head start during the summer months on their electioneering for the general election campaign. In sum, the wisest fund-raising strategy was to avoid public money and its constraints.

Most of the challengers in 2008 thus gave little consideration to the public funding option. In January 2007, a year before the voting in Iowa was to begin, Democrat Hillary Clinton, who began the race as the widely perceived front-runner for her party's nomination, indicated that she would not accept public funding during the primaries.[15] Within a few months, it was evident that the top contenders on both sides of the aisle would not take public money.

The only notable exception in 2008 was John Edwards, who was the Democratic vice-presidential candidate in 2004 but trailed badly behind the front-runners in fund-raising throughout the race. Edwards received $12.9 million in matching funds, which made up about a quarter of the $49.6 million he received during the campaign.[16] A few others received matching funds, but they were all long shots who struggled to raise money and garnered relatively minor sums. In most instances, these individuals resorted to the public option as a last resort and relied on matching money to help pay off their campaign debts after the election. In all, public funding accounted for less than $22 million of the $1.2 billion raised by candidates seeking the presidential nomination.[17] The 2008 contenders made clear that the time of public funding as a means of campaign finance was over.

The Political Context

With candidates free of public funding constraints, it is not surprising that campaign expenditures rose dramatically. But the demise of public funding was not the only factor that contributed to the financial spike that characterized the 2008 nominations. The broader context of the race also encouraged a greater emphasis on fund-raising.

One aspect of the electoral environment that encouraged aggressive fund-raising was the change that took place in the schedule of caucuses and primaries, which exacerbated the front-loading of the presidential calendar.[18] States that felt bypassed by presidential campaigns had been moving their delegate selection contests to earlier dates in the election year since the mid-1980s, but 2008 featured the most heavily front-loaded calendar in party history. In the aftermath of the 2004 election, the Democratic Party gave four states—Iowa, New Hampshire, Nevada, and South Carolina—an exemption from the party rule that required states to hold their delegate selection primary or caucus no earlier than the first Tuesday in February.[19] The party allowed these states to hold their elections in January, thereby creating an initial stage of the selection process in which diverse sections of the country would be represented and the influence of Iowa and New Hampshire might be diminished. In addition, a number of states, including many large, delegate-rich states such as California, Florida, New Jersey, and New York, moved the date of their primaries to the first Tuesday in February, which eventually led to a "Super Tuesday" on February 5 that featured contests in more than twenty states on that one day in both parties.

These changes intensified the financial demands of campaigning. As in other recent presidential races, challengers faced the prospect of having to generate substantial amounts of cash to finance operations and advertising in the crucial first states of Iowa and New Hampshire, as well as the resources to begin to mount operations in as many Super Tuesday states as possible. But in 2008 this strategic necessity was more pressing and complicated. Super Tuesday would take place at the beginning of February, as compared to the beginning of March in 2004, and Nevada and South Carolina would vote in January soon after Iowa and New Hampshire. Most observers expected that the nominations would be decided by the outcome on Super Tuesday. Candidates who hoped to win the nomination therefore had to amass substantial war chests well before the voting took place in Iowa, especially if they hoped to wrap up the nomination by winning big on Super Tuesday.[20] With the states packed so closely together, there would be little time to raise additional money once the voting began. Moreover, candidates who did win early might expect a surge in contributions in response to a victory, but there would be little time to use the money to build a campaign organization or mount an advertising campaign before the voting took place in the next state or, for that matter, before Super Tuesday. Even if a candidate could manage to finance electioneering efforts in most of the Super Tuesday states, it would be a very expensive undertaking. Accordingly, the most rational strategy was to emphasize fund-raising even more than candidates had in the past.

The financial activity also reflected the level of political competition. Candidates in competitive races have a strong incentive to try to gain a financial advantage over their opponents, or at least keep pace with them. Competitive elections also generate higher levels of voter interest, giving individuals incentive to contribute to the candidate of their choice. And the 2008 contests were unusually competitive. For the first time since 1952, no incumbent president or vice president was seeking a party nomination. Given the prospect of open contests in both parties, the race attracted strong candidate fields. These fields featured well-established politicians with high name recognition and proven fund-raising abilities.

After two consecutive defeats in close presidential elections, the Democrats were eager for victory and the party's chance of winning back the White House looked favorable, with public opinion surveys indicating rising disapproval of President Bush, high levels of dissatisfaction with the direction of the nation, and deep opposition to the war in Iraq. A number of prominent Democrats therefore entered the race, led by former first lady and then Senator Hillary Clinton, who had spent years building a political operation, had a broad base of supporters, and began the race with $10 million in cash in her Senate campaign fund which she transferred to her presidential campaign to help launch her candidacy. Other notables included former vice presidential candidate John Edwards and Senator Joseph Biden, who had previously run for president. Barack Obama, though a freshman senator, had been the party's most successful fund-raiser during the 2006 midterm elections and was perceived by many in the party to be a political celebrity, thanks to his highly regarded 2004 Democratic convention speech and two best-selling books.[21]

Senator John McCain, who had lost the 2000 Republican nomination to George Bush and developed a reputation as a maverick on Capitol Hill, was the best-known candidate on the Republican side. Other notable aspirants for the Republican mantle included Rudolph Giuliani, the former mayor of New York, who rose to national prominence in the response to the September 11 terrorist attacks, and Mitt Romney, a former investment firm executive who served as head of the Salt Lake City Organizing Committee for the 2002 Winter Olympic Games and thereafter was elected governor of Massachusetts. Each of these candidates was capable of raising the tens of millions of dollars needed to wage a viable campaign.

The Rise of Web 2.0

Digital technologies are revolutionizing communications and providing candidates with new means of conducting campaign activities.[22] By 2004, presidential candidates were building extensive Internet operations to distribute and gather information, identify and recruit supporters, and solicit and collect campaign donations. Democrat Howard Dean made Internet-based outreach a centerpiece of his campaign for the 2004 presidential nomination, relying on the Internet to garner the support of liberal activists and others who responded to his severe criticisms of the war in Iraq and the administration of President George W. Bush. Dean was not the first presidential contender to make use of the Internet. Candidates had used the Internet since 1992, when Bill Clinton employed it for the limited purposes of internal campaign email and LISTSERV distribution of information.[23] But the Dean campaign revealed the power of the Internet as a tool for organizing and recruiting support. It is therefore often cast as the first Internet campaign.[24]

Dean used the Internet to maintain regular contact with supporters and solicit their ideas for campaign events and volunteer activities. Most important, he highlighted the value of the Internet as a fund-raising tool. He raised $27 million in online contributions, which represented more than half of his $51 million total campaign receipts.[25] He also used an independent social networking website, MeetUp.com, to arrange campaign events and meetings with individuals interested in his candidacy. In all, the Dean campaign ended up with 190,000 enrollees on MeetUp.com and 170,000 supporters on GetLocal, which was his campaign's version of a grassroots-organizing program.[26] These online communities provided Dean with a base of supporters who could be regularly solicited for small contributions.

Though Dean was the candidate most associated with online campaigning in 2004, he was not the only contender to take advantage of the capabilities of the Internet. President Bush and John Kerry, the major-party nominees, made extensive use of the Internet. After he clinched the nomination in March, Kerry raised tens of millions of dollars online, which helped him generate $188 million between March and the party convention in August, and he ended the campaign with a list of three million email addresses.[27] Bush focused on more traditional approaches to fund-raising, such as major fund-raising events and direct mail. While contributions were also solicited online, the campaign did not report the sums raised through its Internet efforts. Bush primarily used his website to distribute information, including videos, and as a portal for organizing volunteers. By the end of the campaign, Bush had recruited 1.2 million volunteers online and constructed a list of six million email addresses.[28]

The 2004 campaign was a harbinger of things to come. But technological innovation continued at a rapid pace, producing a more powerful communications infrastructure and applications than those available in 2004. Specifically, the 2008 contest would be the first held in the world of Web 2.0—the collective term used to refer to the wide range of online activities and applications that provide network-enabled interactive services.[29]

Web 2.0 applications are designed to move away from static web pages to more dynamic, interactive websites that enable online "communities" or "social networks" with virtually seamless interaction and communications among users. Many of the most popular online applications that have come into common use, such as Facebook or YouTube, are based on Web 2.0 capabilities, and most did not gain widespread popularity or great scale until after the 2004 election. For example, MySpace was launched in January 2004 and grew to five million users by November of that year.[30] By the beginning of 2008, it was the largest social networking site on the web. Facebook was launched in 2004 as a site for use by college students and was not opened to anyone with a valid email address until September 2006.[31] By the end of 2007, its user base had grown to twenty-six million.[32] YouTube was opened to the public in November 2005, and was *Time* magazine's "Invention of the Year" for 2006.[33] By July 2006, more than sixty-five thousand videos were being uploaded each day to the site, with one hundred million daily views.[34] Another new application, Twitter, was developed in 2006 and just coming into broad use in 2008. By the time of the November election, 3.5 million accounts had been created.[35]

The rapid growth of these new Internet applications was spurred by the expansion of broadband capability. Broadband or other high-speed Internet connections are essential for Web 2.0 applications, and 2008 was the first election year in which more than half of all Americans had broadband access at home.[36] Expanding access to broadband helped to create a more distributed computing environment, allowing individuals to access the Internet from computers, cell phones, or other mobile communication devices. Consequently, a substantial share of the public was increasingly online, accessing news and other information, watching videos, and participating in social networks. According to surveys conducted by the Pew Internet and American Life Project, 75 percent of adults and 90 percent of teenagers were online by the beginning of 2008, and at least 80 percent of all adults had cell phones.[37]

Technological and behavioral changes thus provided a more dynamic and interactive environment for fund-raising in 2008. As in 2004, individuals interested in making a contribution could easily visit a candidate's website and by clicking through to a contribution form donate money with a credit card. Candidates could gather email addresses from site visitors, those who attended campaign events, and individuals who otherwise came into contact with the campaign, and then solicit donations from these individuals, just as Howard Dean and John Kerry had done in 2004. Presidential hopefuls could now also tap into extensive social networks, interact with supporters and build online relationships, and offer more content to potential supporters by distributing video clips, campaign advertisements, and targeted emails and text messages. The rise of Web 2.0 capabilities empowered candidates to solicit and receive contributions on a scale that was not feasible in previous presidential contests, and they could do so more efficiently and at a fraction of the cost of direct mail or telemarketing, the traditional methods of soliciting large numbers of potential donors. For example, a candidate could email contribution requests targeted to the particular policy concerns or political preferences of thousands of individuals at virtually no cost—and ask these individuals to share these messages with their own networks or the online communities in which they were active.

Technological evolution provided a communications infrastructure that offered candidates a significantly enhanced capacity to raise money. But the availability of this infrastructure did not guarantee that candidates would successfully harness its potential. Candidates still needed to invest the resources needed to build a capacity within their campaigns to make the most of the opportunities offered by this new environment. And individuals still needed the motivation to make a contribution. Obama understood this better than the others, which is one of the reasons why he was able to establish a new standard for fund-raising.

CAMPAIGN FUND-RAISING IN 2008

Presidential contenders in 2008 raised significantly more money than their counterparts in 2004 largely due to the fund-raising of the top two candidates in each of the major parties. Barack Obama and his principal rival Hillary Clinton, and John McCain and his leading opponent Mitt Romney amassed a combined total of almost $990 million, which represented three-quarters of the money raised in the nomination contests (see Table 2.1). Obama led the way, taking in more than $450 million by the time of the party convention, including $41 million in contributions designated for the general election that were received from individuals who had already contributed the maximum $2,300 to his primary campaign. In primary funds alone, Obama garnered $414 million, which was almost twice the amount raised by Clinton ($220 million) or the Republican nominee McCain ($210 million). Romney totaled $105 million, which included $44.7 million of his own money that he invested in his campaign.

These aggregate amounts suggest that Obama and McCain, the respective party nominees, held commanding financial advantages over their opponents. But they obscure the underlying financial portrait of the period when the nominations were still up for grabs. McCain raised most of his money during the bridge period after he clinched the nomination, a period that

Table 2.1. Presidential Nomination Receipts and Expenditures, 2008 (in $ millions)

Candidate	*Receipts*	*Expenditures*
Democrats		
Obama	453.9	376.5
Primary season	287.5	251.3
Bridge Period[a]	125.4	125.2
General Election[b]	41.0	0.0
Clinton	220.1	211.6
Edwards	49.6	43.5
Richardson	22.2	22.1
Dodd	15.1	15.1
Biden	11.9	11.1
Kucinich	5.5	5.3
Gravel	0.5	0.6
Sub-Total:	778.8	685.8
Republicans		
McCain	210.6	177.8
Primary season	61.2	55.7
Bridge period[c]	149.4	122.1
Romney	105.2	105.1
Giuliani	58.7	58.6
Paul	34.5	30.4
Thompson, F.	23.5	23.2
Huckabee	16.1	16.1
Tancredo	8.2	8.2
Brownback	4.2	4.2
Hunter	2.8	2.8
Thompson, T.	1.2	1.2
Gilmore	0.3	0.4
Sub-Total:	465.3	428.0
Total:	**1,244.1**	**1,113.8**

Source: John C. Green and Diana Kingsbury, "Financing the 2008 Presidential Nomination Campaigns," in David B. Magleby and Anthony Corrado, eds., *Financing the 2008 Election* (Washington, DC: Brookings Institution Press, 2011), Table 3-2.
[a]The bridge period for Obama extended from June to August 2008.
[b]Contributions for the general election received during the prenomination period.
[c]The bridge period for McCain extended from March to August 2008.

extended from March through August. At this point, he was raising money in what was, in effect, a general election context, since it was clear he would be the Republican candidate for the presidency. His fund-raising pattern was similar to that of Democrat John Kerry in 2004. Kerry had raised $41 million by the time he clinched the nomination in March and then raised $188 million in the months leading up to the convention.[38] McCain raised $149 million in the months leading up to the convention, which constituted about 70 percent of his total prenomination funding. During the "primary period" when the nomination was still being contested, McCain raised $61 million, as compared to Romney's $105 million and Giuliani's $59 million total.

Obama also raised a substantial sum after he wrapped up the nomination, but the bridge period on the Democratic side was much shorter than that on the Republican side. The race between Obama and Clinton proved to be the most competitive and hard fought contest since 1984, when Walter Mondale reached the delegate majority needed to secure the party's nomination on the day after the final primaries in June. In 2008, the race also lasted until June. By then, Obama had built up an extraordinary base of financial supporters and he took in $125 million in the period from June to the late August convention. He also received $41 million of general election money, most of which was received in the bridge period, after he announced in the third week of June that he would not accept public funding in the general election.[39]

Yet, unlike McCain, Obama held a significant financial advantage over his opponents, especially in the crucial period from January to June when the voting was taking place. In all, he raised $287 million from the start of the campaign through the end of the primaries, as compared to $220 million by Clinton. Moreover, Clinton's total included $10 million that she transferred from her Senate campaign committee at the start of her campaign and $13.2 million in personal funds she loaned to the campaign. Even with these large infusions of cash, Clinton could not keep pace with Obama. In fact, Obama raised more money than the rest of the Democratic field combined, Clinton included.

Early Fund-Raising

From the beginning of the 2008 election cycle, candidates emphasized fund-raising, hoping to enhance their public profiles and establish their viability as contenders by demonstrating an ability to raise large sums of money. Spencer Zwick, national finance director of the Romney campaign, best summarized the prevailing attitude in a simple quip: "We do know in political fund-raising, money talks, but early money screams."[40]

Candidates began to build their war chests early and tried to capitalize on every opportunity available to raise money. By the end of March 2007, aspirants had already taken in $157 million, five times the $30 million total that candidates had received in the first quarter of 2003.[41] The Democrats reported more than $95 million in first quarter receipts, while the Republicans reported close to $62 million. By the end of 2007, the total had soared to $552 million, or more than double the $273 million achieved in 2003, which was the previous high-water mark for off-year presidential fund-raising.[42] The Democratic contenders had garnered $292 million by the end of 2007; the Republicans, $260 million. Even before the election year began, it was clear that fund-raising was soaring to unprecedented heights.

Seeking to raise as much money as possible as quickly and efficiently as possible, candidates focused their early efforts on the solicitation of individual contributions in amounts of $1,000 or more. According to an analysis of FEC filings conducted by the nonpartisan Campaign Finance Institute, 61 percent of the money raised from individuals in 2007 came from contributions of $1,000 or more, including 37 percent that came from individuals who gave the maximum $2,300. In this regard, party affiliation made little difference: 61 percent of the money received by Republican candidates from individual donors came in contributions of $1,000 or more (36 percent from donors who gave the maximum), while 62 percent of the money received by Democrats from individual donors came in checks of $1,000 or more (38 percent from donors who gave the maximum).[43] While the relative importance of large donors varied by candidate, the leading fund-raisers by year's end typically received at least 75 percent of their individual donations from those who gave at least $1,000. The one exception was Obama, but even he raised more than half of his money from large donors, including one out of every three dollars from those who gave his campaign the maximum amount.

No candidate benefited more from the attention the media and public pay to early fund-raising than Obama. As the presidential contest got underway, Clinton was expected to be the outright leader when it came to raising money. She began her campaign with a database of more than 250,000 donors who had contributed to her two U.S. Senate campaigns and was widely expected to be the Democratic front-runner.[44] In the first quarter of 2007, she raised $26 million from individual contributions, which was supplemented by the $10 million from her Senate campaign account for a $36 million total that gave her a significant lead in the money chase. But Obama was the candidate who surprised the prognosticators by keeping pace. He received contributions from 100,000 donors and garnered close to $26 million, which separated him from the rest of the Democratic field and challenged the conventional wisdom concerning Clinton's financial superiority.[45]

Throughout the rest of 2007, Obama continued to show that he could not only match, but also surpass Clinton. By the end of the year, he had raised $99.6 million, slightly more than the $98.7 million accrued by Clinton. None of the other Democrats came close to these sums. Even before the voting had begun in Iowa, the contest was shaping up as a two-person race.

The only Republican who came close to matching the top Democrats was Romney, who reported $90 million by the end of December. But his total included $35.4 million of his own money. The biggest surprise on the Republican side was the weak performance by McCain. As a former presidential contender with a high national profile, McCain was expected to lead the fund-raising race at the start of the campaign and had a good start in the first quarter ($14.8 million). But thereafter his fund-raising ebbed and he ended the year with a total of $40 million in receipts, which left him trailing not only Romney, but also Giuliani, who raised $56 million. McCain's financial problems were evident in the fourth quarter, when his $9.6 million in quarterly receipts even placed him behind conservative Representative Ron Paul, who raised $20 million from October through December as his unorthodox campaign and libertarian policies struck a chord with a segment of conservative activists. McCain's campaign also spent large sums throughout the year on staff and state organizations. So by the end of the year, he was running out of cash, and had to cut his staff and spending in Iowa and rely on bank loans to keep his bid in New Hampshire afloat.

TAKING FUND-RAISING ONLINE

All of the candidates in 2008 recognized that the Internet had become an important means of communication and, as the Dean campaign had demonstrated four years earlier, a valuable fund-raising tool. Candidates used digital technologies in a variety of ways to reach out and connect with supporters. "Donate" click buttons were a common component of candidate websites and online advertisements. Fund-raising appeals were included in most online postings, ranging from advertisements on search sites to YouTube videos to email and text messages. Candidates established pages on Facebook, MySpace, and other social network sites, and sought to collect individual email addresses so that they could solicit contributions in more personal ways.

While all of the major-party contenders sought online contributions, no one was as successful as Obama. Indeed, a key element of Obama's financial strength throughout the election year was the productivity of his online fund-raising, especially his success in attracting contributions from donors who gave less than $200. No candidate had ever raised as much money from small contributions as Obama did, which made his small donor fund-raising the preeminent campaign finance story of the election—this, despite the fact that he also raised a substantial share of his campaign funds from large donors of $1,000 or more, much of which came from more traditional fund-raising approaches.

What distinguished Obama's approach was his emphasis on online politicking and the decision to make Web 2.0 applications an integral component of his political operation. From the start, Obama recognized the potential of the Internet as a means of building a grassroots political effort. As he noted during the campaign, "One of my fundamental beliefs from my days as a community organizer is that real change comes from the bottom up. And there's no more powerful tool for grassroots organizing than the Internet."[46] This emphasis on technology and grassroots politicking was based on the lessons of Dean's 2004 campaign, but also was influenced by the strategic challenge he faced in running against Clinton, whom Obama's campaign manager, David Plouffe, described as "the strongest establishment front-runner in our party's history."[47] To draw a contrast with Clinton and her campaign, Obama cast his campaign as a grassroots, volunteer-driven organization that would rely on technology as a principal means of gathering support.

Before he launched his candidacy in February 2007, Obama retained the services of Blue State Digital, a market research firm specializing in new media founded by four former members of Dean's 2004 campaign.[48] He hired one of the partners, Joe Rospars, to serve as the campaign's director of new media. He was joined on the campaign staff by Julius Genachowski, a former chief counsel at the Federal Communications Commission who served as a senior partner at the Fortune 500 company IAC/Interactive Corp, and Chris Hughes, one of the cofounders of Facebook, who took a sabbatical from the company to join the Obama staff.

These Internet-savvy entrepreneurs oversaw the development of a state-of-the-art website that incorporated Web 2.0 features, including the campaign's own social networking hub, My.BarackObama.com, which became known as MyBO. The goal was to make the hub the central coordinating point for all Internet-related activity that took place during the campaign and use it to build an "online relationship" with supporters that would encourage them to identify with Obama, contribute to his campaign, undertake volunteer activities, and mobilize others to vote. The basic idea was to provide a place online where the campaign could connect and directly interact with supporters, share ideas, distribute information and campaign materials, and assign campaign tasks.

Once MyBO was established, the campaign linked this hub to other social networking sites in order to encourage those who expressed interest in Obama to connect directly with the campaign. Obama profile pages were established in more than fifteen online communities, including Facebook, MySpace, BlackPlanet (a social network for African-Americans), and Eons (a site for baby boomers).[49] Supporters were encouraged to share links to MyBO with their own networks or contacts, thereby creating a viral dimension to Obama's messaging. In addition, they were asked to build personal profiles and pages on MyBO, which provided the campaign with data used to tailor messages to a recipient's particular interests, demographic characteristics, or level of involvement in the campaign. By Election Day, two million supporters had created MyBO profiles, which gave the campaign a wealth of data that could be used to personalize messages and track individuals' activities on behalf of the campaign.[50]

Obama employed a diverse array of tactics to promote online giving that extended well beyond such standard tools as a "donate" click button or email solicitations. The campaign bought advertising on search engines and specific websites, and focused advertising on particular search terms in an effort to reach online users and drive them to MyBO. From January through April alone, the campaign spent close to $3 million on Internet advertising.[51] Obama also used paraphernalia sales, limited edition memorabilia offers, prizes (such as an opportunity to win debate tickets or a chance to meet him), and other inducements to generate initial contributions of $5 or $10 to expand his pool of donors. Those who gave could then be solicited for additional donations and were sometimes asked to make another contribution of $25 or more that would be matched by another Obama contributor. A donor could also enroll in a program that charged a gift of as little as $25 to his or her credit card on a regular basis.

Supporters could further assist Obama by serving as volunteer fund-raisers for his campaign. An application on the MyBO site allowed individuals to set up their own fund-raising pages, establish a personal fund-raising goal, and set up a "fund-raising thermometer" that they could watch rise as friends or contacts gave in response to their requests. The campaign even made it possible for individuals to see how well they were doing as compared to others they knew, thus encouraging friendly competition among Obama supporters. The tactic proved so successful that the campaign established a grassroots fund-raising committee that provided online instruction to train individuals in how to collect donations from friends, relatives, and other associates. Through this effort the campaign developed a corps of seventy thousand volunteer fund-raisers who were willing to solicit their own contacts for campaign dollars. By Election Day, these individuals had brought $30 million into the campaign.[52]

Obama's Internet strategy provided an interactive, Web-based infrastructure that gave him the capacity to make the most of any surges in public support or expressions of interest in his campaign. He was able to immediately process all donations that came his way, and at the same time solicit contributions from millions of individuals through email, text messages, and online ads, thereby expanding the scope of his fund-raising effort far beyond that of any presidential campaign that had come before his. The resources he devoted to this effort began to pay big dividends in the months preceding the Iowa caucuses.

As noted earlier, the leading presidential contenders focused on large contributions for most of their funding throughout 2007. But in the fourth quarter of 2007, Obama began to receive significant sums from small donations. As his popularity rose and as he gained greater recognition as a leading contender for the nomination, his receipts from small contributions started to rise quickly. Obama took in $22.2 million from individual donors in the fourth quarter of 2007 and almost half of this amount, $10.4 million, came from individuals who gave gifts of less than $200. In the same period, Hillary Clinton took in $3.7 million from small contributions. With his win in the Iowa caucuses, his online fund-raising surged, even though he lost the New Hampshire primary to Clinton soon after. In January alone, he took in $32 million, including $28 million in online donations, with 90 percent of this online total coming from individuals who gave $100 or less, and 40 percent from those who gave $25 or less.[53] Thus, in one month, he raised more money through the Internet than Dean had received in his entire 2004 campaign.

Obama's success with small donors in January was the start of an extraordinary period that demonstrated the power of new technologies as tools for campaign fund-raising. In February, the momentum generated by a number of significant victories on Super Tuesday helped Obama generate an astounding $55 million. To put this sum in perspective, no presidential candidate in any election prior to 2008, with the exception of George W. Bush in 2000 and 2004, had raised this much money from the start of a campaign through the end of February. Obama thus took in more money in one month than most previous candidates had amassed in an entire nomination campaign. As in January, most of this money came from small contributions made online, with 90 percent of these online donations consisting of gifts of $100 or less and 50 percent in amounts of $25 or less.[54]

Moreover, Obama was building an extensive base of donors and the vast majority could be solicited for additional donations at relatively little cost. By the end of February, Obama had already attracted more than one million donors, a mark that President Bush, running unopposed for reelection in 2004, did not reach until May of that year.[55] He continued to build support throughout the rest of the nomination campaign and by the time of the convention, he had recruited two million donors, more than any other previous presidential candidate.[56]

Obama's remarkable fund-raising surge, $87 million in two months, gave him a major strategic advantage in the crucial stages of the nominating contest. It provided him with the resources to mount aggressive campaigns in more states than Clinton and outspend her by a significant margin. Obama was therefore able to accumulate the delegates needed to establish a lead after the first month of primary contests, which he never relinquished in his victorious march to the nomination. While Clinton did win some of the big states, including Pennsylvania and Texas, these victories were not enough to overcome the advantage Obama achieved as a result of his small donor online fund-raising.

Obama's resource advantage was most evident with respect to broadcast advertising. Early in the campaign, Obama and Clinton spent relatively equal amounts on ads, but as the contest progressed, the gap between them widened substantially. According to data gathered by the private firm TNS Media Intelligence/CMAG as analyzed by the University of Wisconsin Advertising Project, Obama spent $74.8 million on television advertising by the end of May, as compared to Clinton's $46 million total.[57] Before Super Tuesday, Obama devoted $18.2 million to television advertising as opposed to Clinton's $16.7 million. In the Super Tuesday states, Obama was able to spend more in more states, airing ads in sixteen states at a cost of $14.2 million, while Clinton aired ads in thirteen states at a cost of $11.2 million. In eight of the twelve states where both contenders were on the air, Obama outspent Clinton. Obama had the airwaves to himself in Colorado, Georgia, Kansas, and Minnesota—all states he won—and although he did not purchase ad time in Idaho, where Clinton did, he still won.

After Super Tuesday, Obama was able to seize control of the airwaves. In the remaining February contests held after Super Tuesday, he spent almost four times as much on television as Clinton did ($4.4 million versus $1.2 million). Thereafter, he held a sizable advantage, disbursing $41.6 million on television ads as opposed to $19.7 million by Clinton from the beginning of March through the end of May. This period included selection contests in a number of major battlegrounds, including Ohio, Texas, Pennsylvania, Indiana, and North Carolina, where Clinton needed victories to try to catch Obama in the race for delegates. Even though Clinton won the majority of these battleground states, Obama's financial advantage allowed him to maximize his vote potential in each of these states (and thus win significant numbers of delegates under the Democratic rules that assign delegates based on a candidate's share of the vote) and kept the pressure on Clinton to spend large sums of money, which eventually led her to lend $13 million of her own money to her campaign in an effort to stay financially competitive.

Obama's online fund-raising was beyond compare, but other candidates also raised substantial sums via the Internet. Clinton based her fund-raising on large donations and more traditional methods, but she began to place more emphasis on online giving and small donations once Obama's January surge became apparent. In February she urged supporters to contribute online.

After her campaign revealed that the Senator had used $5 million of her own money to help finance her efforts in the Super Tuesday states, donations on her website rose. Of the $36 million she raised in February, $30 million came from online donors, including gifts received from 200,000 new contributors.[58] More than half of this total came from individuals who gave $200 or less.[59]

Thereafter Clinton continued to rely on the Internet for much needed cash and her victories in key primaries helped to spur donations. For example, within twenty-four hours of her victory in Pennsylvania's April 22 primary, more than 100,000 supporters gave a total of $10 million, which represented her best fund-raising day of the campaign.[60] That a candidate could raise so notable a sum in one day was yet another indication of how greatly the scope of fund-raising had changed as a result of digital communications. Yet, it was not enough to keep pace with Obama.

In 2000, John McCain "put the Web on the political map,"[61] when thousands of his supporters made contributions through his website after his unexpected victory over George Bush in the New Hampshire primary. In the weeks after this win, McCain received $3.7 million through his website, primarily in small individual contributions, which provided him with the funds needed to compete in a number of early March primaries.[62] But in 2008, online contributions played relatively little role in the Republican race.

The McCain campaign understood the value of the Internet as a fund-raising tool. McCain had a website with basic fund-raising tools, linked to Facebook and other social networks, and purchased online ads in an effort to drive Internet users to his site. As Google political ad man Peter Greenberger noted in referring to McCain's fund-raising ebb in mid-2007, "Even in the darkest days of the campaign . . . they never stopped spending on Google AdWords. There were times, corresponding to the political polls, when maybe interest waned in his campaign, but he was ready to capture interest."[63]

McCain's financing did improve after his victory in New Hampshire, and in January he raised $12.7 million. Yet he continued to fall behind Romney, who took in $16.7 million in January, a sum which included almost $7 million of his own money.[64] How much of McCain's January take came from online sources was not disclosed by the campaign. What was apparent throughout the early primary voting was that McCain failed to stimulate the levels of enthusiasm among his supporters that translated into a steady flow of contributions or sizable surges in small donor support. It was not until well after he had wrapped up the nomination that he began to receive substantial sums online and from small contributions. Most of the money he received from small contributions came in after Obama decided to forgo general election public funding and the fall campaigning had essentially begun. In fact, about a third of the money McCain received from small contributions ($19.3 million) was received in August, spurred in part by a rise in contributions received in the days following the announcement of Sarah Palin as his choice for vice president.[65]

One Republican who did raise substantial sums primarily from online supporters was the insurgent challenger, Ron Paul. Although a long shot for the nomination, Paul was able to use the Internet to garner contributions from individuals throughout the country, just as Dean did in his insurgent campaign in 2004. One tactic that produced a significant share of his campaign money was the use of symbolic dates as online fund-raising events. He received $4.3 million on November 5, 2007, the anniversary of the day in British history that Guy Fawkes tried to blow up the British Parliament. Another $6 million was garnered on December 16, the anniversary of the Boston Tea Party.[66] In all, Paul raised $34.5 million, including $21.6 million from small contributions, which was double the amount received by any other Republican contender except for McCain. Even so, Paul's standing in the polls remained low and he never become a serious contender for the nomination.

Large Donor Fund-Raising in 2008

The Obama campaign established a new fund-raising model, one that combined the lessons of the Dean campaign with more traditional approaches. What distinguished Obama's efforts was the extent to which Web 2.0 applications were incorporated into the campaign and the scope of small donor participation he achieved as a result. Yet Obama did not forsake the types of fund-raising events and emphasis on large donors that is typical of presidential campaigns, as reflected in the fund-raising activities of most of the 2008 contenders. Obama's financial strategy thus can best be described as a "hybrid approach," one made possible by technology but still reliant on common fund-raising methods.

In recent elections the best-financed presidential contenders usually have raised a major share of their campaign monies from individuals who gave large contributions, understood as donations of $1,000 or more. Candidates, especially those expected to be front-runners, have a strong incentive to raise large amounts of money and the conventional wisdom among candidates has been that the best way to accomplish this strategic objective is to concentrate on large donations, particularly contributions of the maximum permissible amount. Candidates also seek large contributions because it is the most efficient way to maximize the financial potential of their core supporters, especially early in a race when many challengers are not well known and the public is not yet focused on the election.

In this regard, the 2008 nominations largely followed the patterns of the past. With the exception of Obama, the top fund-raisers received a majority of their campaign funds from large donations. One way to assess the relative role of large donors is to look at the aggregate amount contributed by an individual, rather than individual contributions. Many individuals make more than one contribution during the course of a campaign, so the amount an individual gives in total can differ from the amount of an individual donation. Indeed, this ability to solicit additional contributions was one of the major advantages afforded by Web-based fund-raising. For example, many of Obama's supporters who began by making a small contribution gave repeatedly during the campaign, eventually giving more than the $200 in aggregate that is typically used as a measure for determining a small donor. In fact, according to an analysis by the Campaign Finance Institute, at least 212,000 individuals who initially made a contribution of less than $200 to Obama eventually gave much more, including 13,000 who donated a total of $1,000 or more by the time of the convention.[67]

The role of large donors can be discerned from Table 2.2, which presents data from an analysis conducted by the Campaign Finance Institute on individual contributions in the 2008 nomination campaigns based on the aggregate amounts contributed by donors.[68] In all, 53 percent of the monies given by individuals came from those who gave at least $1,000. Except for Obama, the best-funded candidates received a majority of their individual receipts as a result of the largesse of large donors. Clinton received about $108 million from large donors, which constituted 56 percent of the amount contributed by individuals to her campaign. McCain received $121 million, which represented 60 percent of his total individual receipts. Romney and Giuliani raised even bigger shares of their individual contributions from large donors, with respective shares of 79 percent and 83 percent.

Although Obama received a smaller share of his funding from large donors (43 percent), he raised more money than any other candidate from such contributions. Indeed, his fund-raising was so impressive because of the success he exhibited across the donor spectrum. While he made the Internet a central building block of his campaign, he did not overlook traditional fund-raising techniques geared to soliciting large donors. The Obama campaign held 104 fund-raising events during the primary period and 19 more during the bridge period, ranging from large-scale dinners to small, intimate meetings with high-level donors.[69] In total, he raised $174 million from donors who gave $1,000 or more, almost $67 million more than the sum achieved by Clinton.

Most of these large contributions were solicited with the assistance of "bundlers," a term used to refer to individuals who serve as volunteer

Table 2.2. Source of Individual Contributions to Presidential Candidates, 2008

		Aggregate Amount Contributed by Donor					
		$200 or Less		*$201–999*		*$1000 or More*	
Candidates	*Total Individual Contributions*	*Dollar Amount*	*%*	*Dollar Amount*	*%*	*Dollar Amount*	*%*
Democrat							
Obama	409.2	121.2	30	113.1	28	174.4	43
Clinton	194.0	42.5	22	43.8	23	107.7	56
Edwards	38.6	11.8	31	8.5	22	18.3	47
Richardson	21.8	3.5	16	4.0	18	14.3	66
Dodd	11.8	1.0	8	0.9	8	9.8	83
Biden	9.6	1.6	17	1.3	14	6.7	70
Kucinich	4.4	2.5	57	1.1	25	0.8	18
Gravel	0.5	0.3	60	0.1	20	0.1	20
Sub-Total:	689.9	184.4	27	172.8	25	332.1	48
Republican							
McCain	203.5	42.2	21	40.2	20	121.2	60
Romney	59.8	4.7	8	7.9	13	47.1	79
Giuliani	55.0	3.5	6	5.6	10	45.9	83
Paul	34.3	13.4	39	9.6	28	11.3	33
Thompson, F.	23.2	8.9	38	4.1	18	10.1	44
Huckabee	16.0	4.6	29	3.7	23	7.7	48
Tancredo	4.0	2.2	55	1.1	28	0.7	18
Brownback	3.5	1.2	34	0.8	23	1.5	43
Hunter	2.3	1.1	48	0.4	17	0.8	35
Thompson, T.	1.0	0.1	7	0.1	10	0.7	70
Gilmore	0.3	0.0	10	0.0	7	0.3	100
Sub-Total:	402.9	81.9	20	73.5	18	247.3	61
Total:	**1092.8**	**266.3**	**24**	**246.3**	**23**	**579.4**	**53**

Source: Campaign Finance Institute. Amounts noted in millions of dollars.

fund-raisers and gather numerous large dollar checks on behalf of a candidate. These individuals "bundle" together checks they have received—often for the maximum $2,300—and deliver them or direct them to the candidate. This is usually done by selling tickets to fund-raising dinners, sponsoring fund-raising events, or simply soliciting donations from their own fund-raising networks and business associates.

The reliance on bundlers was not a new development. Since the early 1980s, candidates have relied on such individuals, often naming their top fund-raisers as members of their "finance committee," "business council," or a group given some other designation. But bundlers became more prominent in recent elections, particularly due to their role in the Bush campaigns and the voluntary disclosure of his "Rangers" and "Pioneers," the nomenclature given to those who raised at least $100,000 or $200,000 for his campaign.

In 2008 the top contenders relied on bundlers to help them gather the large sums of money that they were seeking. Those whose names were disclosed by the campaigns were primarily involved in securities and investments, real estate, lobbying, law firms, or the entertainment industry. Based on the disclosures made by the Obama and McCain campaigns, the nonpartisan Center for Responsive Politics determined that Obama had recruited at least 509 bundlers as of August 2008 who had raised a minimum of $63 million, while McCain had recruited 534 bundlers who brought in at least $75 million. The top bundlers each raised at least $500,000, a level met by 47 of Obama's supporters and 65 of McCain's.[70] However, the Center estimated the total amounts raised by these bundlers based on the fund-raising threshold each individual had achieved (e.g., $100,000 or $250,000), not the actual amount they may have raised (e.g., $120,000 or $270,000). Consequently, the totals reported represent conservative or minimum sums.

The Center for Responsive Politics' study did not include Clinton, but she also recruited a significant number of bundlers. In all, at least 311 individuals qualified as "Hillraisers," with each raising at least $100,000 for her campaign.[71] These bundlers thus gathered a minimum of $31 million and, more realistically, much more.

Table 2.2 also indicates the role of small donors in 2008. In this regard, Obama's overwhelming advantage is readily apparent. Obama received $121 million from individuals who gave a total of $200 or less, which was more than the rest of the Democratic field combined and almost $80 million more than the $42 million received from small donors by Clinton or the $42 million received by McCain. Obama thus raised a larger share of his prenomination monies from small donors than either Bush (26 percent, $66 million) or Kerry (20 percent, $44 million) did in 2004. Dean took in 38 percent of his individual funding from small donors in 2004, but the total amount received, $28 million, paled in comparison to Obama's total.[72] No matter the level of donor involved, Obama set new standards for presidential nomination finance.[73]

LOOKING AHEAD TO 2012

The 2008 nominations took place in a context that promoted an intensive chase for campaign dollars, which produced high spending on both sides of the aisle. But the outcomes offered mixed signals concerning the role of money in election victories. On the Democratic side, the race followed the patterns of the past and conformed to the view that money is a key determinant of nomination outcomes. The challengers with the biggest war chests broke away from the rest of the field and the eventual winner was the candidate who raised the most money. Obama was able to wage a better-funded, more extensive campaign and held a major financial advantage at crucial stages in the contest. In fact, he attained the biggest financial advantage over his principal opponent of any presidential candidate since the adoption of the FECA in 1974.

However, the results of the Republican contest indicated that money is not the most important factor in determining election outcomes. The top fund-raisers faltered once the voting began. Mike Huckabee won Iowa, even though he trailed far behind in the money race and only raised $16 million in his entire campaign. John McCain, who began as an expected front-runner and fell to so low a point that he had to borrow money from a bank to get through the New Hampshire primary, resurrected his campaign by winning that state, even though he was outspent significantly by Mitt Romney, who had once served as governor of the neighboring state of Massachusetts. Giuliani raised $59 million, an impressive sum, but his campaign never gained traction. His decision to focus his efforts on one of the first big states to vote, Florida, instead of Iowa and New Hampshire, proved to be the path to a quick exit from the race. In the end, Huckabee was one of the last candidates standing and McCain clinched the nomination despite Romney's $40 million-plus financial advantage.

One lesson of 2008 is that money can help establish a candidate's viability and front-runner status early in a race, and can play a crucial role in helping a candidate survive the rigors of the front-loaded presidential selection process. But a candidate with major weaknesses or one who does not excite a following of passionate supporters cannot resolve these problems by simply spending money. As Howard Dean demonstrated in 2004, fund-raising success, in and of itself, is not enough to guarantee victory. Nomination contests are political contests; the politics of the process, a candidate's ability to secure political endorsements and voter support, and the strategic decisions made in a campaign often matter more than money.[74]

Future aspirants, however, are unlikely to pursue strategies based on the outcome of the 2008 Republican primaries. To the extent that they do take something away from the 2008 Republican experience, it will be to question McCain's decision to accept public funding in the general election and thereby cede a significant financial advantage to his opponent. Obama demonstrated that it is possible to finance a primary and general election without public money and by doing so, raise significantly more money than public funding provides. His approach will dictate the strategic thinking in 2012, making it a virtual certainty that the Republican nominee will not only forgo public funds in the primaries, but also in the general election. If so, the 2012 race will sound the death knell of public funding in presidential elections.

The Obama campaign now stands as the new model of presidential campaign finance. Candidates will seek to emulate his tactics, hoping to use the Internet as a means of building extensive bases of support and thereby gain a financial advantage over their opponents. In this regard, they will be aided by the further evolution of technology and the continuing spread of broadband, smart phones, tablets, and other devices throughout the electorate. The 2012 election will take place in a more dynamic, distributed, and mobile communications environment. This will make it possible for candidates to reach large numbers of prospective voters in interactive ways and enhance their capacity to capitalize on popular support.

The availability of more powerful communications technology will further aid popular front-runners in their quest to raise funds, since individuals who wish to make a contribution will find it easier than ever before, no matter where they are physically located. Insurgent candidates, those outside the party establishments, who rely on clear ideological or issue appeals, nontraditional election tactics, or unorthodox views, will also benefit. As John Green and Diana Kingsbury have noted, a major challenge for candidates who pursue these "outside strategies" is finding and tapping new sources of money.[75] Dean's outsider candidacy in 2004 and Paul's in 2008, although conducted in different parties and appealing to opposite ends of the political spectrum, indicate that outsiders who offer a message that resonates with even a small share of the electorate may raise substantial amounts of money.

But the availability of technology alone does not mean that candidates will succeed in raising large sums online or experience the levels of success that Obama achieved in 2008. Individuals still need to have the motivation to give and certain dimensions of Obama's 2008 candidacy will be difficult to replicate. He began as a charismatic and inspiring underdog, seeking to make history as the first African-American president. He emerged as the candidate representing change, in an election defined by an electorate anxious for change. He embraced new technologies, and stimulated the passions of a new generation of young activists and voters who made his candidacy their own. His campaign capitalized on an extraordinary level of voter enthusiasm and engagement, which was a key element in the scope of his financial success. Future candidates will attempt to engage voters in their campaigns in ways similar to those employed by Obama. If they do so successfully, they too should be able to tap into the resources that can come from broad-based giving online.

The political context of the 2012 race will differ from that of 2008. An incumbent president will be seeking reelection and his opponents can expect that he will run without public money. President Obama will begin his quest for reelection with an unparalleled base of potential donors. By the end of 2008,

Obama had received contributions from 4 million individuals and constructed a list of 13 million email addresses.[76] After the election, Obama sought to maintain communications with these supporters by converting his campaign organization into "Organizing for America," which was established as a "special project" of the Democratic National Committee.[77] This organization, which maintained the My.BarackObama.com website, remained active throughout Obama's first term, distributing information on administration policies, building grassroots support for policy initiatives, recruiting organizers in the fifty states, offering volunteer training, and raising money. Although this organization did not prove to be the grassroots-lobbying powerhouse that some expected at the beginning of Obama's term, it nonetheless provided an infrastructure for keeping in touch and updating information on his core supporters.[78]

Prior to the start of the 2012 nomination campaigns, political observers were predicting that Obama might raise the previously unthinkable sum of one billion dollars in his bid for reelection.[79] Should he approach this lofty mark, it is a virtual certainty that all of the candidates will again be chasing Obama in the race for campaign dollars. Obama will benefit from the power of incumbency and the advantage of a well-established donor base. But he will also be facing a weak economy and a nomination process that in all likelihood will not feature an unusually competitive, dramatic battle for the party standard and the high level of partisan interest that characterized the 2008 contest.

Given the dynamics of presidential fund-raising in a post-public funding environment, Obama—or any other future incumbent with a strong base of political support—will begin the race in an enviable position. Although an incumbent advantage is not a new aspect of campaign finance, in a world without spending limits an incumbent can better capitalize on the opportunity to raise money more efficiently and start general election fund-raising earlier in the election cycle. The individual contribution limit in 2012 is set at $2,500 per election ($200 more than in 2008), which means that a candidate can receive a maximum of $5,000 from an individual donor.[80] A candidate may begin soliciting these maximum donations from the start of the campaign, raising primary election funds at the same time that general election funds are solicited. For example, fund-raising events may be held at which individuals are asked to give $5,000, including $2,500 for the primary and $2,500 for the general election. In this way, a candidate—or a candidate's bundlers—can raise large sums quickly and efficiently. While any candidate may engage in this practice, it is easier for an unchallenged incumbent or an individual who has quickly wrapped up a nomination to do so, since candidates engaged in a competitive nomination contest must be cognizant of the possibility that an early start to general election fund-raising may be perceived by voters as a sign of overconfidence or as an act indicative of a lack of respect for other party hopefuls.

Moreover, any monies left over in a candidate's primary campaign account at the time of the nominating convention can be spent in the general election campaign, since there are no limits on spending. In 2008, Obama raised more than $40 million in general election money during the nomination period and had more than $35 million in unspent primary money at the time the delegates cast their votes in convention and formally chose him as the party's nominee. Thus, he began his 2008 general election campaign with $77 million in cash, a sum that was almost equivalent to the $84 million public grant accepted by McCain.[81]

The return to private financing of presidential campaigns may therefore serve to enhance the advantages an incumbent or unchallenged aspirant for the nomination has with respect to campaign funding. Such a contender can spend unlimited amounts of money during the prenomination period on activities largely designed to get a head start on general election campaigning or build up large reservoirs of cash for use in the fall election while continuing to raise and spend primary funds. Such activity will drive campaign fund-raising and place additional pressures on candidates involved in competitive nomination contests to raise funds, especially in the bridge period before the formal commencement of the general election period.

Another change taking place in the campaign finance system may also serve to spur an emphasis on fund-raising. In recent elections, organized groups have spent significant sums to influence the White House race, including a rising amount of money expended during the primaries. These groups include PACs, Section 527 committees (political organizations established under Section 527 of the Internal Revenue Code whose major purpose is to influence elections), and nonprofit advocacy groups (organizations established under Section 501(c) of the Internal Revenue Code whose major purpose is to promote policy ideas or educate the public on policy issues). Not all of the monies spent by these groups are subject to federal disclosure rules or contribution limits. Groups do, however, have to disclose the amounts they spend on certain types or categories of spending, such as the amounts spent on broadcast advertisements that expressly support a candidate or ads that feature a federal candidate and are aired close to an election.[82] The ability of most groups to operate outside of the confines of federal contribution restrictions and the amounts they have disclosed in recent elections suggest that group spending is becoming a more prominent component of the financial activity that takes place in nominating contests.

In 2004, organized groups reported $61 million in disclosed spending on the presidential race during the nomination phase of the election. More than two-thirds of this total ($47 million) was disbursed after the nominations had been clinched, with most of this amount spent by pro-Democratic political committees opposing President Bush's reelection.[83] In 2008, prenomination spending by organized groups totaled at least $79 million, with most of this amount ($51 million) spent during the primaries, rather than during the bridge period.[84] Much of the spending in 2008 was focused on the Democratic contest. Groups spent at least $15 million in support of Obama and $3 million against him, as well as $22 million in support of Clinton and almost $2 million against her. During the bridge period, political organizations spent more than $10 million opposing Obama and more than $10 million supporting him, while spending more than $6 million opposing McCain and more than $1 million supporting him.[85]

In 2012, interest groups and nonparty organizations will be able to finance election activity free of many of the constraints that governed their activity in the past as a result of court rulings issued after the 2008 election. The most important was the Supreme Court's decision in *Citizens United* v. *Federal Election Commission*, which led to a major change in federal campaign finance law.[86] Citizens United, a conservative nonprofit advocacy group, produced a feature-length film, *Hillary: The Movie*, to be distributed in theaters, as a DVD, and through a video-on-demand cable service in January and early February 2008. The group wanted to use its own funds, including corporate contributions, to finance the advertising and distribution of the film. This raised the question of whether *Hillary* should be viewed as an election communication that opposed Hillary Clinton, who at the time was a candidate for the presidential nomination. In a highly controversial decision released in January 2010, the Supreme Court in a five-to-four vote ruled that a ban on the spending of corporate money for independent communications that advocated the election or defeat of a candidate violated the First Amendment's right of free speech. The Court did not overturn federal contribution restrictions or the prohibition on the use of corporate or labor union treasury funds to make contributions to federal candidates or party committees. But the Court did strike down the long-standing ban on corporate spending in federal elections and the BCRA provisions that prohibited corporate or labor treasury monies from being used to pay for electioneering communications. If corporations or labor unions wanted to spend their own monies independent of a candidate on election communications or other activities that advocated the election or defeat of a particular candidate, the Court declared that they had a right to do so. In the view of the Court's majority, the First Amendment did not allow restrictions on speech based on the identity of the speaker. Thus, government regulations could not privilege some viewpoints or speakers (for example, individuals or PACs) over others (for example, corporations) since this "deprives the public of the right and privilege to determine for itself what speech and speakers are worthy of consideration."[87]

Following the decision in *Citizens United*, the U.S. Court of Appeals for the District of Columbia issued an opinion in March 2010 in *SpeechNow.org* v. *Federal Election Commission*.[88] SpeechNow.org, a nonprofit, unincorporated political organization established under Section 527 of the Internal Revenue Code, was formed by individuals who wanted to make independent expenditures in support of candidates. The group did not intend to make contributions to candidates and therefore turned to the courts to determine whether they would have to abide by the limits and other requirements imposed on contributions to PACs under federal law. SpeechNow.org argued that they should not be required to register as a political committee with the FEC and thus be limited to raising individual contributions of $5,000 per year (the limit established for federal PACs under the FECA). They contended that independent expenditures did not pose a risk of corruption, which prior court rulings had established as the sole constitutional rationale for regulating campaign funding, since no monies would be given to candidates. Citing the Supreme Court's analysis in *Citizens United*, the appeals court agreed, noting that there was no government interest in regulating the contributions made to independent expenditure groups.

Thus, organizations now have broader leeway to raise and spend money in presidential campaigns. As in the past, federal PACs are limited in the amount of money they can contribute directly to a candidate or party, but they may spend unlimited amounts from the monies they raise on independent efforts to promote or support candidates. Other organizations, including 527s, corporations, nonprofit groups, and labor unions, can raise and spend money in unlimited amounts, including funds from sources prohibited from making contributions to candidates or national party committees, such as corporations and labor unions. In the past, interest groups and other organizations could spend such funds on activity that was not considered election activity, such as issue advertisements or broadcast communications that were aired more than 30 days before a primary. Now they may spend these funds specifically advocating the election or defeat of a candidate without restriction, so long as they do not coordinate their efforts with the candidate.

As a result of these judicial rulings, nonparty political organizations will have greater opportunities to raise and spend money than they have had in the past. To note but one example that reflects the changes taking place in the regulatory environment, two conservative organizations, American Crossroads and Crossroads GPS, announced more than a year before the 2012 election a fund-raising goal of $120 million to finance efforts to defeat President Obama and elect Republicans to Congress.[89] If other organizations follow suit, group electioneering is certain to rise, which in turn will influence candidate fund-raising, as contenders pursue the dollars needed to defend themselves against such efforts, as well as the efforts of their opponents.

Presidential campaign finance is in the midst of a period of dramatic change. The 2008 election demonstrated the transformative effects of the changes underway. The financing of the 2012 campaigns will be shaped by the experience of 2008 and the strategies and innovations likely to arise from a heightened demand for campaign dollars. The continuing evolution of digital communications and a less stringent regulatory framework will also have significant effects on the financial activity in 2012. The consequences of these developments are not easy to predict, but they raise a central question: how will this affect the sources of funding in presidential campaigns? Does the experience of Obama in 2008 suggest that small donors will play a greater role in the financing of future campaigns? Or will large donors and groups relying on unregulated contributions continue to be a major source of money in presidential elections? Political observers will be looking to the 2012 election for answers.

ACKNOWLEDGMENT

Andrew Wade of Colby College assisted in the research and preparation of this chapter.

NOTES

1. According to Federal Election Commission (FEC) data, Democratic and Republican candidates in the 2004 prenomination contests raised a total of $678 million. In 2000, the total was $329 million.

2. In the 2004 election, President Bush raised $356.4 million, including $74.6 million of general election public funding. John Kerry raised $318.1 million, including $74.6 million in general election public funding. See FEC, "2004 Presidential Campaign Financial Activity Summarized," press release, February 3, 2005, Table: Overview of Presidential Financial Activity 1996–2008, www.fec.gov/press/press2009/20090608Pres/1_OverviewPresFinActivity1996–2008.pdf (accessed February 27, 2011).

3. Eliza Newlin Carney, "The Death of Public Financing," *National Journal*, June 16, 2007, 34.

4. The totals for the presidential prenomination campaign receipts as of December 31, 2003 can be found on the FEC website at http://www.fec.gov/press/bkgnd/pres_cf/atm1231/presreceiptsye2003.pdf (accessed February 27, 2011).

5. Carney, "The Death of Public Financing," 34.

6. For a detailed discussion of the provisions of the presidential public funding program, see Anthony Corrado, "Public Funding of Presidential Campaigns," in Anthony Corrado et al., *The New Campaign Finance Sourcebook* (Washington, DC: Brookings Institution Press, 2005), 180–204.

7. Anthony Corrado, *Paying for Presidents* (New York: The Twentieth Century Fund Press, 1993), 40–41.

8. David B. Magleby and William G. Mayer, "Presidential Nomination Finance in the Post-BCRA Era," in William G. Mayer, *The Making of the Presidential Candidates 2008* (Lanham, MD: Rowman & Littlefield, 2008), 149–152.

9. Ibid., 152; and Anthony Corrado, "Financing the 1996 Elections," in Gerald M. Pomper et al., *The Election of 1996* (Chatham, NJ: Chatham House Publishers, 1997), 145.

10. Prior to 2000, Republican John Connally in 1980 opted out of public funding in order to avoid the spending limit in New Hampshire. In 1996, three Republicans, Malcolm "Steve" Forbes, Maurice Taylor, and Robert Dornan did not take public funds. Forbes and Taylor financed their campaigns primarily from personal funds. In 2000, Forbes again refused public funds and once again spent substantial sums of his own money on his campaign. Republican Orrin Hatch also did not accept public funds in 2000.

11. Anthony Corrado, "Financing the 2000 Elections," in Gerald M. Pomper et al., *The Election of 2000* (New York: Chatham House Publishers, 2001), 105.

12. John C. Green, "Financing the 2004 Presidential Nomination Campaigns," in David B. Magleby et al., *Financing the 2004 Election* (Washington, DC: Brookings Institution Press, 2006), 115.

13. Ibid., 105 and 116–117.

14. FEC, "2004 Presidential Campaign Financial Activity Summarized," www.fec.gov/press/press2005/20050203pressum/20050203pressum.html (accessed February 28, 2011).

15. Jeff Zeleny and Patrick Healy, "Obama Shows His Strength in a Fund-Raising Feat on Par with Clinton," *New York Times*, April 5, 2007; and "Fix Federal Aid for Presidential Races," *Christian Science Monitor*, editorial, January 26, 2007.

16. FEC, "FEC Approves Matching Funds for 2008 Presidential Candidates," press release, January 23, 2009, www.fec.gov/press/press2009/20090123Matching.shtml (accessed February 28, 2011).

17. Ibid. Besides Edwards, the other Democrats who received matching funds (and the amount each received) were Joseph Biden ($2 million), Christopher Dodd ($1.9 million), Dennis Kucinich ($1.1 million), and Mike Gravel ($216,000). Two Republicans also took matching funds: Tom Tancredo ($2.2 million) and Duncan Hunter ($454,000).

18. For a detailed discussion of the front-loading phenomenon, see William G. Mayer and Andrew E. Busch, *The Front-Loading Problem in Presidential Nominations* (Washington, DC: Brookings Institution Press, 2004).

19. Tad Devine, "Obama Wins the Nomination: How He Did It," in Dennis W. Johnson, *Campaigning for President 2008* (New York: Routledge, 2009), 32.

20. Rachel Kapochunas and Marie Horrigan, "Primary Shift Could Mean Christmas on Campaign Trail for White House Hopefuls," *CQPolitics.com*, August 9, 2007; and Kristin Jensen, "Primary Shifts Complicate Leading Candidates' Plans," *Bloomberg.com*, August 9, 2007, www.bloomberg.com/apps/news?pid=newsarchive&sid=a_F6pDONxt8g&refer=home (accessed March 2, 2011).

21. Barack Obama, *Dreams of My Father* (New York: Three Rivers Press, 1995); and Obama, *The Audacity of Hope* (New York: Crown, 2006).

22. This section draws on the discussion found in Anthony Corrado, "The Obama Campaign Revolution: Presidential Electioneering in the Digital Age," in Carol McNamara and Melanie M. Marlowe, eds., *The Obama Presidency in the Constitutional Order* (Lanham, MD: Rowman & Littlefield, 2011), 4–6.

23. John Allen Hendricks and Robert E. Denton, Jr., "Political Campaigns and Communicating with the Electorate in the Twenty-First Century," in John Allen Hendricks and Robert E. Denton, Jr., eds., *Communicator-in-Chief* (Lanham, MD: Rowman & Littlefield, 2010), 3.

24. Michael Cornfield, *The Internet and Campaign 2004: A Look Back at the Campaigners*, Pew Internet and American Life Project, Commentary, www.pewinternet.org/~/media/Files/Reports/2005/Cornfield_commentary.pdf.pdf (acccessed May 28, 2010), and Joe Trippi, *The Revolution Will Not Be Televised* (New York: Regan Books, 2004).

25. David Talbot, "The Geeks Behind Obama's Web Strategy," *Boston Globe*, January 8, 2009, www.boston.com/news/politics/2008/articles/2009/01/08/the_geeks_behind_obamas_web_strategy/ (accessed May 28, 2010); and Green, "Financing the 2004 Presidential Nomination Campaigns," 100.

26. Trippi, *The Revolution Will Not Be Televised*, 88.

27. Green, "Financing the 2004 Presidential Nomination Campaigns," 100; and Melissa Smith, "Political Campaigns in the Twenty-First Century: Implications of New Technology," in *Communicator-in-Chief*, 142.

28. John F. Harris and Jonathan Martin, "The George W. Bush and Bill Clinton Legacies in the 2008 Elections," in Janet M. Box-Steffensmeier and Steven E. Schneider, eds., *The American Elections of 2008* (Lanham, MD: Rowman & Littlefield, 2009), 7–8.

29. Jenn Burleson McKay, "Gadgets, Gismos, and the Web 2.0 Election," in *Communicator-in-Chief*, 23–24.

30. "MySpace," www.crunchbase.com/company/myspace (accessed June 2, 2010).

31. Steven Levy, "Facebook Grows Up," *Newsweek*, August 20 and 27, 2007, 44.

32. Jody C. Baumgartner and Jonathan S. Morris, "Who Wants to Be My Friend? Obama, Youth, and Social Networks in the 2008 Campaign," in *Communicator-in-Chief*, 54.

33. Hendricks and Denton, "Political Campaigns and Communicating with the Electorate," 9.

34. Larry Powell, "Obama and Obama Girl: YouTube, Viral Videos, and the 2008 Presidential Campaign," in *Communicator-in-Chief*, 84.

35. Frederic I. Solop, "'RT @BarackObama We Just Made History': Twitter and the 2008 Presidential Election," in *Communicator-in-Chief*, 38 and 40.

36. John Horrigan, *Home Broadband 2008*, Pew Internet and American Life Project, July 2, 2008, www.pewinternet.org/Reports/2008/Home-Broadband-2008.aspx (accessed March 8, 2011).

37. Susannah Fox, *Privacy Implications of Fast, Mobile Internet Access*, Pew Internet and American Life Project, March 5, 2008, www.pewinternet.org/Reports/2008/Privacy-Implications-of-Fast-Mobile-Internet-Access.aspx (accessed March 8, 2011).

38. Green, "Financing the 2004 Presidential Nomination Campaigns," 100.

39. Michael Luo and Jeff Zeleny, "Obama, in Shift, Says He'll Reject Public Financing," *New York Times*, June 20, 2008. In response to an advisory opinion request submitted to the FEC by the Obama campaign in 2007, presidential candidates were allowed to solicit and receive private contributions for use in the general election during the prenomination period, yet retain the option of accepting public funding in the general election. If a candidate did decide to accept public funding, these general election donations would have to be returned to the donor or designated for some other permissible purpose, such as being used to finance a candidate's general election legal, accounting, and compliance costs. See FEC, Advisory Opinion 2007–3, March 1, 2007.

40. Quoted in Adam Nagourney, "Romney Makes It Official and Asks for '08 Cash in a Big Way," *New York Times*, January 9, 2007.

41. Campaign Finance Institute, "Big, $1,000+ Donations Supply 79% of Presidential Candidates' Early Money," press release, April 16, 2007, www.cfinst.org/Press/PReleases/07-04-16/Big_Donations_Supply_79_of_Presidential_Early_Money.aspx (accessed March 10, 2011).

42. Campaign Finance Institute, "Presidential Fund-raising in 2007 Doubles 2003," press release, February 11, 2008, www.cfinst.org/Press/PReleases/08-02-11/Presidential_Fund-raising_in_2007_Doubles_2003.aspx (accessed March 10, 2011).

43. Ibid.

44. Jeff Zeleny and Patrick Healy, "Obama Shows His Strength in a Fund-raising Feat on Par with Clinton," *New York Times*, April 5, 2007.

45. Unless otherwise noted, the discussion of 2007 year-end fund-raising totals that follows is based on the data contained in this Campaign Finance Institute release cited in note 42 above.

46. Quoted in Brian Stelter, "The Facebooker Who Friended Obama," *New York Times*, July 7, 2008.

47. David Plouffe, *The Audacity to Win* (New York: Viking, 2009), 21.

48. The description of Obama's Web operations in this section is based on the description found in Corrado, "The Obama Campaign Revolution," 6–8 and 11–12.

49. Jose Antonio Vargas, "Obama Raised Half a Billion Online," washingtonpost.com, November 20, 2008, voices.washingtonpost.com/the-trail/2008/11/20/obama_raised_half_a_billion_on.html (accessed March 9, 2009).

50. Baumgartner and Morris, "Who Wants to Be My Friend?" 58.

51. Kate Kaye, *Campaign '08: A Turning Point for Digital Media* (n.p.: Kate Kaye, 2009), 20.

52. Vargas, "Obama Raised Half a Billion Online."

53. Michael Luo, "Small Donations Add Up for Obama," *New York Times*, February 20, 2008.

54. Jeff Zeleny and Katharine Q. Seelye, "More Money Is Pouring in for Clinton and Obama," *New York Times*, March 7, 2008.

55. Anthony Corrado, "Fund-Raising Strategies in the 2008 Presidential Campaign," in James A. Thurber and Candice J. Nelson, eds., *Campaigns and Elections American Style*, 3rd ed. (Boulder, CO: Westview Press, 2010), 116.

56. Foon Rhee, "Obama Reaches 2 Million Donors," *Boston Globe*, August 14, 2008, www.boston.com/news/politics/politicalintelligence/2008/08/obama_reaches_2.html (accessed June 3, 2010).

57. TNS Media Intelligence/CMAG and Wisconsin Advertising Project, "Nearly $200 Million Spent on Presidential Campaign TV Ads to Date," press release, June 2, 2008, http://wiscadproject.wisc.edu/wiscads_pressrelease_060208.pdf (accessed March 11, 2011). All figures cited in this section are from this source.

58. Corrado, "Fund-Raising Strategies in the 2008 Presidential Campaign," 119.

59. Ibid.

60. Fredreka Schouten, "Small Amounts Add Up for Candidates," *USA Today*, May 2, 2008.

61. Kaye, *Campaign '08*, 1.

62. Anthony Corrado and Heitor Gouvea, "Financing Presidential Nominations Under the BCRA," in William G. Mayer, ed., *The Making of the Presidential Candidates 2004* (Lanham, MD: Rowman & Littlefield, 2004), 61.

63. Quoted in Kaye, *Campaign '08*, 78.

64. John C. Green and Diana Kingsbury, "Financing the 2008 Presidential Nomination Campaigns," in David B. Magleby and Anthony Corrado, eds., *Financing the 2008 Election* (Washington, DC: Brookings Institution Press, 2011), 116.

65. Small contributions figure based on the unitemized contributions reported in McCain's August monthly FEC report. See also Kaye, *Campaign '08*, 78–79.

66. Stephen J. Wayne, "When Democracy Works: The 2008 Presidential Nominations," in William J. Crotty, ed., *Winning the Presidency 2008* (Boulder, CO: Paradigm Publishers, 2009), 59–60.

67. Campaign Finance Institute, "Reality Check: Obama Received About the Same Percentage from Small Donors in 2008 as Bush in 2004," press release, November 24, 2008, www.cfinst.org/Press/Releases_tags/08-11-24/Realty_Check_-_Obama_Small_Donors.aspx (accessed March 13, 2011).

68. Campaign Finance Institute, "All CFI Funding Statistics Revised and Updated for the 2008 Presidential Primary and General Election Candidates," press

release, January 8, 2010, www.cfinst.org/Press/Releases_tags/10-01-08/Revised_and_Updated_2008_Presidential_Statistics.aspx (accessed March 13, 2011).

69. Green and Kingsbury, "Financing the 2008 Presidential Nominations," 99.

70. Cited in Corrado, "Fund-Raising Strategies in the 2008 Presidential Campaign," 122–123.

71. Seth Colter Walls, "Hillraisers Donated Less Than $20,000 to Obama in June," *Huffington Post*, July 21, 2008, www.huffingtonpost.com/2008/07/21/hillraisers-donated-less_n_114100.html (accessed March 13, 2011).

72. Campaign Finance Institute, "All CFI Statistics Revised and Updated."

73. Obama raised $113 million from individuals who gave an aggregate donation of $201–999, as compared to $43.8 million for Clinton and $40.2 million for McCain. In 2004, Bush received $37.7 million from donors in this range, while Kerry received $51.5 million. Ibid.

74. On this point, see Marty Cohen, David Karol, Hans Noel, and John Zaller, "The Invisible Primary in Presidential Nominations, 1980–2004," in Mayer, ed., *The Making of the Presidential Candidates 2008*, 1–38.

75. Green and Kingsbury, "Financing the 2008 Presidential Nomination Campaigns," 91.

76. David Plouffe quoted in the Institute of Politics, John F. Kennedy School of Government, Harvard University, *Campaign for President: The Managers Look at 2008* (Lanham, MD: Rowman & Littlefield, 2009), 181; and Vargas, "Obama Raised Half a Billion Online."

77. Chris Cillizza, "Obama Announces 'Organizing for America,'" *The Fix* Weblog, entry posted January 17, 2009, voices.washingtonpost.com/thefix/white-house/obama-announces-organizing-for.html (accessed June 4, 2010).

78. See, for example, Micah Sifry, "Section I: Year One of Organizing for America: The Permanent Field Campaign in a Digital Age," www.techpresident.com/ofayear1/I (accessed June 6, 2010), and Jeremy Bird, "Organizing for America: Looking Back, Marching Ahead," *Huffington Post*, January 6, 2010, www.huffingtonpost.com/jeremy-bird/organizing-for-america-lo_b_413000.html (accessed March 14, 2011).

79. Chris Cilliza, "Obama's Reelection Campaign Could Hit the Billion-Dollar Mark," *Washington Post*, December 12, 2010.

80. FEC, "FEC Announces 2011–12 Campaign Cycle Contribution Limits," press release, February 3, 2011.

81. Anthony Corrado and Molly Corbett, "Rewriting the Playbook on Presidential Campaign Financing," in Dennis W. Johnson, ed., *Campaigning for President 2008* (New York: Routledge, 2009), 141.

82. These include: (1) independent expenditures, which are monies spent by a group or individual on advertising or other election activities that directly advocate the election or defeat of a candidate; (2) electioneering communications, which are broadcast ads that feature a federal candidate and are aired within 30 days of a primary or 60 days of a general election, but do not specifically ask viewers to vote for or against a candidate; and (3) communications costs, which are the costs incurred by a union or corporation to communicate with members. According to the

rules operative in the 2008 election, independent expenditures had to be disclosed to the Federal Election Commission and paid for with monies subject to federal contribution requirements. Electioneering communications also had to be disclosed if the amount spent exceeded $10,000 in a calendar year. These communications could not be financed with corporate or labor union treasury contributions, but unlimited individual contributions were permissible. Communication costs had to be disclosed if the amount spent on a communication exceeded $2,000.

83. Green, "Financing the 2004 Presidential Nominations," 103.

84. Green and Kingsbury, "Financing the 2008 Presidential Nominations," 102. Green and Kingsbury provide a detailed discussion of organized group spending in the 2008 presidential nomination campaign.

85. Ibid. These totals are based on the data reported by Green and Kingsbury in Table 3–3.

86. *Citizens United* v. *Federal Election Commission*, U.S. Supreme Court, No. 08-205, January 21, 2010, 558 U.S. ___ (2010). All citations herein are to the slip opinion.

87. Ibid., 24 and 26.

88. *SpeechNow.org* v. *Federal Election Commission*, U.S. Court of Appeals for the District of Columbia, No. 08-5223, March 26, 2010.

89. Dan Eggen, "GOP Groups Seek to Raise $120M to Spend Against Obama, Other Democrats in 2012," *Washington Post*, March 1, 2011.

Chapter 3

Political Movements, Presidential Nominations, and the Tea Party

Andrew E. Busch

When CNBC financial analyst Rick Santelli took to the airwaves on February 19, 2009 to call for a modern "Tea Party" to protest government bailouts of financial institutions and overextended mortgage-holders, he set off a political movement that quickly became a major force in American politics. The "Tea Party" movement that resulted engaged thousands of Americans across the country. The movement has been called by *Washington Post* political correspondent and presidential biographer Lou Cannon "a movement that is more truly grassroots than any other of our time"[1] and by four *Wall Street Journal* correspondents "the most dynamic political force of 2010."[2] By the end of 2010, the movement had not only organized scores of chapters and sponsored numerous rallies, some of them drawing tens or hundreds of thousands of participants, it had also directly affected numerous primary and general election contests. What sort of influence might the Tea Party exert on the 2012 presidential race, and how should its efforts be judged within the context of other powerful political movements in American history?

The place to start is by defining what exactly is meant by a political movement. There are at least six broad characteristics of significant political movements in the American context. First, they are actually or potentially broadly-based but are not (yet) a majority and are driven by a relatively small hard core of activists. Second, they are organized and exhibit at least a loose hierarchy, making them an identifiable entity to outside observers, but their organization typically features a decentralized collection of both competing and collaborative structures that are less institutionalized than an existing political party. Third, they are motivated by at least a rough ideology, or generally coherent political vision of the world. Fourth, they have come (sometimes after a lengthy process of recruitment, education, and politicization of members) to promote change based on their ideology though political action, hence making them political, and not merely social, movements. Fifth, while not a permanent feature of the political landscape, they are not merely ephemera but have staying power beyond a single election. Finally, although their fortunes often become intertwined with particular political leaders, they are not synonymous with those leaders but rather have independent organizational existence. Genuine movements have substance beyond the individuals who serve as their standard-bearers. Although aimed at changing the political establishment, successful outside movements often forge an alliance with sympathetic insurgents within the establishment.[3]

Historically, political movements have exerted two kinds of influence in the area of presidential nominations. First, they have often influenced the outcome of presidential nomination races and, through those races, influenced the future direction of one or both of the major parties. That influence can be direct, exercised through involvement in the major parties, or indirect, exerted through a third party. Second, political movements have sometimes used their weight to push successfully for a change in the rules of the nomination game.

POLITICAL MOVEMENTS AND PRESIDENTIAL NOMINATIONS IN HISTORY

Before looking seriously at the Tea Party and its potential for influencing the 2012 presidential nominations, it is useful to survey previous major political movements in American history since two-party competition and decentralized party nominations were regularized in the 1830s. The movements that bear examination in this period include the Free Soil movement, Populists, Progressives, conservative movement, New Politics, and religious right.

Free Soil: The Free Soil movement, aiming to prevent the expansion of slavery into the western territories, operated in the pure convention system, a system characterized by "party-activist control of nominations and platforms through the convention."[4] The system revolved around party committees chosen through local party meetings usually called "primaries" (though more like what we would today call "caucuses"). Although the character of the nominating system made it difficult for movements to operate within the major parties, lack of state-controlled ballots and ballot access laws meant that it was relatively easy to start a third party.

As the issue of the expansion of slavery became more salient in the 1840s, Americans in both major parties who wanted to stop that expansion joined forces through what became known as the Free Soil movement. However, the movement quickly turned to the third party route. In 1848, former Democratic president Martin Van Buren was nominated for president by the Free Soil Party, whose convention chose the Whig (and son and grandson of former presidents) Charles Francis Adams as the party's vice presidential candidate. The Free Soil movement and party in 1848 drew strength from both major parties in varying places (as well as from the defunct Liberty Party), probably delivering New York's electoral votes to Whig candidate Zachary Taylor and possibly tilting other states to Taylor or Democrat Lewis Cass. (It turned out that Taylor, though himself a slaveholder, had Free Soil convictions when it came to extension of slavery into the West, but took pains during the campaign to obscure this fact.)[5]

The Free Soil Party continued organizing and ran a presidential ticket again in 1852. Free Soil ideas also continued to advance within the Whig Party among Whig politicians (like Abraham Lincoln and Thaddeus Stevens) who never joined the party. The Free Soil Party and the broader movement it represented then collapsed into the new Republican Party after 1854, guaranteeing its long-term significance.

Populists: The Populist movement of the late nineteenth century was the culmination of a series of agrarian reform movements such as the Grange, the Greenback movement, and the Farmers' Alliances. Historian Lawrence Goodwyn has called the Populists "the largest democratic mass movement in American history."[6] Concentrated in the South, West, and prairies, the Populists demanded government ownership of the railroads and telegraphs—the farmers' means of communication and transport with the outside world—as well as an inflationary currency policy. Based in the Farmers' Alliances—which had a northern wing with two million members and a southern wing with three million—the Populist movement was well-organized and had a ready-made lecture system and national reform press consisting of some one thousand journals to get their message out.

Like the Free Soilers, the Populists operated in an environment characterized by relatively difficult access into the major parties and relative easy formation of third parties. They initially pursued a strategy of influencing the major parties from the inside as much as possible, especially in the Democratic Party in the South. When operating within the major parties, the movement's supporters flooded local "primaries," sometimes overwhelming the local party establishments that normally controlled those meetings. However, the party regulars were able to reestablish control in most places within a couple of years. As a result, the Populists did ultimately form a national third party in 1892—the People's Party, or Populist Party—which ran candidates for offices from the U.S. presidency to municipal mayors. Populists and their sympathizers inside and outside of the major parties were able to maximize their strength because of the widespread allowance in state law of "cross-listing," in which candidates could be listed as the nominee of more than one party, a practice that facilitated "fusion" tickets between major and minor parties. Although the regulars had driven most outright Populists from the major parties, the growing electoral strength of the Populist Party aided the cause of many who remained in the major parties but were sympathizers of the movement for either principled or tactical reasons. Consequently, both Democrats and Republicans in the 1890s included wings that hewed to some key Populist planks, especially currency inflation.

By 1896, pro-Populist and pro-inflationary forces had gained control of the Democratic Party in many places, and most congressional Democrats also fell in that camp—much to the consternation of Democratic president Grover Cleveland, a staunch defender of the Gold Standard.[7] Cleveland had already served two (non-consecutive) terms in the White House and was unable to steer his party's nomination to a like-minded successor. As a result, that year's Democratic nomination went to William Jennings Bryan, a Populist-leaning pro-silver congressman from Nebraska, who also received the People's Party presidential nomination. The Democratic convention approved a platform that adopted many Populist positions and was judged by one noted scholar to be "more radical than any presented to the people by a major party within the memory of any but the oldest living men."[8] Bryan lost to William McKinley, but succeeded in giving a new cast to the Democrats. By 1900, the Populist Party was shriveled and Populist-leaning Republicans had either returned to the fold or become Democrats; the Bryan forces remained in control of the Democratic Party for most of the next decade and permanently transformed its philosophical approach toward the use of government power in the economic realm. Bryan himself was nominated again by the Democrats in 1900 and 1908, and his intraparty successes laid the groundwork for the Progressive movement.[9]

Progressives: Following hard on the heels of the Populist movement, the Progressive movement also worked in both major parties. Starting at the municipal level and working up to the state level and finally the federal level, the Progressives shared the Populists' support for more active government regulation and political reform, but were strongest in the urban middle class. The movement melded together (with some tensions) varying strands of reform, including some elements of populism, "good government" political reform as represented by the liberal Republicans of the late nineteenth century (the "Mugwumps"), civil service reform, "muckraking" journalism, the Christianity of the "Social Gospel," and advocates of social reforms for the urban immigrant populations.[10] Progressive mayors met with labor representatives at the National Social and Political Conference in Buffalo, New York in 1899, and the resulting call for direct democracy, redistribution of income, and control of monopolies served as "the very heart of Progressivism" for the next twenty years.[11]

When President McKinley was assassinated in 1901, Theodore Roosevelt became the first president who aligned himself with the Progressive movement, though he was never fully trusted by some Progressives. In 1912, Progressives in both parties sought their presidential nominations. Republican Progressives organized under the banner of the "National Progressive Republican League" while their Democratic counterparts formed the "Democratic Federation." Democratic progressives prevailed by obtaining the nomination of Woodrow Wilson (with the endorsement of William Jennings Bryan); GOP progressives were divided between Wisconsin Senator Robert LaFollette and Roosevelt, who was seeking a third term after sitting out for four years. In the end, Republican President William Howard Taft won renomination despite the Progressive challenge, and Republican Progressives bolted the party and nominated Roosevelt under the label of the Progressive (or "Bull Moose") Party. In the multi-candidate general election that followed, Wilson won and Roosevelt finished second, relegating Taft to a distant third.

Not only did the Progressives succeed in moving national, state, and local policy toward more activist government, contributing to the intellectual groundwork for the New Deal two decades later, but they also succeeded in changing the character of the presidential nominating process. The Populists had endorsed innovations like the direct primary, in which nominations would be decided directly by party voters rather than through representative processes usually controlled by party leaders, but it was the Progressives who enacted them in many places. By 1912, 14 states used primaries for the selection of national convention delegates, often instituted by Republican Progressives with the hope that the reform would make it easier for insurgents to block Taft.[12] The backlash against Taft's convention triumph—which he won despite the victory of Roosevelt or LaFollette in all the Republican primaries—led even more states to adopt some form of the presidential primary. Progressives redoubled their efforts, believing that Taft's nomination was "stolen by gross fraud in brazen defiance of the mass of the Republican voters throughout the country."[13] After the system stabilized around 1920, about one-third of the states (with about two-fifths of the convention delegates) typically held primaries, producing what is now often called the "mixed system." The rest continued electing delegates through local meetings ("caucuses") and state conventions.

Conservatives: In the aftermath of World War II, a new political movement arose that sought to challenge the assumptions and policies of New Deal liberalism as well as the advance of communism abroad. This "conservative movement" represented a coalition among organizations and individuals with three broad orientations: economic conservatives (or, as they often called themselves, classical liberals) whose primary concern was the maintenance of a free market economy and limited government; cultural traditionalists; and strong anticommunists.[14] The magazine *National Review*, founded by William F. Buckley in 1955, helped to glue these elements together.

In the era of the mixed nominating system, the major parties were more open to outside movements while the third party route had become more difficult due to restrictive ballot access requirements. Prominent conservatives believed that their greatest prospect of exerting influence was to work within a major party (rather than forming a third party), and saw the Republican Party as more receptive. Upset that northeastern liberal Republicans had come to dominate the party's presidential nominations, conservatives were determined to organize on behalf of a conservative aspirant to the GOP nomination. By 1960, Senator Barry M. Goldwater of Arizona stood out as a candidate who could articulate the conservative case and inspire conservative activists and voters. Shortly after Richard Nixon's 1960 defeat, conservatives formed a "Draft Goldwater" effort in order to pull the reluctant senator into a run. The effort was successful, and Goldwater won the 1964 Republican nomination largely on the basis of superior organization.[15] He won some crucial primaries—above all California, with the aid of nearly 25,000 volunteers on primary election day alone[16]—but won principally by dominating the caucus/convention states, where early organization by the movement was decisive.[17] The conservative movement did not formally change the nomination process, but it did pioneer a new way of gaining the votes of caucus/convention state delegates, by trying to elect committed supporters as delegates rather than persuading delegates after they had been chosen.

Although Goldwater lost the 1964 general election to Lyndon Johnson in a landslide, his nomination was a crucial step in turning the GOP into a more consistently conservative party with a strategy focusing on the "Sunbelt" states of the South and West. As scholar Nicol Rae notes, after 1964, "[T]he liberal wing would not again control the presidential Republican party."[18] Indeed, conservatives continued organizing inside and outside of the party, allowing Ronald Reagan to come within a hair's breadth of winning the nomination against incumbent Republican president Gerald Ford in 1976. When Reagan won the presidency in 1980 and turned public policy significantly to the right, he owed a considerable debt to Goldwater and the conservative movement.

New Politics: In the turmoil of the late 1960s, another important political movement arose that seriously affected presidential nominations, this time from the left. Drawing heavily from more moderate elements of the anti-Vietnam War movement (especially among students), the New Politics movement also endorsed redistributionist economics, new concerns such as environmentalism and feminism, a permissive social ethos, strong attention to the concerns of racial minorities, and political reforms such as campaign finance reform and the 18-year-old vote. The New Politics lay somewhere between "establishment" Democrats who represented the old New Deal-labor-anticommunist consensus and New Left radicals such as Students for a Democratic Society (SDS). The New Politics shared the general direction of the New Left, but with less radicalism and a commitment to work within "the system."[19]

There were stirrings of the New Politics in 1966 and 1967, by the end of which the dominant faction in the liberal group Americans for Democratic Action (ADA) had decided to attempt to deprive Lyndon Johnson of renomination. Spearheading the "Dump Johnson" effort was liberal activist Allard Lowenstein, a member of ADA and former president of the National Student Association, who organized three key groups: "Dissenting Democrats," aimed at the antiwar movement; "Concerned Democrats," focusing on insurgent Democratic politicians; and a student network. The movement sprang fully to life to back the presidential candidacy of Senator Eugene McCarthy of Minnesota in 1968. McCarthy struck his first blow in the New Hampshire primary, where as many as 4,500 student volunteers had gone "Clean for Gene" and contacted up to 60,000 voters. McCarthy came within 8 percentage points of defeating Lyndon Johnson. In the next primary state, Wisconsin, McCarthy established 41 student headquarters to coordinate volunteers who rang 800,000 doorbells.[20] Meanwhile, four days after McCarthy's unexpectedly strong showing in New Hampshire, Robert Kennedy also entered the Democratic nomination race as an antiwar candidate, drawing much of his support from New Politics constituencies as well. Facing likely defeat in Wisconsin and a protracted struggle to the Democratic convention, on March 31 Johnson declared that he would not seek renomination.

Appealing to many of the same constituencies, McCarthy and Kennedy split the remaining primaries, though Kennedy won almost all of their head-to-head battles. But on the final night of primaries, minutes after declaring victory in the important California contest, Kennedy was assassinated. In late April, Vice President Hubert Humphrey joined the race as a traditional labor/anticommunist Democrat. In the end, Humphrey won the Democratic nomination, despite having entered the race too late to participate in any of the primaries. In the "mixed system," however, he did not have to. Instead, he relied on his strength in the non-primary states, which still selected a solid majority of the delegates to the national convention. (This does not mean he had less support than his opponents, though; a Gallup Poll taken on the eve of the national convention showed Humphrey with the support of 53 percent of Democratic voters nationwide to 39 percent for McCarthy.) For his part, McCarthy did well in some non-primary states, such as Minnesota, Iowa, and Colorado, where New Politics forces were well-organized and his campaign worked energetically. Otherwise, party regulars took advantage of their position in the system and of McCarthy's negligence. Key McCarthy organizer Ben Stavis later revealed that toward the end of the primary season the campaign "suddenly realized" that the number of delegates chosen in primary states, where McCarthy had focused his energy, was "quite low."[21]

However, the New Politics movement was not finished. Like the Progressive movement before it, the New Politics leveraged outrage over a particular nomination outcome into reform of the system itself. At the 1968 convention, New Politics supporters succeeded in banning the unit rule (which some state delegations used to allocate all of their votes for the candidate who was preferred by a majority of the delegates within the state). More importantly, the convention authorized the creation of a reform commission with a mandate to "give all Democratic voters . . . a full, meaningful, and timely opportunity to participate in the selection of national convention delegates. Once named in 1969, the Commission on Delegate Selection and Party Structure (more commonly known as the "McGovern-Fraser Commission" after its two chairmen) rewrote the Democratic Party's presidential nomination rules. The eighteen guidelines it promulgated compelled all states to adopt explicit, written rules governing delegate selection, prevented delegate selection in the year before the national convention, required delegates to announce which presidential candidate they were supporting, and made it much harder for party officials to control precinct caucuses. Altogether, the commission aimed to make the nominating process more directly democratic (or, to put it another way, less based on the principle of indirect representation) and more open to popular forces like the New Politics. As political scientist William J. Crotty argued, "Reform of the party's nominating process became the vehicle through which the eventual policy and leadership changes the reformers held to be so important could be realized."[22]

Meanwhile, the McCarthy-Kennedy wounds were healed and the New Politics reorganized under the banner of the "New Democratic Coalition." When McGovern ran for the Democratic presidential nomination in 1972 as the consensus representative of the movement, he won. The degree to which the new rules aided McGovern is a matter of some dispute, but two things are clear.[23] McGovern won because he had a highly-motivated, well-organized, matured movement behind him—a movement that had benefited from the organizational sinews cultivated by the reform commission itself.[24] And, despite his crushing general election defeat at the hands of Richard Nixon, his nomination changed the Democratic Party forever, shifting its center of gravity away from labor and the lower class and toward such groups as affluent professionals, who were more culturally liberal, more secular, and more anti-anticommunist—the "new class" that was at the heart of the New Politics.

Religious Right: Religious conservatives, especially evangelical Protestants, began organizing for political action on a wide scale in the 1970s after decades of relative quietude. These voters were outraged by a number of secular liberal advances, including Supreme Court decisions banning school prayer, striking down laws against pornography, and establishing (or, as they saw it, inventing) a constitutional right to abortion; agitation by feminists for an Equal Rights Amendment to the Constitution, which opponents saw as a potential means of assaulting the family and imposing an androgynous social model; and proposed federal policies threatening the survival of independent Christian schools. By the late 1970s, evangelicals had become increasingly politicized and hundreds of national, state, and local organizations sprung up to defend the traditional family and religious liberty against "secular humanism." At the same time, Catholics were energized around the abortion issue in particular, and evangelicals began tentatively exploring alliances with Catholics, Mormons, and Orthodox Jews.[25] The resultant movement was often called the "religious right" (or sometimes the "Christian right").

To channel these efforts, Baptist pastor and "televangelist" Jerry Falwell formed the Moral Majority in 1980. The Moral Majority quickly gained prominence, as it aided Ronald Reagan's 1980 election and successfully targeted a number of liberal Democratic senators. After Falwell's group closed down in 1989, the Christian Coalition was formed by Pat Robertson. Robertson, also a Baptist pastor and televangelist (though, unlike Falwell, from the "charismatic" strand of the evangelical world), had run unsuccessfully for the Republican nomination for president in 1988, but used his extensive lists of campaign volunteers and contributors to build the Christian Coalition.[26] Much more than the Moral Majority, the Christian Coalition was a grassroots organization which aimed at influencing politics at the local level, then translating that success into influence at the national level.

Both Falwell and Robertson saw the Republican Party as inherently more hospitable to social conservatism, and their organizations worked primarily within the GOP (and served to bring no small number of socially conservative former Democrats into the party). By the 1994 midterm elections, the Christian Coalition claimed 1.4 million members; by one journalistic estimate, the Christian right was "dominant" in 18 state Republican parties and a "substantial force" in 13 more.[27] By the end of the decade, the Christian Coalition was also facing organizational difficulties, though it still operates. Although the Moral Majority and Christian Coalition received the lion's share of media attention in the 1980s and 1990s, the religious right movement was and continues to be much broader and deeper, featuring a variety of organizations such as the Family Research Council, Focus on the Family, American Family Association, Traditional Values Coalition, and many others at the national, state, and local levels.

As three prominent scholars of the religious right note, "[T]here have been numerous obituaries for the movement—followed by dramatic revivals of its fortunes."[28] Though it has had mixed success in obtaining its public policy objectives, the religious right movement has been highly successful at assuring that the Republican Party remains committed to a socially conservative platform, including support for conservative judges and opposition to abortion and (more recently) gay marriage. Unlike the conservatives in 1964 or the New Politics in 1972, the religious right has been unable to unite its forces behind a single standard-bearer in recent Republican presidential nomination fights. Even in 1988, when Pat Robertson himself was a candidate, Jerry Falwell endorsed George H. W. Bush in the Republican primaries while candidates such as Jack Kemp and Pete du Pont also received considerable support from Christian right voters and activists. Instead, key figures and activists in the movement have typically divided their support among a number of aspirants.[29] In 2008, for example, Robertson endorsed Rudy Giuliani, James Dobson of Focus on the Family supported Mike Huckabee, and the National Right to Life Committee backed Fred Thompson. In spite of this lack of unity (or perhaps because of this diffusion of effort), Republicans have not nominated a pro-choice candidate for president since the religious right became active.

Other Movements in Recent History: These movements are far from the only social/political movements to have actively influenced the presidential nominations of major parties in recent years. The feminist movement has been the mirror image of social conservatives, swinging the Democratic Party to an uncompromising pro-choice position on abortion. This movement's influence within Democratic circles has been sufficient that many big-name Democratic presidential aspirants, including Edward Kennedy, Al Gore, Richard Gephardt, and Jesse Jackson, moved from a pro-life to a pro-choice position as the price of remaining viable contenders. Feminists also got the Democrats to adopt a rule that compelled state parties to select national convention delegations that were equally divided between men and women.

Jackson, a black minister and civil rights leader, also stood at the head of something of a movement that he called the Rainbow Coalition—a coalition of black activists, affluent white leftists, and the radical edge of organized labor. Particularly essential were the organizational resources of the black churches and portions of the civil rights movement. Although it was more dependent on Jackson's personality than a real movement would have been, the Rainbow Coalition survived his two presidential runs (in 1984 and 1988) to play a small role in the 1992 Democratic nomination race and in some local elections. (As a candidate in 1992, Jerry Brown—who came in second behind Bill Clinton in delegates—sometimes succeeded in tapping into the Rainbow Coalition for support.)[30] Jackson, who was strong enough to finish third in delegates in 1984 (behind Walter Mondale and Gary Hart) and second in 1988 (behind Michael Dukakis), was able to force Democrats to modify their nominating rules again, reducing the threshold percentage required for a candidate to win delegates, delaying the election of "superdelegates" until after primary voting begins, and (after 1988) abolishing non-proportional primaries.

In 2008, Barack Obama's campaign was sometimes likened to a movement, insofar as it drew intense support from broad masses of voters, organized those supporters into a grassroots army, and benefited from the spontaneous growth afforded by the innovative use of social media. In some sense, Obama's support was also undergirded by the recent development of the progressive "netroots," which shared certain characteristics of a movement. However, Obama's drive to the presidency was ultimately a highly personalistic one. His supporters—however intense and well-organized—were drawn to him much more than he latched on to a preexisting movement that had substance before and beyond him.[31]

THE TEA PARTY MOVEMENT

The most recent major political movement on the American scene is the Tea Party movement. It emerged in a complicated context which was defined above all by the financial crisis of 2008 and the Great Recession, and the policies devised by the federal government to combat those economic ills. Throughout 2008, the George W. Bush administration fought an *ad hoc* battle against the impending collapse of a number of important financial institutions. Things came to a head in mid-September when Lehman Brothers declared bankruptcy and the dam appeared ready to break, threatening the entire financial system. No longer convinced that it was workable to handle these problems on a case-by-case basis, Treasury Secretary Henry Paulson proposed that Congress establish a large fund that could be used to shore up threatened banks and other financial institutions.

After considerable debate and one failed attempt, Congress finally passed the $700 billion Troubled Assets Relief Program (TARP). It had been proposed by a Republican administration and supported by both the Republican and Democratic presidential candidates (John McCain and Barack Obama) in the midst of the campaign, but Republicans in Congress were considerably less enthused by what they preferred to call the "bailout bill." To many conservative politicians and commentators, the "bailout" was of a piece with the fiscal recklessness that they had come to see as a hallmark of the Bush administration. Even before the financial crisis exploded, a slowing economy (later deemed to have entered recession in December 2007) had led Bush and Congress to agree on a $160 billion stimulus package.

Obama was elected in November 2008 largely on a promise of "change," but the primary change in economic policy instituted by the new administration was to accelerate the sort of interventionist measures begun by Bush. Obama embraced and distributed TARP, took a controlling share in General Motors and Chrysler to prevent their bankruptcy, and proposed both a mammoth economic stimulus package valued at $787 billion and a new plan to provide financial aid to homeowners threatened with foreclosure. Subsequently, Obama sought to make good on his promise to "transform America" by promoting (and ultimately winning) passage of a federal government takeover of health care, federal takeover of all federally subsidized student loans, and budget policies that ballooned federal spending to 25.4 percent of Gross Domestic Product in 2010 (it had been less than 20 percent as recently as 2007), threatening to add $9 trillion or more to the national debt over the next decade.

To many observers, the roots of the discontent that turned into the Tea Party could be found in the TARP proposal and in Bush's subsequent declaration that "I've abandoned free-market principles to save the free-market system."[32] As a movement, the Tea Party itself can be traced to the debate over the Obama stimulus and mortgage relief proposals in February 2009. First, with the aid of author and blogger Michelle Malkin, conservative blogger "Liberty Belle" Keli Carender hosted a "Porkulus Protest" in Seattle to rally against the controversial programs. Then, on February 19, an on-air commentary by CNBC financial analyst Rick Santelli did more than any other event to spark the movement. Broadcasting live from the floor of the Chicago Mercantile Exchange, Santelli harshly criticized Obama's aid to financial institutions and delinquent homeowners, called the latter an injustice to those paying their mortgages on time, and called for a "Chicago Tea Party" where derivative securities would be dumped into Lake Michigan. Santelli's call went "viral" online and inspired a key conference call the next day among about 20 activists to plan a response. The call would lead to about 50 Tea Party protests around the country on February 27 and a much larger set of Tax Day Tea Party protests on April 15, which were primarily promoted online but also received publicity from talk radio and from such Fox News commentators as Sean Hannity and Glenn Beck. The Tax Day protests drew hundreds of thousands of participants in more than 800 cities. A burgeoning nationwide movement had been launched.[33]

WHO IS IN THE TEA PARTY?

Every political movement has leaders and followers—in other words, people who organize and coordinate the movement and the ordinary voters who support it in various ways. The Tea Party, like other major political movements, is a decentralized coalition rather than a single hierarchical group. Nevertheless, it is possible to identify key leaders and organizations that have helped coordinate its efforts at a national level.

In response to Rick Santelli's impassioned plea (or rant, as some preferred to call it), an *ad hoc* coalition was formed by the leaders of three online social media groups: Top Conservatives on Twitter, American Liberty Alliance, and Smart Girl Politics. The group called itself the National Tea Party Coalition and promoted the first national day of Tea Party protests on February 27. A month later, former House Speaker Newt Gingrich's organization, American Solutions for Winning, became the fourth member of the Coalition. In May, the umbrella group Tea Party Patriots was incorporated, claiming 2,800 local affiliates across the country by November 2010. [34] Then, in the summer of 2009, Republican political consultant Sal Russo and several associates formed the Tea Party Express, a national bus tour to drum up support for the Tea Party. The Tea Party Express also tapped into Russo's political action committee, the Our Country Deserves Better PAC, to fund sympathetic candidates.[35] Other groups such as Americans for Prosperity and FreedomWorks, headed by former Republican House majority leader Richard Armey, helped fund and coordinate some Tea Party activities. Later in the year, the for-profit group Tea Party Nation took its place in the movement, organizing social networking and a national Tea Party convention, though it was criticized by many in the movement for straying from the original spirit of the movement by charging for the event.

Although House Speaker Nancy Pelosi and a number of other Democrats accused the Tea Party of being "Astroturf"—that is, driven from the top down with only a pretense of grassroots support—the individuals and organizations at the top always seemed to be more in a support and coordination role rather than a controlling one. They were attempting to ride and channel a genuine outburst of public sentiment. In fact, state and local Tea Party committees usually sprang up spontaneously and sometimes even in competition with each other, often headed by new activists with little experience in politics. In this, the Internet played a crucial role, with social networking sites often serving as magnets for activism. Indeed, it may be more accurate to call this cluster of organization and activities the Tea *Parties*, rather than the Tea *Party*, given its fundamentally decentralized character.

So what were the ordinary activists and supporters of the Tea Party like? A number of surveys taken throughout 2010 helped to clarify the profile of Tea

Party supporters. It is not as easy as it might seem to determine how many Americans were Tea Party supporters. At the broadest level, Americans were frequently asked by pollsters whether they had a "favorable" (or sometimes "positive") or "unfavorable" (or sometimes "negative") view of the Tea Party. In 36 surveys taken between November 2009 and September 2010, an average of about one-third of Americans said they had a "positive" or "favorable" view of the Tea Party (32.2 percent); slightly fewer had an "unfavorable" or "negative" view (30.5 percent), and the rest had no opinion or did not know. [36] In other surveys, a slightly smaller proportion (usually around one in four, though sometimes more) called themselves "supporters" of the Tea Party, an ambiguous phrase that could be interpreted as providing some active support (rather than merely passive approval). Other surveys asked more directly whether respondents considered themselves "members" of the Tea Party movement or "part of" that movement. These surveys usually showed that somewhere between 8 percent and 18 percent of Americans considered themselves members in or part of the movement (the average in ten surveys was 14 percent).[37] Finally, when asked whether they had taken specific actions to aid the Tea Party movement, one CNN poll showed that 2 percent of Americans had contributed money, 5 percent had attended a Tea Party rally, and 7 percent had taken "other active steps"; a Democracy Corps survey showed that 2 had given cash, 3 percent had rallied, and 3 percent had done both.[38] As Scott Rasmussen and Douglas Schoen have noted, public opinion about and participation in the Tea Party can best be seen as a series of concentric circles that include (moving from the periphery to the center) "sympathizers," "supporters," "members," and "activists."[39]

Survey results of Tea Party members or supporters must be viewed cautiously partly because of these uncertainties in how to define the group, and partly because most of the data are from national surveys, in which Tea Party affiliates make up only a small subset of the respondents and which are therefore subject to high margins of error. Nevertheless, some patterns can be identified. Politically, only a handful of Tea Partiers are Democrats. Most surveys show that a majority are Republicans, but they are joined by a strong representation of Independents. For example, an in-depth *New York Times*/CBS News survey indicated that 54 percent were Republicans, 36 percent Independents, and 5 percent Democrats (the rest refusing to state or in third parties, most likely Libertarian and American Constitution Party).[40] Three out of four Tea Party activists at a major Washington, D. C. rally voted for John McCain in 2008 and George W. Bush in 2004. However, it is clear that the Tea Party has been fueled by dissatisfaction with both parties. Of those same activists at the rally—who identified 43 percent Republican, 36 percent Independent, and 9 percent Democrat—more than half said they did not trust either party.[41] Indeed, when top Republicans, such as Republican National Committee chair Michael Steele, sought to bring the movement under their wing, Tea Party Patriots published a "Tea Party Declaration of Independence" from the GOP, which it accused of consistently betraying conservative principles.[42] In this respect, the Tea Party can be considered the revolt of fiscally conservative Republicans and Independents who were angered by George W. Bush's assault on the principles of limited government, even if they voted for him as the lesser of evils, well before Obama's leftward lunge pushed them over the edge. In the tradition of many prior political movements, they were "not a wing of the GOP but a critique of it,"[43] mobilizing not merely to support the Republican Party but to transform it from within.

Geographically, most surveys showed particular strength for the Tea Party in the South and the West, particularly the Plains and Mountain states (rather than the West Coast) with relative weakness in the Northeast. Demographically, the average Tea Partier is disproportionately likely to be a non-Hispanic white, though there is disagreement among analysts over whether the movement is much more white than the population as a whole or only slightly so.[44] Tea Party members are also a bit more likely to be men (around 55–60 percent), though women play key leadership roles in the Tea Party Express, the Tea Party Patriots, and many local organizations. Most (but not all) surveys show them to be older on average than the general population; most surveys also show them to be considerably more likely to be married and to have a college degree or some post-graduate education than the average American. Evidence was mixed regarding the average incomes of Tea Party members, but it seems clear that those incomes are at least as high as the average and very possibly quite a bit higher. (For example, one CNN survey showed that two-thirds of Tea Party members had incomes over $50,000, compared with only 42 percent of all Americans, but most studies showed a smaller gap or none at all.[45]) Significantly, it appears that an outsized proportion of Tea Party members own their own small businesses. In general, much of this picture is not unexpected given the general profile of the politically-active in America.

WHAT DOES THE TEA PARTY BELIEVE?

The Tea Party starts from an ideology which is generally hostile to centralized, activist government. Somewhere between two-thirds and three-fourths of Tea Party members identify themselves as "conservative" and no more than 10 percent as "liberal."[46] Over 90 percent of movement members nationwide say they prefer smaller government providing fewer services to a larger government providing more services. A *Politico* survey of participants in a large Washington, D.C. Tea Party rally on April 15, 2010, though not a representative national sample, also indicated that 88 percent thought government was trying to do too many things and 81 percent thought that cutting taxes and spending were more important than maintaining government services.[47] Most self-identified Tea Party members also express a willingness to accept some social inequalities as a price for the maintenance of liberty and limited government.[48]

These general principles lead to a definite set of policy priorities and positions. While sharing the general national concern with jobs and economic conditions, Tea Partiers are significantly more likely than are Americans more generally to list the deficit and spending as top issues. Tea Party members nationwide told a *New York Times*/CBS News survey that the main goal of their movement should be to "reduce the federal government" generally, cut the budget, or lower taxes.[49] Likewise, the Tax Day protestors listed the national debt, the rate of growth of government, the recently-passed health care reform bill, and "government intrusion" as the chief objects of their anger (in that order).[50]

Their positions on specific issues follow from these general principles and priorities. According to a variety of surveys:

- Tea Party members favor significant cuts in government programs, including entitlement programs such as Social Security and Medicare.
- They were twice as likely as most Americans to think the stimulus bill made the economy worse, and three-quarters thought it would be better for the government to cut spending than to spend more money attempting to create jobs.[51]
- Three-quarters also believed the bank "bailouts" were unnecessary.[52]
- Tea Partiers were considerably stronger than the average American in their opposition to the health care reform bill. Over 80 percent opposed the bill as a whole, opposed the "individual mandate" requiring that Americans purchase health insurance, and thought the passage of the bill was a "bad thing." Before the vote, nine in ten thought that Obama should scrap the bill and start over again.[53]
- At a time when Americans favored increased bank regulation by a 56-32 percent margin, Tea Party supporters opposed it by a 48-42 percent margin.[54]
- Tea Partiers were skeptical of other sorts of government regulation as well. Surveys showed that they were more than twice as likely as the general

populace to say that global warming either had "no serious impact" or did not exist.[55]

- As a movement, the Tea Party has embraced the "Repeal Act," a proposed constitutional amendment that would allow two-thirds of the states to overturn a federal law.

As these data indicate, Tea Party participants were mobilized into the movement as a result of economic policy issues and concerns about the growth of government, not social issues. The *Politico* survey of Washington ralliers showed that gay marriage was dead last on the list of things driving the anger of the crowd, and in the wake of the 2010 midterms some Tea Party leaders cautioned Republicans against emphasizing social issues.[56] However, this de-emphasis on social issues should not be taken as meaning that Tea Partiers are not socially conservative. To the contrary, although there is a libertarian wing to the movement, the evidence shows that Tea Party members are significantly more likely than the average American to call themselves "pro-life," to consider the *Roe v. Wade* decision a bad thing, to favor restrictions on abortion, and to oppose gay marriage.[57] (In fact, one survey showed Tea Party members more likely to oppose gay marriage than self-identified Republicans.[58]) Other social issues show a similar pattern, with Tea Partiers more supportive of gun rights and more concerned about illegal immigration than other Americans.[59] An extensive survey conducted by the Public Religion Research Institute concluded that on most dimensions Tea Party members were considerably more traditionalist than most Americans, though less so than white evangelicals. Nearly half (47 percent) of Tea Party members considered themselves also part of the Christian conservative movement, and Tea Party members were even more likely than white evangelicals to say that the United States is a "Christian nation."[60]

Altogether, throughout 2010, Tea Party members were more likely than most Americans to say the nation was headed in the wrong direction, more likely to distrust Washington D.C., more likely to hold negative views of the state of the economy, and less likely to approve of the performance of the Democratic Congress or President Obama. (It should be pointed out that their responses here differed only in degree, not in kind, from those of their fellow Americans.) In one *New York Times*/CBS News survey, a whopping 96 percent of Tea Party members disapproved of the job Congress was doing, while 88 percent disapproved of Obama's job performance and 94 percent declared themselves either dissatisfied or angry with Washington.[61] Three of four Tea Party members saw Obama as failing to share the basic values of most Americans, while overwhelming majorities consistently expressed a belief that Obama was pursuing a "socialist agenda" and had expanded government power "too much."[62]

Another common theme among Tea Party participants has been a fear that government was ceasing to represent the people, a concern shared by the large majority of Americans who told pollsters in 2010 that they believed the nation was no longer run on the basis of the "consent of the governed."[63] This fear was particularly inflamed by the health care bill, which Obama and the Democratic congressional leadership pushed through despite voluminous evidence that most Americans opposed it. It was also undergirded by significant evidence that a wide gulf existed between the views of (as Rasmussen and Schoen put it) the "political class" and "mainstream Americans" on issues ranging from taxes to immigration.[64]

This belief added a dimension to the Tea Party agenda that was not easily quantifiable, though it was arguably at the heart of the movement. Aside from specific issues of economic or other policy, the Tea Party was driven by broad constitutional concerns about the role of government, particularly the federal government, in national life and by the fear that it has strayed far from the wise design of the Founding Fathers. As Scott Rasmussen and Douglas Schoen note, those who participated in the Tea Party protests "felt their very liberty was at stake."[65] Broadly speaking, the movement believed that the federal government had overstepped its legitimate powers as outlined in the enumerated powers of the Constitution and, as a natural concomitant, unduly infringed on the rights of the states and of the people. These views might be said to represent "Large C" constitutional concerns. A parallel set of "small c" constitutional concerns accompanied them, having to do less with an interpretation of the written Constitution than with the informal distribution of power and the overall character of the government and the people. Here, the Tea Party feared a concentration of government power that would threaten to turn America into a European-style social democracy, with a very large welfare state, very high taxes, and an enervated and dependent population. In this view, Obama and the liberal Democrats who controlled Congress, if left to make policy unhindered, would turn America into Sweden in twenty years; France, where infantilized citizens were rioting in the streets to protest an increase in the retirement age from 60 to 62, in thirty years; and Greece, tottering on the edge of complete insolvency, in forty years. In the end, much of what the Tea Party is about is American Exceptionalism—or the idea that America is a special nation with a different and better way—and the perception that Barack Obama does not believe in it.

As with every significant political movement seeking change, the Tea Party was not free of a fringe, which its opponents liked to emphasize. Tea Partiers were slightly more likely than other Americans to express doubts about Obama's citizenship and to say that violence against the government might sometimes be justified. However, the differences were not large. While 20 percent of Americans expressed doubts that Obama was born in the U.S., 30 percent of Tea Partiers did so; where 16 percent of all respondents said violence might sometimes be justified, 24 percent of Tea Partiers did so.[66] The Tea Party's opponents were concerned enough (or unscrupulous enough) that on several occasions acts of political violence were immediately—and it turned out, incorrectly—blamed on the Tea Party.[67] In response, the national leadership of the Tea Party has taken steps to keep "birthers" and other extremists from using the movement as a platform for their views, including banning them from organizational websites.[68] Despite a total lack of evidence connecting the Tea Party to the shooting of Arizona Congresswoman Gabrielle Giffords, polls taken in its aftermath showed that the attacks were having a negative effect on the movement's popularity.[69]

The Tea Party movement as a whole was also accused by its opponents of racism, and polls showed that about a quarter of Americans were likely to ascribe a significant amount of racism to the movement.[70] The evidence for this charge, however, was thin. In one case, Tea Party Express spokesman Mark Williams, a Sacramento radio host, resigned after caricaturing a black person in a blog post. Another Florida Tea Party activist was drummed out of the movement after forwarding an email depicting Obama as an African witch doctor with a bone through his nose. Of greater note, shortly before the final health care vote in Congress, members of the Black Congressional Caucus claimed to have had racial slurs shouted at them and to have been spit at while walking through a Tea Party protest on Capitol Hill. Video evidence confirmed uncivil conduct by some protestors, but no independent evidence surfaced to corroborate the claims of racist comments, despite a $100,000 reward offered by conservative new media figure Andrew Breitbart. In surveys, Tea Party members were more likely than others to hold that blacks and whites had an equal chance in today's America and that too much has been made of the problems of racial minorities, though such views are at least as consistent with color-blindness as with racism.[71] And, as we will see below, Tea Parties backed several racial minorities as candidates in the 2010 elections.

WHAT HAS THE TEA PARTY MOVEMENT DONE?

The Tea Party movement has been active in two main ways: organizing wide scale protests against federal policy and involving itself in a number of primary and general election races in 2009 and 2010. Each type of activity deserves a detailed examination.

Protest: The modern Tea Party—like the original 1773 version—was first and foremost a protest movement. From the first Tea Party protests on February 27, 2009, a major focus of the movement has been to express anger at federal policies and exert pressure on federal policymakers from the president on down. The protest character of the Tea Party movement was made clear in its adoption as its unofficial emblem of the Revolutionary War "Gadsden Flag," the famed yellow banner sporting a coiled rattlesnake and the motto "Don't Tread on Me." After the first waves of protests, the summer of 2009 saw increased activity. Most notably, Tea Party protests were prominent on Independence Day and Tea Party activists made a major show of force during town meetings held by members of Congress home for the August recess.

On July 4, 2009, a coordinated wave of Tea Party rallies reached an estimated 1500 cities.[72] During the August recess, Tea Party Patriots, FreedomWorks, and others worked to motivate supporters to turn out for congressional town meetings. Tea Party Patriots also provided instructions for those attending, including directions to be loud and to question the representative's support of a "socialist agenda." Heavily focused on the pending health care bill, town meetings across the country provided many Democratic congressmen with an immediate taste of the unhappiness simmering among many of their constituents. Many of the meetings received national media attention as unruly crowds confronted their representatives. Some Democratic members canceled their sessions, and some prominent Democrats and media figures expressed fears about violence from the outraged audiences. (However, the worst violence that was recorded in this period came when a pro-Obama member of the group MoveOn.org bit a finger off of a Tea Party protestor at a rally in Thousand Oaks, California.[73]) Of course, the Tea Party was not the only force driving public protest at congressional town meetings, but it was the force whose efforts were most organized and coordinated.

Further major protests surrounded the health reform legislation. Above all, a major rally held in Washington, D.C. on September 12, 2009 mobilized a new cohort of Tea Party activists. The Taxpayer March on Washington, also known as the 9-12 Project, was the brainchild of Fox commentator Glenn Beck and was subsequently organized and implemented by FreedomWorks and national and local Tea Party groups. The protest, held a few days after President Obama's health care speech to a joint session of Congress, drew at least 75,000 demonstrators according to mainstream media reports (some conservative bloggers claimed the attendance may have been closer to a million). As Congress drew close to a final vote on the legislation in March 2010, a new round of rallies was held, drawing thousands more to Washington to plead with representatives to "kill the bill."

2010 Elections: When Massachusetts Senator Edward Kennedy, sometimes called the "liberal lion of the Senate," passed away in late 2009, it was widely assumed that a Democrat would be elected in the special election to fill the vacancy. Republican state legislator Scott Brown's surprising victory in the vacancy election in January 2010 owed more than a little to the Tea Party movement, which rallied around Brown's pledge to be the "41st vote against health care reform" in the Senate. The Tea Party Express took a lead in organizing support for Brown, and for many around the country Brown's election became a catalytic event. As one Tea Party sympathizer from Georgia related, the Massachusetts special election produced "this feeling of solidarity, that people are finally waking up. It was this feeling that 'Yeah, we can make some changes. We can make a difference.'"[74]

With the passage of the health care bill in March 2010 in spite of the strenuous efforts of the Tea Party, the movement refocused its efforts on electoral politics. In a large number of states, Tea Parties threw their weight behind selected candidates in the upcoming Republican congressional primaries. In U.S. Senate primaries, local and/or national Tea Party organizations got behind insurgent Republican contenders such as Marco Rubio in Florida, Rand Paul in Kentucky, Mike Lee in Utah, Joe Miller in Alaska, Sharron Angle in Nevada, Ron Johnson in Wisconsin, Ken Buck in Colorado, and Christine O'Donnell in Delaware. In each of these cases, the insurgent Tea Party-supported candidate won. Rubio drove popular Republican governor Charlie Crist from the primary and into an independent campaign; Lee and Miller defeated Republican incumbents; the rest won against an assortment of establishment-backed Republicans. One of the most dramatic instances came in Delaware, where Tea Party favorite O'Donnell beat the incumbent at-large Congressman and former Governor Mike Castle, a more moderate Republican who nevertheless had voted against both the stimulus and health care reform. Castle had been widely considered a shoo-in in the general election. Not all Tea-Party supported insurgents won their Senate primaries: former NFL star Clint Didier in Washington state and Ovide Lamontagne in New Hampshire both fell short. And not all Tea Party-supported candidates even had a primary: Republicans Pat Toomey in Pennsylvania and Rob Portman in Ohio seriously cultivated Tea Party support, but stored it up for the general election, having no serious primary opponents. Indeed, local Tea Parties showed the ability to work with the Republican organization and to support more established and experienced candidates, such as Toomey, Portman, Roy Blunt of Missouri, and Dan Coats of Indiana, even when they had provoked considerable displeasure in the past. (In the case of Blunt, who had voted for TARP and George W. Bush's Medicare prescription drug entitlement, the candidate had to sign a "tea party treaty" pledging himself to support spending cuts and health care repeal.)[75]

At the other end of the spectrum, Ron Johnson represented perhaps the purest form of a Tea Party candidate. A successful businessman, Johnson rose from obscurity on the basis of a short speech that he delivered at a Tea Party rally. The speech was picked up by conservative talk radio in Wisconsin, leading to an upsurge in support for a Johnson candidacy. He decided to throw his hat into the ring, ran a strong primary campaign, and won going away with 85 percent of the vote.

Tea Parties also played a role in gubernatorial primaries in many states. Notably, in South Carolina, they backed Nikki Haley, an Indian-American woman who faced and defeated three establishment Republican aspirants. In New York, Tea Party-supported Buffalo businessman Carl Paladino defeated former Republican congressman and 2000 U.S. Senate nominee Rick Lazio by a 2-1 margin in the gubernatorial primary. And in Colorado, an obscure figure by the name of Dan Maes, a local Tea Party activist, won the Republican nomination after the campaign of his opponent, former congressman Scott McInnis, imploded due to a plagiarism scandal.

Not least, local Tea Parties involved themselves heavily in a significant number of U.S. House primaries, successfully supporting (for example) Kristi Noem in South Dakota, Tim Scott in South Carolina, Allen West in Florida, Jesse Kelly in Arizona, and Jeff Landry in Louisiana. Scott would become the first Republican African-American congressman from South Carolina since Reconstruction; West the same in Florida. Working in concert with Tea Party organizations were some big-name Republicans, especially 2008 vice presidential nominee Sarah Palin and South Carolina Senator Jim DeMint, who backed insurgent candidates with important primary endorsements at all levels. Although the vast majority of the primaries in which Tea Parties intervened were Republican, not all were. In Florida's 11th district, Tea Party member Tim Curtis defeated incumbent Kathy Castor in the Democratic primary.

Local and national Tea Party organizations remained active in the general election. In Senate races, the results were a mixed bag from a Tea Party standpoint, though one that tilted in a positive direction. Toomey, Portman, Rubio, Johnson, Paul, and Lee all won. O'Donnell lost in a landslide, Angle and Buck lost nail-biters, and Miller was defeated in the general election by the Republican he had beaten in the primary—Lisa Murkowski—when she successfully ran a write-in campaign to hold her seat. Likewise, in gubernatorial races, Haley won, while Paladino and Maes behaved erratically and were crushed. Maes collapsed so thoroughly that former Republican congressman Tom Tancredo, running as the gubernatorial candidate of the American Constitution Party, filled the vacuum and finished a strong second behind the Democratic winner (John Hickenlooper). Maes was ultimately repudiated by his local Tea Party chapter and finished with 11 percent of the vote. In House races, Tea Party candidates—like other Republican candidates—caught the national wave and rode it to considerable success. Indeed, House Republicans took positive action to catch the wave in September, when they unveiled a campaign document called "The Pledge" which embraced the movement's key themes. No fewer than 32 Republican House seat pick-ups, about half the total, were made by candidates who had received significant Tea Party support.[76] Overall, the Tea Party Express, just to cite one group, compiled a donor list of more than 400,000 and spent more than $5 million on advertising for candidates.[77]

These results led immediately to a debate in Republican circles about whether the Tea Party had been a net plus or a net minus for the party in the 2010 elections. On the minus side, critics pointed to the Delaware Senate race, where O'Donnell's primary victory almost certainly cost the GOP a seat, and to Nevada and Colorado, where the more polished establishment candidates who were defeated in the primaries might well have succeeded against the unpopular Democratic incumbents. The weaknesses of the Tea Party candidates allowed their opponents to paint them as "extremists" and to turn the election from a "referendum" into a "choice." Former George W. Bush speechwriter and commentator David Frum consequently argued that "three ridiculously winnable Senate seats" were "thrown away."[78] Critics could also point to the Paladino and Maes disasters as examples of the Tea Parties' poor judgment in candidate selection, though in New York it was unlikely that any Republican nominee could have won.

On the positive side of the ledger, Tea Party-backed candidates won more swing Senate races than they lost, and not only in conservative states but in blue states such as Wisconsin and Pennsylvania (as well as Massachusetts, if one includes Scott Brown's January 2010 special election victory). Tea Parties backed a number of candidates likely to prove attractive spokespersons for the Republican Party in the future, such as Nikki Haley, Marco Rubio, and Tim Scott. As noted above, about half of Republican House gains were attributable to Tea Party-supported candidates.

Less quantifiably, the Tea Party mobilized a crucial segment of the electorate for Republicans nationally. As one news account noted, "the movement re-energized—and in some cases, scared—conservatives demoralized and dispirited in the aftermath of the Bush presidency and Obama victory."[79] Nearly three in five Tea Party members had not been active in campaigns before 2010.[80] The Tea Party leadership also made a crucial decision to work within the GOP rather than pursue a third party strategy, which would have been catastrophic to Republican chances. In a handful of local cases, third party candidates ran under a Tea Party label of some sort, but these were rare instances, not supported by Tea Party organizations and never very serious (although Sharron Angle was worried enough about the third-party "Tea Party" candidate in Nevada to try to convince him to leave the Senate race). The potential harm to Republicans of a third-party Tea Party was evident in a number of surveys throughout 2010 that showed that Democrats would win a plurality of the House vote if a generic Tea Party candidate was on the ballot, but were invariably outvoted by the combination of Republican and Tea Party supporters.[81]

Finally, as former Reagan speechwriter and *Wall Street Journal* columnist Peggy Noonan pointed out, the Tea Party succeeded in forcing Republicans back to their traditional themes of limited government and constitutionalism, after the interlude of "compassionate conservatism" or "big government conservatism," just as those traditional themes were gaining resonance with the broader electorate. In Noonan's view, the Tea Party rescued the GOP.[82] Altogether, exit polls showed that Tea Party supporters outnumbered Tea Party opponents among House voters on Election Day by a 41-30 percent margin.[83]

THE TEA PARTY AND 2012

By most of the criteria that define political movements, the Tea Party clearly qualifies. It is broadly-based but not (yet) a majority and is driven by a modest hard core of activists. It is organized enough to make it an identifiable entity to outside observers, but its organization is a decentralized collection of both competing and collaborative structures. It is motivated by a fairly well-defined set of political principles, and is seeking to promote change based on that ideology though political action. It is not synonymous with any political leaders, much less at their service, but rather has independent organizational existence. Like other influential movements, the Tea Party has been ridiculed and disdained by its opponents; like other movements, it has combined a vigorous populist appeal to the "outside" with substantial support from within the party structure by insurgent figures such as Senator Jim DeMint. Aided by modern technology, the Tea Party has blossomed more quickly than past movements like the Populists, Progressives, or conservatives.

By definition, movements are not fully institutionalized, permanent fixtures in the political landscape. Rather, although they have some staying power, they tend to arrive with great passion and fade as the issues that gave rise to them are either resolved or prove intractable and give way to new concerns. While not a permanent feature of the political landscape, they have staying power beyond a single election. Thus a key question in the 2012 presidential election—and especially in the Republican presidential primaries—is what role the Tea Party will play. In this regard, it is almost certain that the Tea Party will indeed continue to be active through at least the 2012 election. The issues that have given rise to the movement—national debt, federal spending, and fears of a move toward democratic socialism crystallized by health care reform—were not extinguished by the 2010 elections, and will doubtless continue to be salient at least as long as Obama remains in the White House.

A movement's two greatest enemies are failure and success. Consistent and complete failure leads to discouragement and dissolution; too much success leads to complacency by supporters and perhaps even the eclipse of the mobilizing issues. In the 2010 elections, the Tea Party experienced enough success for activists to remain engaged, but not enough to lead to complacency. If anything, the movement seemed energized and eager for the next round. On election night 2010, Tea Party Patriots national coordinator Jenny Beth Martin proclaimed that, "No one in this movement is stopping today. This is not an endgame. This is just a beginning."[84] Tea Party activists remain primarily interested in policy change, not in electoral activity as an end in itself, and they consistently express the intention of holding the 2010 congressional winners to their promises of lower spending, lower taxes, and health care repeal.

Moreover, although the movement is controversial, it is clearly tapping into real concerns held by millions of Americans who do not consider themselves part of the movement. In the last half of 2010, pollsters frequently found a small plurality of respondents disapproving of the Tea Party. Yet when respondents were asked in ten polls whether they agreed or disagreed with the concerns raised by the movement, a plurality always agreed.[85] The movement has reflected a more general trend toward greater conservatism in the electorate. Though this could change, the movement has been swimming with the current, not against it, even if it has been swimming faster than the current requires.

As in 2010, Tea Party activists will have to decide whether to support a third party or, in the words of one organizer, work to "co-opt the Republican Party" through the primary and precinct caucus process.[86] When the movement involves itself in the 2012 Republican presidential primaries, it is far from clear what the effect will be. For the time being, the movement is focused on substantive policy and electoral outcomes. However, based on past movement experience, one should not rule out the possibility that it might direct its energies toward procedural reform if its members feel unfairly treated through the 2012 process.

Among frequently-mentioned potential candidates, Sarah Palin is often assumed to be the favorite among Tea Party supporters. In 2010, Palin stood out for her early and enthusiastic embrace of the movement and her endorsement of many of the movement's preferred primary candidates. Nevertheless, surveys of Tea Party members or supporters in 2010 showed no clear front-runner among prospective Republican presidential aspirants. A *New York Times*/CBS News survey taken in April 2010 showed that among Tea Party members, the most admired political figure living today was Newt Gingrich with 10 percent, followed by Sarah Palin with 9 percent, Ron Paul with 5 percent, and a wide smattering of others. One out of four respondents did not offer a name. While Palin was rated higher by Tea Party members than by other Americans, only 40 percent of members held that she would make an effective president (to 47 percent who said she would not).[87]

The *Politico* survey of participants in the April 15, 2010 Tax Day Tea Party protest revealed a similar diffusion of support and seeming disenchantment with the options. Palin was named the politician today who best exemplifies the Tea Party by 15 percent, followed by Paul with 12 percent, Representatives Michelle Bachmann and Paul Ryan with 8 and 6 percent respectively, and a collection of others in low single digits. Here, one in three offered no name. When asked which of a list of potential candidates they might consider supporting for president, Palin and Gingrich tied with 44 percent—but 53 percent said they would not consider them. Mitt Romney would be considered by 42 percent, but not by 55 percent. Other political figures went down from there. If forced to establish a presidential preference, the Tax Day protestors named Palin (15 percent), Paul (14), Romney (13), Gingrich (9)—and Obama (8).[88] And, while they rarely place very high in national surveys, Senators Jim DeMint of South Carolina and John Thune of South Dakota, former Governor Tim Pawlenty of Minnesota, Governor Rick Perry of Texas, Representatives Mike Pence of Indiana and Michele Bachmann of Minnesota (founder of the congressional Tea Party Caucus), and some others attracted noticeable support among Tea Party activists as possible presidential contenders. (As of this writing, Thune, DeMint, and Pence have all announced they would not be running for president in 2012; Perry finally entered the race in August 2011.)

In other words, as the midterm elections settled and the presidential race began, the Tea Party constituency was wide open. Although some potential contenders (including Romney and Gingrich) would have to overcome the disadvantage of close association with the party establishment, Tea Party Patriots national coordinator Mark Meckler declared that, "I don't think anyone's disqualified," while Amy Kremer of the Tea Party Express echoed that, "I don't think there's anybody we should rule out, or anybody we should rule in. I think it's a completely level playing field."[89] This meant that every Republican aspirant was likely to try to attract Tea Party support. Indeed, potential candidates such as Palin, Gingrich, Romney, and Huckabee were already busy courting the movement even before the midterm elections were over.[90] A key question will be whether the movement will end up coalescing behind a single candidate, as conservatives got behind Barry Goldwater and the New Politics behind George McGovern in 1972, or will spread its support around as the New Politics did in 1968 and as the religious right has typically done since 1988.

Within the Republican Party as a whole, surveys in late 2010 pointed to an electorate split three ways. One-third of Republicans said they did not support the Tea Party movement. Another one-third said they supported the movement but identified more as Republicans than Tea Partiers. The final one-third considered themselves part of the movement and actually identified with it more than with the party. Moreover, these three groups evaluated Republican leaders differently, with Romney considered the "most important leader" among the first group, Palin and Huckabee among the second group, and Gingrich among the third group.[91]

In early 2011, it was not clear whether national Tea Party groups would endorse anyone, though it seemed probable that at least some local groups would do so. National organizations planned a variety of other efforts to influence the Republican race. The Tea Party Express arranged to co-host (with CNN) a presidential primary candidates debate focusing on issues of particular interest to the Tea Party. Tea Party Patriots invited all the candidates to an American Policy Summit in February 2011, while FreedomWorks established a Political Action Committee to assist candidates.[92] Complicating the picture further will be the degree to which the Tea Party is a decentralized, grassroots phenomenon not subject to easy hierarchical control. The national Tea Party Patriots and Tea Party Express could easily wind up as less important in the nomination process than the local Tea Parties in Iowa, New Hampshire, and South Carolina, key early caucus and primary states. Moreover, as political scientist Zachary Courser argues, continued extreme decentralization of the movement may limit its effectiveness as it attempts to affect elections and policy.[93]

Whether it backs one candidate or many, the Tea Party will also face the perennial dilemma posed to every ideological movement: how to manage the tradeoff between ideological purity and stylistic compatibility on the one hand and electability and governing ability on the other. Movements such as the Populists, conservatives, and New Politics changed their parties and American politics in dramatic ways, but they did so in a long process that included running candidates who were notably unsuccessful in the short run: Bryan lost three times, while Goldwater and McGovern were each at the losing end of historic landslides. If that history is any indication, there is a real possibility that the Tea Party will saddle the GOP in 2012 with a nominee who inspires the movement and articulates its message but who cannot win. Indeed, it already did exactly that in a number of cases at lower levels in 2010. Yet the movements that obtained long-term change also learned how to meld ideology and pragmatism; it was a key moment in the conservative movement when *National Review* founder William F. Buckley declared that the guiding dictum of the movement should be to support the most conservative primary candidate who could win. A key test of 2012 will be whether the Tea Party (or Tea Parties) will follow the Delaware model, where the movement preferred losing with a Christine O'Donnell rather than winning with a Mike Castle, or the Missouri model, where the movement made peace with a Roy Blunt and sailed to easy victory in a swing state. Some analysts predicted that the Tea Party would help re-elect Obama by pressuring Republicans to nominate someone who could be portrayed as an extremist.[94] Discussing the upcoming presidential primaries, Brendan Steinhauser of FreedomWorks predicted to the contrary that "[P]eople are going to be very prudent about this. Who do we have who can beat Obama that agrees with us on 75 to 80 percent of the issues? We're going to have a lot of hard choices to make as a movement."[95] One of the biggest questions of the 2012 Republican nomination fight will be whether he is proved right.

*****

I would like to acknowledge the research assistance of Hannah Burak and Laura Sucheski, whose aid was invaluable. Thanks are also due to the Salvatori Center for the Study of Individual Freedom in the Modern World.

NOTES

1. Lou Cannon, "The Conservatives Come Back From the Dead," *Politics Daily*, October 31, 2010, http://www.politicsdaily.com/2010/10/31/the-conservatives-come-back-from-the-dead (accessed December 12, 2010).

2. Douglas A. Blackmon, Alexandra Berzon, Jennifer Levitz, and Lauren Etter, "Rebel Movement Takes Center Stage," *Wall Street Journal*, November 2, 2010, A6.

3. See Andrew E. Busch, *Outsiders and Openness in the Presidential Nominating System* (Pittsburgh, PA: University of Pittsburgh Press, 1997), 22.

4. Walter Dean Burnham, *Critical Elections and the Mainsprings of American Politics* (New York: W. W. Norton, 1970), 72.

5. Holman Hamilton, "Election of 1848," in Arthur M. Schlesinger, ed., *History of American Presidential Elections*, 2 vols. (New York: Chelsea House, 1971), 2:865–918.

6. Lawrence Goodwyn, *The Populist Moment* (New York: Oxford University Press, 1978), vii.

7. J. Rogers Hollingsworth estimates that by April 1896, 60 percent of congressional Democrats were pro-silver. *The Whirligig of Politics: The Democracy of Cleveland and Bryan* (Chicago, IL: University of Chicago, 1963), 38, 43.

8. James Sundquist, *Dynamics of the Party System* (Washington, DC.: Brookings Institution, 1973), 142, 138–139.

9. On these points see, for example, Roscoe Martin, *The People's Party in Texas* (Austin: University of Texas Bulletin Number 3308, 1933), 266; Paul W. Glad, *McKinley, Bryan, and the People* (Philadelphia, PA: J. B. Lippincott, 1964), 207; Fred E. Haynes, *Third Party Movements with Special Reference to Iowa* (Cedar Rapids: Torch, 1916), 382–386.

10. Sundquist, *Dynamics of the Party System*, 156; Richard Hofstadter, *The Progressive Movement, 1900–1915* (Englewood Cliffs, NJ: Prentice-Hall, 1963), 7–8; Richard Hofstadter, *The Age of Reform* (New York: Alfred A. Knopf, 1955), 164–172; Stanley P. Caine, "The Origins of Progressivism," in Lewis L. Gould, ed. *The Progressive Era* (Syracuse, NY: Syracuse University Press, 1974); John J. Broesamle, "The Democrats from Bryan to Wilson," in Gould, *The Progressive Era*, 86–92; Benjamin Parke De Witt, *The Progressive Movement* (Seattle, WA: University of Washington Press, 1968 [1915]), 26–35.

11. Caine, "The Origins of Progressivism," 31.

12. Louise Overacker, *The Presidential Primary* (New York: Macmillan, 1926).

13. Amos R.E. Pinchot, *History of the Progressive Party, 1912–1916* (New York: NYU Press, 1958), 165.

14. William A. Rusher, *Rise of the Right* (New York: William Morrow, 1984); Paul Gottfried and Thomas Fleming, *The Conservative Movement* (Boston, MA: Twayne, 1988); George Nash, *The Conservative Intellectual Movement since 1945* (Wilmington, DE: ISI Books, 1996).

15. See F. Clifton White, *Suite 3505: the Story of the Draft Goldwater Movement* (New York: Arlington House, 1967); Nicol Rae, *Decline and Fall of the Liberal Republicans from 1952 to the Present* (New York: Oxford University Press, 1989); Theodore H. White, *The Making of the President 1964* (New York: Atheneum, 1965).

16. Lee Edwards, *Goldwater: The Man Who Made a Revolution* (Washington, DC: Regnery, 1995), 216–218; White, *The Making of the President 1964*, 132.

17. See Busch, *Outsiders and Openness in the Presidential Nominating System*, chap. 3.

18. Rae, *Decline and Fall of the Liberal Republicans*, 46.

19. Arthur Herzog, *McCarthy for President* (New York: Viking, 1969); Theodore H. White, *The Making of the President 1968* (New York: Pocket, 1970); Stephen C. Schlesinger, *The New Reformers: Forces for Change in American Politics* (Boston, MA: Houghton Mifflin, 1975); George McGovern, "The New Politics," in James A. Burkhart and Frank J. Kendrick, ed., *The New Politics: Mood or Movement?*

(Englewood Cliffs, NJ: Prentice-Hall, 1971); Stewart Burns, *Social Movements of the 1960s: Searching for Democracy* (Boston, MA: Twayne, 1970).

20. White, *Making of the President 1968*, 107, 148–150.

21. Ben Stavis, *We Were the Campaign: New Hampshire to Chicago for McCarthy* (Boston: Beacon, 1968), 150. See also Eugene McCarthy, *The Year of the People* (Garden City: Doubleday, 1969), chap. 11; Lewis Chester, Godfrey Hodgson, and Bruce Page, *American Melodrama: The Presidential Campaign of 1968* (New York: Viking, 1969), 201.

22. William J. Crotty, *Party Reform* (New York: Longman, 1983), 47–48.

23. Busch, *Outsiders and Openness*, chap. 4.

24. Byron Shafer, *Quiet Revolution: The Struggle for the Democratic Party and the Shaping of Post-reform Politics* (New York: Russell Sage Foundation, 1983), 158–159; George McGovern, *Grassroots* (New York: Random House, 1977), 136, 159.

25. Samuel S. Hill and Dennis E. Owen, *The New Religious Political Right in America* (Nashville, TN: Abingdon, 1982).

26. Alan Hertzke, *Echoes of Discontent: Jesse Jackson, Pat Robertson, and the Resurgence of Populism* (Washington, DC: CQ Press, 1993).

27. John F. Persinos, "Has the Christian Right Taken Over the Republican Party?" *Campaigns & Elections*, September 1994.

28. John C. Green, Mark J. Rozell, and Clyde Wilcox, "The Christian Right's Long Political March," in Green, Rozell, and Wilcox, ed., *The Christian Right in American Politics* (Washington, DC: Georgetown University Press, 2003), 1.

29. See Duane M. Oldfield, "The Christian Right in the Presidential Nominating Process," in William G. Mayer, ed., *In Pursuit of the White House: How We Choose Our Presidential Nominees* (Chatham, NJ: Chatham House, 1996).

30. Hertzke, *Echoes of Discontent;* Lorn S. Foster, "Avenues for Black Political Mobilization:The Presidential Campaign of Reverend Jesse Jackson," in Lorenzo Morris, ed., *The Social and Political Implications of the 1984 Jesse Jackson Presidential Campaign* (New York: Praeger, 1990). On Brown and the Rainbow Coalition, see Lou Cannon, "Brown Vows He Would Back Clinton," *Washington Post*, April 12, 1992, A25; Busch, *Outsiders and Openness*, 155–159.

31. Indeed, some commentators expressed concern that his campaign had introduced a sort of personalistic political idolatry seldom seen in American politics but often seen in the Middle East and Latin America. See Fouad Ajami, "Obama and the Politics of Crowds," *Wall Street Journal*, October 30, 2008.

32. Douglas A. Blackmon, Jennifer Levitz, Alexandra Berzon, and Lauren Etter, "Birth of a Movement," *Wall Street Journal*, October 29, 2010, A1.

33. For a history of the origins of the Tea Party movement, see Blackmon, Berzon, Levitz, and Etter, "Rebel Movement Takes Center Stage"; Scott Rasmussen and Douglas Schoen, *Mad as Hell: How the Tea Party Movement Is Fundamentally Remaking Our Two-Party System* (New York: Harper, 2010); Kate Zernike, *Boiling Mad: Inside Tea Party America* (New York: Times Books, 2010).

34. Jennifer Levitz, Cameron McWhirter, and Douglas A. Blackmon, "As Races End, Tea Party Plans for Next Phase," *Wall Street Journal*, November 3, 2010, A10.

35. Matea Gold, "Ad Man Fueling the 'Tea Party,'" *Los Angeles Times*, September 19, 2010, A1.

36. Included in this number were surveys from Democracy Corps, NBC News/*Wall Street Journal*, *New York Times*/CBS News, CNN, Fox News, Pew Research, Common Cause, ABC News/*Washington Post*, Quinnipiac, Gallup/*USA Today*, Associated Press/Gfk, George Washington University, and Bloomberg News.

37. *New York Times*/CBS News survey, February 5–10, 2010 (18 percent); The Winston Group survey, February 22–23, 2010 (16 percent); Public Religion Research Institute survey, "Religion and the Tea Party in the 2010 Election," October 2010 (11 percent); Quinnipiac University survey, March 16–21, 2010 (13 percent); ABC News/*Washington Post* survey, April 22–25, 2010 (8 percent); Fox News/Opinion Dynamics survey, April 20–21, 2010 (17 percent); Quinnipiac University survey, April 14–19, 2010 (15 percent); Quinnipiac University survey, July 13–19, 2010 (12 percent); Center for American Progress, "Doing What Works" survey, May 10–22, 2010 (18 percent); Quinnipiac University survey, August 31-September 7, 2010 (12 percent). Unless otherwise indicated, this and other survey data provided by the Roper Center for Public Opinion Research, University of Connecticut.

38. Democracy Corps/Campaign for America's Future survey, July 26–29, 2010; CNN Opinion Research, February 12–15, 2010.

39. Rasmussen and Schoen, *Mad as Hell*, 137–141.

40. *New York Times*/CBS News survey, "National Survey of Tea Party Supporters," April 5–12, 2010.

41. *Politico*/TargetPoint survey, April 15, 2010.

42. Rasmussen and Schoen, *Mad as Hell*, 177.

43. Peggy Noonan, "Why It's Time for the Tea Party," *Wall Street Journal*, September 18–19, 2010, A15.

44. At one extreme, one CBS/New York Times poll indicated that 95 percent of Tea Party members were white, as opposed to 77 percent of the full national sample; at the other end, a Gallup survey showed only 79 percent of Tea Partiers—as opposed to 75 percent of all Americans—were white.

45. See CNN, February 2010; NYT/CBS, April 2010 and Gallup, March 2010 also showed Tea Partiers as more affluent. NYT/CBS February 2010 and Winston Group February 2010 showed no difference between Tea Partiers and the national average.

46. See Winston Group, February 2010; CNN, February 2010; Gallup, March 2010; NYT/CBS, April 2010; and Public Religion Research Institute, October 2010.

47. *Politico*, April 2010; NYT/CBS, April 2010.

48. The Public Religion Research Institute poll (October 2010) showed that 64 percent of Tea Party identifiers agreed that it is not too big a problem "if some people have more of a chance in life than others."

49. In this April 2010 survey, 45 percent of Tea Party members said the main goal should be to reduce the federal government, 6 percent said cut taxes, and

6 percent said cut the budget, adding up to 57 percent. Nine percent said create jobs, 7 percent electing candidates, 7 percent "something else," and 18 percent "all of them." This means that altogether at least 75 percent included reducing the federal government as their top priority. See also WinstonGroup, February 2010.

50. *Politico*, April 2010.

51. NYT/CBS, April 2010.

52. NYT/CBS, April 2010.

53. Winston Group, February 2010; Gallup, March 2010; NYT/CBS, April 2010.

54. NYT/CBS, February 2010.

55. NYT/CBS, April 2010.

56. Ben Smith and Byron Tau, "GOP Is Urged to Avoid Social Issues," *Politico*, November 14, 2010, http://www.politico.com/news/stories/1110/45110 .html (accessed January 21, 2011).

57. Gallup, March 2010; NYT/CBS, April 2010.

58. Kathleen Hennessey, "Republicans Seek to Address Issues of 'Values Voters,'" *Los Angeles Times*, September 18, 2010, A8–A9; Michael M. Phillips, "Social Conservatives Line Up To Get a Seat at the Tea Party," *Wall Street Journal*, September 18-19, 2010, A4.

59. NYT/CBS, April 2010.

60. Public Religion Research Institute, October 2010.

61. NYT/CBS, February 2010; NYT/CBS, April 2010.

62. NYT/CBS, April 2010; *Politico*, April 2010.

63. Rasmussen polls in February and July 2010 showed only about one in five Americans believed the country operated on the basis of consent of the governed. See http://www.rasmussenreports.com/public_content/politics/general_politics/february _2010/only_21_say_u_s_government_has_consent_of_the_governed; http://www .rasmussenreports.com/public_content/politics/general_politics/july_2010/23_say _u_s_government_has_the_consent_of_the_governed (accessed January 11, 2011).

64. Rasmussen and Schoen, *Mad as Hell*, 81–109.

65. Rasmussen and Schoen, *Mad as Hell*, 127.

66. NYT/CBS, April 2010.

67. In one instance, in September 2010, a man named James Lee invaded the Discovery Channel headquarters and took hostages before being shot by police. Although some commentators assumed he was somehow connected with the Tea Party, he was actually a mentally disturbed individual espousing an extreme environmental manifesto. Then, in January 2011, the horrific shooting of Arizona Congresswoman Gabrielle Giffords and 18 others by Jared Loughner led to a similar outpouring of commentary until it became clear that he was a mentally disturbed loner with no coherent ideology or record of political activism. Ranting about "conscious dreaming" and government control of grammar, identifying the *Communist Manifesto* and *Mein Kampf* among his favorite books, it turned out that the only tea party Loughner was affiliated with was the one presided over by the Mad Hatter and the Red Queen.

68. Kenneth P. Vogel, "Conservatives Target Their Own Fringe," *Politico*, February 27, 2010, http://www.politico.com/news/stories/0210/33621.html; Kenneth P. Vogel, "Weak Tea? Partiers Fear Fallout," *Politico*, March 22, 2010, http://www.politico.com/news/stories/0310/34790.html (accessed January 11, 2011).

69. Dan Balz and Jon Cohen, "Poll Shows High Marks for Obama on Tucson, Low Regard for Political Dialogue," *Washington Post*, January 18, 2011, http://www.washingtonpost.com/wp-dyn/content/article/2011/01/17/AR2011011703262.html?hpid=topnews (accessed January 21, 2011).

70. The April 2010 ABC News/*Washington Post* poll showed that 19 percent of Americans thought that racial prejudice accounted for "a great deal" of the Tea Party's antipathy to Obama, while another 9 percent believed prejudice accounted for "a good amount," 21 percent said "just some," and 43 percent said "not at all." In a July 2010 CNN/Opinion Research poll, 10 percent replied that "almost all" Tea Party members were prejudiced against minorities and another 15 percent judged that "most" were; 35 percent said "some" and 38 percent said "just a few" or "almost none."

71. NYT/CBS, April 2010.

72. http://www.cnn.com/2009/POLITICS/07/04/tea.party/index.html (accessed January 11, 2011).

73. Ben Smith, "MoveOn: California Fracas, Finger-Biting 'Regrettable,'" *Politico*, September 3, 2009, http://www.politico.com/blogs/bensmith/0909/MoveOn_California_fracas_fingerbiting_regrettable.html (accessed January 11, 2011).

74. Blackmon, Berzon, Levitz, and Etter, "Rebel Movement Takes Center Stage,"A1.

75. James Oliphant, "GOP Insiders Hitch a Ride on 'Tea Party' Bandwagon," *Los Angeles Times*, October 29, 2010, A23; Neil Ling, Jr., "Tea Parties Forge Alliances in Bid to Advance Agendas," *Wall Street Journal*, October 6, 2010, http://online.ws.com/article/SB10001424052748704847104575532693771514772.html (accessed October 7, 2010).

76. "Repainting the House," *New York Times*, November 4, 2010, 16.

77. Gold, "Ad Man Fueling the 'Tea Party,'" A25.

78. "The Tea Party's Impact: Will Newcomers' Influence Derail Any Compromising?" *USA Today*, November 4, 2010, 2A. See also James Rosen, "DeMint Earns Praise, Rebukes after Election," *The Post and Courier*, November 7, 2010, http://www.postandcourier.com/news/2010/nov/07/demint-earns-praise-rebukes-after-election (accessed January 11, 2011).

79. Blackmon, Berzon, Levitz, and Etter, "Rebel Movement Takes Center Stage," A6.

80. NYT/CBS, April 2010.

81. At least five such surveys were taken, with the following results: 31 percent Democratic (D), 26 percent Republican (R), 8 percent Tea Party (TP) (*National Review* Institute, January 19-20, 2010); 46 D, 32 R, 16 TP (CNN, February 2010); 36 D, 25 R, 15 TP (Quinnipiac, March 2010); 36 D, 24 R, 13 TP (Fox News, April 2010); 34 D, 27 R, 16 TP (Fox News/Opinion Dynamics survey, August 10–11, 2010).

82. Peggy Noonan, "Tea Party to the Rescue," *Wall Street Journal*, October 22, 2010.

83. National House exit polls, www.cnn.com/ELECTION/2010/results/polls (accessed November 2010).

84. Levitz, McWhirter, and Blackmon, "As Races End, Tea Party Plans for Next Phase," A10.

85. NYT/CBS, February 2010; *Washington Post*, March 2010; Pew, March 2010; AP, April 2010; AP, May 2010; Pew, May 2010; Pew, June 2010; Pew, July 2010; AP, August 2010; and AP, September 2010.

86. "After Election Victories, Tea Party Activists Look Ahead to 2012," Fox News Channel, http://www.foxnews.com/politics/2010/11/05/election-victories-tea-party-activists-look-ahead (accessed January 20, 2011).

87. NYT/CBS, April 2010.

88. *Politico*, April 2010.

89. Michael O'Brien, "2012 Republican Presidential Hopefuls Getting a Jump on the Tea Party Courtship," *The Hill*, December 24, 2010, http://thehill.com/blogs/blog-briefing-room/news/135069-2012-gop-hopefuls-have-tea-party-courting-to-do-groups-say (accessed January 11, 2011).

90. See O'Brien, "2012 GOP Presidential Hopefuls"; Peter Wallsten, "Tea Party Already Shapes '12 Race," *Wall Street Journal*, October 25, 2010, A1; Michael Kranish, "Tea Party Success Could Hurt Romney's Chances at a Presidential Bid in 2012," *Boston Globe*, November 6, 2010.

91. Wallsten, "Tea Party Already Shapes '12 Race."

92. O'Brien, "2012 GOP Presidential Hopefuls."

93. Zachary Courser, "The Tea Party at the Election," *The Forum*, Vol. 8, Issue 4. Article 5. http://www.bepress.com/forum/vol8/iss4/art5 (accessed January 13, 2011).

94. Andrew Rawnsley, "Why Barack Obama Is Looking Good for a Second Term in 2012," *The Guardian*, November 7, 2010 http://www.guardian.co.uk/commentisfree/2010/nov/07/barack-obama-second-term-2012/ (accessed January 20, 2011).

95. O'Brien, "2012 GOP Presidential Hopefuls."

Chapter 4

The Experience of Running for President

Michael S. Dukakis

One doesn't make the decision to run for the presidency lightly. In fact, it is probably the single most important decision anybody in public life in America will make.

The reasons for this seem obvious, but going through the process of making the decision, launching a campaign, and then campaigning virtually nonstop for a year and a half will be the toughest experience anybody in American politics will ever have. At the same time, win or lose, it will be the most inspiring experience one will ever have.

I took a long time to make the decision in 1987. In fact, I had never even thought of running for the presidency until after I was reelected to a third term as governor of Massachusetts in November of 1986. Massachusetts was in great shape. We had fought our way out of a brutal Northeast recession in the mid-1970s. A region that some were calling the New Appalachia was beginning to awaken again after it had lost a huge chunk of its historic industrial base in shoes and textiles. Knowledge was now the currency of economic growth, and a state with 120 colleges and universities, including Harvard and MIT, had only itself to blame if it wasn't leading the pack.

By 1986, we were up there with the best of them. The Massachusetts Miracle wasn't just a slogan. Unemployment, which had been in the 12 percent range in the mid-1970s, had dropped to below 3 percent by 1987. Thanks to our economic revival and a serious economic game plan, our older, severely depressed industrial communities were coming back to life. Revenue growth was strong; and as I looked forward to a third term, I had an unfinished agenda that I was anxious to tackle. Oh sure, some people had talked to me occasionally about the 1988 presidential race, but I didn't pay much attention to them. I wanted to win a third term decisively and make my final gubernatorial term my best.

Then, the Iran-Contra scandal broke just days after the November 1986 election, and I and millions of Americans were appalled. The spectacle of a president and a vice president defying the law and deliberately misleading Congress while their subordinates were shredding documents in the basement of the White House was beyond anything we had ever seen, and for me, at least, those events first got me thinking about a presidential run. Maybe I wasn't the guy to do it, but somebody had to run and win and turn the White House into something we could be proud of.

Even so, however, I was highly skeptical about a lot of things that would be entailed in a presidential race. I wasn't particularly concerned about the physical requirements for running—and they are formidable. If you aren't in excellent physical shape and ready for the simple physical demands that a national race places on you, then you have no business running.

At a minimum, you will be on the campaign trail, one way or the other, for eighteen consecutive months. You will be crossing time zones repeatedly—a not insignificant factor when it comes to getting a good night's sleep. In states like Iowa and New Hampshire, you will be making six or seven speeches a day, and while you try to eat three reasonably decent meals a day, the chances are that you will be bolting them down and end up eating chili or chicken wings on the campaign plane as you head for the next day's destination.

Moreover, your campaign staff may overreact to an occasional expressed preference for a particular food. I remember in the late stages of the campaign I expressed a strong desire one day to have a coffee milk shake when I arrived at my hotel in the late evening. For the next two weeks I found about a dozen coffee milk shakes waiting for me every time I wrapped up the day. I finally told somebody that the fact that I wanted a milk shake didn't require a daily dozen of them, that this was costing us a lot of money, and that milk shakes that went untouched weren't much good for anything the following day.

Fortunately, the physical demands of the campaign were not a problem for me. I had been a pretty good athlete in my youth. I either jogged or power walked on a regular basis. In fact, when I did decide to run, light heavy-hand weights were always packed in my bag so I could do my power walking while swinging the weights when I was on the campaign trail. Admittedly, I wasn't in the kind of condition that made it possible for me to run and finish the Boston Marathon when I was a senior in high school, but for a busy fifty-four-year old, I was in excellent shape and did my best to eat sensibly and exercise regularly.

The impact on my family of making the decision to run was another matter, however. In fact, had even one of our children still been in high school, I would never have thrown my hat in the ring. Being there for my kids has been a very important part of my life, and leaving our younger daughter pretty much on her own or with her grandparents to finish high school was not something I was prepared to do under any circumstances.

Don't get me wrong. I have a lot of admiration for the Carters and the Clintons and the Obamas and their apparent ability to combine good parenting with nearly two years of non-stop campaigning and their years in the White House, but I was simply not prepared to do that. Fortunately, Kara, our youngest, was a sophomore in college, and our two oldest children had either finished college or were already deeply engaged in the adult world. Andrea graduated from Princeton in May of 1987, and John had gone off to be an actor—and a good one—after a year at Brown.

That didn't mean, however, that we didn't have long discussions about the pressures and burdens on them of a presidential campaign and on Kitty, too. We have two very attractive daughters. " How," I said to them," do you feel about the prospect of never being able to go out on a date without a Secret Service person tagging along if I win this thing?" And while Kitty and I had had two hard-and-fast rules from the time we were married about home and our time together—dinner at home at 6 p.m. without fail and no politics on Sunday—a national campaign would obviously require that those rules be waived for the duration.

Interestingly enough, my wife and children were considerably more enthusiastic than I was about the prospect of a national campaign. In fact, I remember Andrea, our older daughter, looking across the kitchen table at me and saying, "Dad, very few people have the opportunity to do something like this, especially in the middle of this current White House mess. You have a responsibility to do it."

Unquestionably, our family discussions dispelled some of my own concerns about how a presidential campaign would affect the most important people in my life—Kitty, our son, and our two daughters. But trying to make sure that we didn't lose what was very special about our family was something I took very, very seriously.

I can't say enough, however, for the effort and energy and determination that Kitty and our children brought to the campaign. She was terrific—and turned out to have a lot more staying power than I did. In fact, I have often said that if she had been the candidate, we would have won in a walk.

The same was true of our children. John had been an actor—and a successful one—for seven years, and in addition to handling formidable organizational chores in the campaign, he was often a surrogate for me—and an extremely effective one—both on the campaign trail and on national and local television.

Andrea, who while strongly committed to the campaign and a full-time campaign worker, started out by saying that she did not want to do any serious public speaking, ended up being as effective on the stump as anybody we had—a transformation that led her after the campaign to pursue a career in broadcast journalism where she has worked ever since on both national and regional public radio.

Kara had plenty of work to do as a student at Brown, but I will never forget the standing-room-only rally she and Patrick Kennedy, himself then a student at Providence College, put together for me on the Brown campus before the Rhode Island primary. They moved around that hall like a couple of real pros, and the rally itself was a huge success.

I was equally concerned about another question: Was I qualified and equipped to be the most important political leader in the world? I remember meeting with a group of Washington-based journalists at the time I was trying to make the decision and making that precise point, and I remember Jack Germond telling me that they had been having these kinds of meetings with prospective presidential candidates for a long time, and I was the first candidate ever to raise that question.

I told him that if a candidate had never asked himself that question, he didn't deserve to be in the race—and I still feel that way. Moreover, the Cold War was by no means over, and whoever sat in the Oval Office might have the awesome responsibility of making the decision to use nuclear weapons and blow up civilization. I couldn't imagine a potential candidate not at least asking himself the question of whether or not he was prepared to do that.

I spent a lot of time in the approximately three months I set for myself before I made the decision asking people whose judgment I trusted, some of whom had worked previously in the White House, if they thought I had what it took to do the job. And I made it clear to them that I was not interested in idle flattery. I wanted them to level with me and tell me what they thought and whether or not I had the right stuff.

For obvious reasons, I was also very concerned about my ability to continue to do the job to which I had just been reelected while running a national campaign. I had just been elected overwhelmingly to a third term. I had been thrown out of the governor's office after my first term and had to claw my way back in 1982 to defeat the guy who had beaten me in 1978. I had been a far better governor the second time around than I had been in my first term, and when one has been as deeply involved in state politics and governing as I had been since my election to the legislature in 1962, one develops both a personal commitment to one's state and a stake in its success which are powerful indeed.

Furthermore, the state government I entered as a young legislator in the early 1960s had been one of the three or four most corrupt in the country. We had done a lot to change that over the previous couple of decades, and I did not want to see us slip back to the time when at least some of my fellow Bay Staters used to say, "Republicans in Massachusetts bore you to death, and Democrats steal you to death."

Fortunately, I had a great team of people working for me. They were strongly committed to continuing on the path that we had set for ourselves, and I was in a position to delegate responsibility with a lot more confidence in my third term as governor than I would have been in my first. Moreover, I was determined that, at least during the primaries, I would spend four full days a week in the State House and campaign for the nomination essentially on nights and weekends.

Being from Massachusetts helped. For one thing, it put me very close to New Hampshire, and campaigning in Manchester or Nashua wasn't that much different from making a speech in Worcester or New Bedford. A plane could get me down and back to the New York metropolitan area in an evening. In fact, one night I left the State House at 5 p.m., flew to South Bend, Indiana to speak to a national meeting of the bricklayers' union, and was back in my bed in Brookline, Massachusetts by midnight.

But paying attention to the job I had was a very important part of my candidacy for the presidency. I was running in large part on my record as governor. Any sense that I was neglecting that job or, worse still, that what I hoped and believed was effective leadership was weakening or showing signs of wear and tear would have a direct effect on people's perception of me as somebody who had what it took to run the country.

And so, after many weeks of discussions with my family and with people whose judgment I trusted, I made the decision in March of 1987 to be a candidate and announced my candidacy on the Boston Common in April after a rare overnight snow storm. It was there that my 85-year-old mother, who had immigrated to America from central Greece in 1913, turned to Chris Spirou, the Democratic minority leader of the New Hampshire House of Representatives and, like my mother, an immigrant from central Greece, and said to him about the snow, "Christo, to lipasma tou ftohou." "Chris, poor man's fertilizer."

So now I was a candidate. What does one do in that role? It's important to remember that most of us who run for the presidency have been in elective politics at the local, state, or national level for a long time. We have run in many campaigns. None of them will ever compare with a presidential campaign, but none of them are easy, and over time one accumulates a lot of experience and learns a lot of lessons. My local and state campaigns had always emphasized grassroots organizing and grassroots fund-raising and, not surprisingly, that's exactly what I focused on as we began putting a national campaign together. My campaign staff was largely made up at the beginning of people that had been with me for many years.

Some of them had been involved in national campaigns and gradually began encouraging talented people they had met in those campaigns to join mine. I don't believe, for example, that I had ever met Madeleine Albright before my presidential campaign, but a number of people close to me had met her during the 1984 Mondale campaign, and she became my principal foreign policy advisor. The same was true on the organizational front as we began putting together what we hoped would be a national effort that could build a national grassroots network as quickly as possible.

A number of my core staff quickly identified people with whom they had worked in previous national campaigns who they believed were exceptionally good and could be attracted to the campaign. I myself had been very active in the National Governors Association and as chair of the Democratic Governors, and I talked with a lot of my Democratic gubernatorial colleagues about the really talented campaigners and organizers in their states. I wanted a campaign that "looked like the country," something that often is not the case, and so we made a concerted effort to recruit state and regional coordinators who gave us good geographical, racial, and ethnic balance and either were part of or understood important Democratic constituencies like the labor movement and social services network. I was particularly focused on people who understood grassroots organizing—something that I thought would be the key to success in the primaries. And our fund-raising efforts strongly emphasized relatively small contributions from a broad base of donors, just as my state campaigns had done.

Getting up to speed also involved a good deal of homework on those issues with which I was less familiar than the ones I had worked on for years as a state legislator and governor. Occasionally, that involved boning up on things like agricultural subsidies which were not a part of my daily life in Massachusetts, and to this day I still can't tell you precisely how we regulate and subsidize dairy products. In fact, I wish somebody would tell my why these days I am paying twice as much for a gallon of milk in Massachusetts as I pay for the same thing in southern California where I teach at UCLA during the winter quarter.

Defense and national security issues were other areas where I spent a lot of time studying and being briefed. Don't get me wrong—I had very strong views on foreign policy and national security and I wasn't happy with a lot of what was coming out of the Reagan administration in those areas, but trying to decide whether I favored the Midgetman or the MX missile is not something a busy governor is likely to ponder at any great length unless they are manufactured in his state. I had serious doubts about both of them as a credible deterrent to a Soviet missile attack, but I finally decided I would go with the MX, largely because it was designed to move around the country twenty-four hours a day on trains, and I figured that this might be the only way we could get President Reagan, who regularly tried to zero out the Amtrak budget, to get serious about building a first-rate national passenger rail system!

All of this policy work may be dangerous, however. For some reason, I began developing a reputation for being a bloodless technocrat—a reputation I apparently still can't shake. As recently as May 2011, I found myself referred to in the pages of the *New York Times* as "wonkish." I have my strengths and my weaknesses, but you don't get elected governor of Massachusetts three times because you are wonkish.

Intensive state-by-state efforts were at the top of our to-do list, however, and given the way the states line up, Iowa and New Hampshire loomed large. I had an obvious advantage in New Hampshire. People in New Hampshire often read Boston newspapers and watch a lot of Boston television. Furthermore, then-New Hampshire Governor John Sununu and I had been locked in a continuing controversy over the advisability of building a nuclear power plant in Seabrook, New Hampshire, and that debate had been covered heavily by both the Massachusetts and New Hampshire press. In fact, at one point the *Boston Herald*, for reasons best known to itself, decided to do a poll on whether the people of New Hampshire favored Sununu or me for governor of New Hampshire, and when I beat him by 10 points in the poll, I sensed a decided cooling on his part in what had been a friendly but often contentious relationship.

Of course, the downside of the picture was that if a candidate from Massachusetts couldn't carry New Hampshire—and by a decisive margin—he was probably dead nationally. So even though people up there knew me and a lot of them seemed to like me, it was a state that clearly could not be taken for granted. I spent a lot of time there, but so many Massachusetts people had moved there that I always felt as if I was campaigning on home territory when I headed north.

Iowa was an entirely different story. I had only been there a few times. It was, and is, a lot different from New England, although I remember going by the Horace Mann Junior High School somewhere in Iowa and suddenly feeling very much at home. What was a school in Iowa doing named for the founder of public education in the country and a former president of the Massachusetts State Senate? Apparently, before Iowa even became a state, the territorial governor had asked Mann to come to Iowa and help him set up a system of free public education for the territory.

I can't say enough for the people of Iowa and the kind of reception I received there, but you have to work if you want to win Iowa—and work we did. I remember asking John Sasso, my campaign manager, how many campaign days I would have to spend in Iowa. He said at the time that it would be sixty-five. I ended up spending eighty-five campaign days in that state alone. I was in every one of the state's ninety-nine counties at least once and lots of times in many of them. Kitty campaigned in seventy-five of them. But given the peculiar dynamics of the primary process, somebody from the Northeast or the West, for that matter, had better do well there. And it was a battle, because both Dick Gephardt and Paul Simon, who were also running hard for the nomination, came from states which literally bordered Iowa.

When, in fact, I finished third, albeit a close third—Dick got 31 percent of the vote, Paul got 27 percent, and I got 22 percent—there were a lot of long faces in my hotel room the night of the caucuses as we began getting the results. In the meantime, a crowd of hundreds was gathering downstairs in the hotel ballroom, and in a relatively few minutes I was going to have to go downstairs, face the crowd, and, more importantly, millions of Americans who were just tuning in to the nomination battle for the first time.

There wasn't a lot of happy conversation in that hotel room. Many of my closest advisors said that I would now "have to go negative" on my opponents even though I had vowed from the beginning that I wouldn't do that. In fact, I said at the time in no uncertain terms that if I had to go negative in reaction to the Iowa results when I hit New Hampshire, I'd wrap up the campaign and go back to the State House full-time.

Nobody was coming up with anything worth saying, and time was wasting until Marty Kaplan, who was then married to Susan Estrich and was there with us, said, "Well, it's an Olympic year, and you did win the bronze." "That's it," I said. "Let's go downstairs and face the nation." I'm not sure what that small group of people who had worked their heads off for nearly a year thought I was about to do, but, thanks to Marty, I delivered one of the better sound bites of the campaign when I spoke to the crowd in the ballroom and to millions of Americans who were watching across the country.

"Tonight," I said, "we won the bronze. Next week, [in New Hampshire] we're going to win the gold." And sure enough, a week later, Kitty was putting a gold medal around my neck as we won a decisive victory in the Granite State.

Doing pretty well in Iowa and winning in New Hampshire hardly guarantees victory. Winning a presidential nomination contest is a long slog—a marathon, I often called it—and one is going to have his ups and his downs. But we did have a national strategy of sorts in those early contests. In addition to solid showings in the first two states, I wanted to do well in the next two states—Minnesota and South Dakota—and then win "at the corners" on Super Tuesday. That meant doing everything we could on what was then the biggest Super Tuesday in history to win Maryland, Florida, Texas, and Washington. They were not only delegate-rich states in their own right, but if I could win them all, that would demonstrate that I had at least some kind of national appeal.

Winning those and other Super Tuesday states meant starting early, and many months before Super Tuesday, we had deployed some of my best organizers to those four states. They did a superb job, and on Super Tuesday I did, in fact, "win at the corners," as we had hoped and planned. Those victories were by no means decisive, because at that point the primary contest becomes a war of attrition. Who can hang on and keep moving forward as others bow out? Does one have the combination of a field organization and sufficient funds that can help one absorb the inevitable losses and continue to make progress?

Even after our successes on Super Tuesday, I took some big hits. Despite a lot of effort in Illinois, I was virtually wiped out by Paul Simon and Jesse Jackson in their home state. Then, I lost Michigan to Jackson in that state's so-called firehouse primary (in terms of turnout, it was actually more like a caucus), when all the polls said I was leading the field by a comfortable margin. Flying home from Detroit that night was not the most pleasant trip I have ever taken.

Fortunately for me, other candidates were falling by the wayside at the same time, and I was able to win Wisconsin and head for New York in mid-April with only Al Gore and Jesse Jackson left in the field. Winning New York ended the Gore candidacy, and by the following week and the Pennsylvania primary, it was pretty clear that I had sown up the nomination. Jesse continued to battle right down to the last primary in June and on to the convention, but we had the votes and the nomination was ours.

How does one try to run a busy state and campaign in primaries on a nearly weekly basis? Each week I would return to the State House on the particular primary day, leaving it to my field organization to get out the votes, spend the next few days doing my job as governor, and then head out on Friday for the next battleground—and then repeat the process again and again.

It goes without saying that doing it that way requires a superb organizational effort and a superb fund-raising effort, and thanks to some remarkable people, I had both. Bob Farmer and his fund-raising crew were extraordinary, and John Sasso and Jack Corrigan were the principal architects of our grassroots field strategy. Unfortunately, I had to replace John in the fall of 1987—a decision I have regretted ever since—but Susan Estrich and our team never faltered as they executed our primary strategy to perfection. The self-styled very, very long shot had won the Democratic nomination for the presidency of the United States.

Because Jesse insisted on contesting every primary, however, we had to mount an effort in all of the subsequent primary states. In some ways, however, he did me a favor because it required us to keep working and campaigning in state after state, and the fact that he continued to run gave us the opportunity to expand and test our field operation in every one of those states. And because he contested each primary, I never permitted myself the luxury of thinking about running mates until after the final primaries in California, New Jersey, Montana, and New Mexico on the first Tuesday in June.

How does one pick one's running mate? If you have any sense, very carefully. And while I made a lot of mistakes in the course of the campaign, the process we put in place to select a running mate established a model that, at least on the Democratic side, has been used by every Democratic nominee ever since. I asked my campaign chair, Paul Brountas, to head up the search. We invited suggestions from anybody and everybody. We gradually narrowed the field to four prospects, any one of whom would have been an excellent running mate and a fine vice president. Paul then organized teams of volunteer lawyers and accountants who went into the background, career, and finances of each of the final four. I met with them. He met with them and their families. And when all was said and done, Lloyd Bentsen was the logical choice. He was a great running mate, and he would have been a terrific colleague and advisor. I only regret that we spent too much time campaigning and not enough time conferring in those final months. After all, he had beaten George H. W. Bush for the United States Senate, and he knew him, his strengths and his weaknesses, a lot better than I did.

What's it like to go from a moving series of primary contests to the final head-to-head round? Tough, more difficult than I imagined, and, believe it or not, increasingly boring. That may sound strange to those who haven't been through one of these campaigns, but imagine what it is like to start campaigning seriously at least a year and a half ahead of the November election; run against a field of six or seven candidates; engage in dozens of debates—we had forty-five scheduled primary debates in 1987 and 1988, and I made thirty-nine of them—and then, having won the nomination, start the process all over again.

There may be ways to spice up a campaign, and I could have done a better job of trying to come up with them, but by the time you win the nomination, you've said just about all you can possibly say about the great issues of the day. Trying to make your platform—and yourself—sound fresh and interesting for the five or six months after you have clinched the nomination and before you reach the finish line is not easy. The routine is pretty much the same. Up early in the morning; out on the campaign trail for a morning speech; back in the plane and up in the air for a second one in the afternoon; back in the plane and up in the air for still another one in the evening before you wrap it up.

And while in a gubernatorial campaign you are always energized by your contact with voters as you campaign in streets and neighborhoods across your state in a very personal way, that just isn't possible in a presidential campaign, where security is very tight and where personal contact at the rope line is largely staged and nowhere near as much fun or as real as it is in a campaign closer to home.

I personally found the security situation to be very difficult. I had never had security as governor. Massachusetts doesn't have a governor's mansion, and I wouldn't have lived in it if we did. Our kids went to the neighborhood schools; I took public transportation to work; and if I wanted to buy a new suit, I walked from the State House down to Filene's Basement and had plenty of conversations with my pals on the Basement sales force who have been selling me suits for years. They had always freely dispensed political advice to me during my legislative days, and they didn't stop when I became governor—and some of those guys had very smart political heads on them.

None of that easy informality and contact is possible if one becomes one of two major-party nominees for the presidency. For one thing, the job of the Secret Service is to protect you and they do it exceedingly well, but that doesn't allow for much easy informal contact with potential voters. And the threats are real. Our current president has been the subject of a record number of them, and in my case the Secret Service arrested a man who had a fifteen-year history of mental illness; bought a gun in a gun shop in Springfield, Missouri; flew to Boston and took up residence in a Holiday Inn a few blocks from the State House; and was caught with the gun when he went through the metal detector at Logan Airport on his way to my second debate with George H. W. Bush. What he was planning to do with it is beyond me, but I was very grateful to those Secret Service people for making sure he wasn't stalking me from one coast to the other.

In retrospect, there were ways that we might have made the daily campaign routine a lot more interesting for both me and the people whose votes I was seeking. Bill Clinton and Al Gore hit upon one idea almost by accident in the 1992 campaign which I wish we had thought about. They decided to get on a bus with their spouses and do a three-day bus tour from New York to St. Louis right after the Democratic convention in New York. Thousands of people poured out of their homes and businesses to see them, and the first three days were so successful that they decided to continue to campaign by bus for another three days. In fact, there were very few weeks when they didn't spend two or three days on a bus together in a different part of the country, and if seventy-five or a hundred people wanted to meet them on the route, they would stop and talk with them. I'm sure it made the Secret Service detail with them very nervous, but it had a profound and energizing effect on them and was a huge hit with the people who had a chance to see and meet them. In fact, I remember Al Gore at a fund-raiser in Boston in September 1992 talking about the impact these bus tours had on him as a candidate, particularly as people came up to him to talk about health care and how they either couldn't pay for it, had lost it, or weren't getting it from their employers.

Bill Clinton's TV question-and-answer sessions were another hit with folks and another way to liven up the often deadening routine of day-after-day speechmaking. At first he had to pay for them, and then the networks decided there was something to them and invited both him and President Bush to do them on their morning shows. Bush refused, but Clinton seized the opportunity and made the most of it. And taking questions from real people on national television beats three or four set speeches a day anytime.

Unfortunately, I didn't have the good sense to do those kinds of things. I was a guy who always loved campaigning at the local and state level, and that includes the state-to-state campaigns one wages during the nomination process. I didn't love the much less spontaneous final campaign, and I am afraid it showed.

Of course, one has to have a pretty well thought-out game plan, too, and we did a lot better job of that in the primary than we did in the final. I—nobody else—made the decision that I was not going to respond to the Bush attack campaign, and that turned out to be a terrible mistake. If there is one major lesson we all learned from the 1988 campaign, it is that you have to anticipate an attack campaign; be prepared for it; come up with a strategy for dealing with it that not only blunts the attacks but turns them into a character issue on the guy that is making them; and keep yourself in a position where you can emphasize the positive in a way that draws a clear contrast between the two of you.

The Willie Horton attack campaign was a case in point. Forty-five out of the fifty states had furlough programs in 1988. The Massachusetts furlough version was the product of the Republican administration that I succeeded in 1975. It was as loose as marbles when I inherited it, and my administration did a lot to tighten it up. Unfortunately, Horton went out on a furlough and did some terrible things, and I ended furloughs for people like him, but the fact of the matter was that the Reagan-Bush administration had a furlough program far more liberal than ours. Their furloughs could extend for up to forty-five days compared to a maximum of no more than three days under the Massachusetts program. In fact, one of their inmates, while on an extended furlough, murdered a young pregnant mother in the Southwest, and Ronald Reagan himself as governor had a furlough program he continued to defend even though two California inmates out on furlough during his state administration committed murders.

I doubt very much that the then-vice president even knew his administration had the most liberal furlough program in the country, but it was my responsibility—not his—to tell people about it and describe the hypocrisy in the Willie Horton attack ads. Bill Clinton never made the mistake I made. He had a special unit in his 1992 campaign that referred to itself as the Defense Department, and all they did all day long was ferret out and respond to the Bush attacks on him that were equally as tough as those on me. Admittedly, 1992 might have been a better year for a Democrat to run for the presidency because the country was in the middle of another Republican recession, but that's no excuse for my failure to plan for and deal with the attacks that were leveled at me.

My second big mistake in the 1988 campaign was not to make a fifty-state, precinct-based, grassroots organization the heart and soul of the campaign. I had always won elections with that kind of effort. The 1978 gubernatorial campaign that I lost was the only one where I didn't because we were much too overconfident, and I never forgot that lesson in my two subsequent gubernatorial campaigns. But I spent too much time talking to people at the national level who I thought knew more about winning the presidency than I did, and for the most part they rejected the notion that that kind of effort could make a difference in a presidential campaign. Maybe if you were running for city council, but for the presidency?

It took twenty years and Barack Obama to prove them wrong, but there was no excuse for my ignoring the lessons of my own political experience which told me that personal contact by people in neighborhoods on a systematic precinct-by-precinct basis can make a huge difference in a campaign. Has my party learned that lesson as a result of the president's victory in 2008? I am not sure. We lost a lot of congressional seats in the 2010 midterm elections, and there were very few Democrats in those congressional and Senate races that had a precinct captain and six block captains making personal contact with every single voting household in their precincts. A good grassroots campaign is worth 5 to 10 percentage points in a competitive race, and Democrats lost dozens of seats in the Congress by a lot less than that.

So do I have any advice for would-be candidates who are thinking of entering the presidential race? I sure do.

First, make sure you understand the magnitude of what you are about to do. It is, to be sure, an extraordinary experience unlike any other you will ever undertake in American politics, but make sure you also understand just how tough it is. You will be surrounded by all kinds of friends and self-styled political experts who will tell you that you are just the candidate for the job. Take that advice with a grain of salt; consult with people whose judgment you respect and who will give it to you straight; make sure your family is solidly behind you; and then, and only then, seriously consider running. Second, remember that you will be subject to a degree of public exposure by the press and others that you have never experienced, no matter what office you have previously held. And the closer you get to the brass ring, the more intense will be your exposure and the energy and zeal of those whose job it is to cover you as you work your way through the campaign.

Third, stick with the values and the philosophy that got you to where you are. That doesn't mean that you can't change your mind or that you won't learn a lot in the course of the campaign that will shape your views, but don't try to be somebody you are not. It doesn't work, and it will make life difficult indeed.

Finally, expect the attacks and prepare for them. Politics is a contact sport. That doesn't mean it's unfair or inherently down and dirty. You will be running for the most important political office in the world, and if you have strongly held views, there are inevitably going to be people who disagree with them and are going to go after you because of them. Just make sure you have a carefully thought-out plan for dealing with them. To do otherwise will leave you where I was—in second place . . . and you don't win the presidency in second place.

Chapter 5

More: Digital Media and the Densification of Presidential Campaign Discourse

Michael Cornfield

This chapter considers a long-term media-borne trend in presidential campaign discourse: that candidates, managers, journalists, and citizens are saying more and more in public about the race for the presidency. "In public" is a crucial qualifier. There is no way to tell whether the number of utterances about a presidential contest has increased, remained steady, or fluctuated from cycle to quadrennial cycle with the coming of digital networks, channels, and devices. But it is beyond dispute that the volume of readily available communications has skyrocketed. Even in a non-presidential election year, which is to say, in three of every four years, anyone who wishes to keep current with the available material about the next presidential election would have a tremendous amount of reading, viewing, and listening to do. In the middle of election night 2000, a relatively small number of online members of the engaged public kept hitting the "refresh" button and toggling from site to site to keep pace with the snarling of the Florida returns. That kind of frenetic checking is now a regularly available experience, applying not only to vote counting, but to the ordinary dialogue about the parties, the candidates, their policies, and their campaigns. It is this explosion in the sheer volume of political and campaign communications that I mean by the term *densification*. The purpose of this chapter is to document this important trend and explore its implications for American politics in general and the presidential selection process in particular.

The increasingly dense environment for political communication has strategic and civic implications. I will argue that more time and attention from campaign professionals is needed for content management than message development, two strategic processes that I explain more fully below. I will also argue that while gaining a rhetorical advantage in rapid-fire exchanges can confer benefits to presidential candidates, parties, and other players who seek political power by influencing the discussion, it is important for participants to resist the temptation to win each and every conversational moment so that they can maintain focus on their campaign goals. The same advice will be offered to citizens who, I contend, have a greater responsibility to participate in this discourse more frequently, transparently, and civilly. We face in 2012 and beyond a digital Tower of Babel which can obscure and befuddle our choices as voters, donors, volunteers, commentators, and political actors. Yet if we keep our wits about us we can draw on a wealth of knowledge both lodged and on the loose inside the digital grid, and make smarter choices more in line with our political ideals and preferences.

A DISCOURSE ONE HALF CENTURY IN "THE MAKING"

By *presidential campaign discourse*, I mean public communication about an enduringly popular cluster of discussion topics: the field of candidates, the state of the race, the issues in play, the personal characteristics of those prominently involved, and the compositions of electoral constituencies (eligible voters) and coalitions (likely/actual voters). A convenient starting point from which to view the expansion and thickening of this discourse is fifty years ago, in 1961, when magazine journalist Theodore H. White published his account of how John F. Kennedy out-campaigned several Democratic rivals for the presidential nomination and then defeated Republican Richard M. Nixon in the 1960 presidential contest. *The Making of the President 1960*, which was both a huge best-seller and a winner of the Pulitzer Prize, established a narrative template for what many people find interesting and important about presidential elections—indeed, its title is echoed in the title of the present book. White drew on many sources, from insider interviews to Census Bureau data. But the book essentially reflected one man's perspective on what happened of significance in connection with the campaign and election process. That mode of influence—one author communicating in a long uninterrupted stretch to millions of readers—is a relative rarity in our day, the rising popularity of e-books notwithstanding.

By 1982, when the fifth and final book in White's series was published (he did not publish an account of the 1976 election), many other alternatives vied for public and elite attention. Other national journalists competed for White's share of the book market. In 1972, Harvard University's Institute of Politics began publishing the transcripts of a conference held shortly after each election in which the campaign managers talked about their experiences in the just-completed campaign, giving these favored journalistic sources a direct, albeit edited, outlet for their views apart from what the media chroniclers distilled from them. But readers did not have to wait for these books. Stories about the backstage activities, significant events, and public reactions to presidential campaigns were available, installment by installment, in mass media news outlets often within hours of their occurrence. Journalists at news weeklies, large daily newspapers, wire services, and radio and television networks produced narrative accounts nourished by the latest managerial spin and leaked, media-sponsored, and academic poll data. A cultural rhythm was established: presidential election spectators followed the discourse as it described the entourages that travelled the campaign trail, and then, if they were really enthralled by the topic, they could peruse synoptic accounts after the election.

The debut of onetime political consultant Doug Bailey's news service *The Hotline* in 1987 proved that there was sufficient material and interest in the discourse for a daily digest of mass media entries, distributed by fax to those willing to pay thousands of dollars a year. Along with the lengthening presidential race, *Hotline* also aggregated material about other campaigns and elections and related Washington goings-on. Subscribers numbered in the thousands, enough to make it profitable. *Hotline* migrated to the Internet in the 1990s, where it was joined by other discourse digests, which soon became bulletin services as well: *The Note, First Read, Taegan Goddard's Political Wire, Real Clear Politics*. As online services became more technically sophisticated, these discourse aggregators developed the additional benefit of linking their readers to campaign transcripts, podcasts, photographs, and videos, which widened and prolonged public exposure to messages that formerly had to be consumed at broadcast or publication time on their channels of origin.

Original and reproduced, there was a lot more information to absorb as the Internet settled into the media mix. Yet a broader change was also in the works: digital media enabled lay people to join journalists and politicos in publishing their observations on the cluster of topics first delineated by Theodore White. Some of these popular expressions resided on rarely visited websites and hosted pages; some were delivered to subscribers via email and then RSS feeds and social networks. By the mid-2000s, blogs were a staple part of political discourse, and the concept of the political "blogosphere" as a sort of cyclotron of commentary became a commonplace term. Google dominated search directories and chat rooms gave way to Facebook. As a larger proportion of the population could take part in presidential campaign discourse, the discourse grew more informal. The stilted speech of news releases and campaign oratory and the smoothly crafted stories produced by journalists were joined by a cornucopia of rumors, wisecracks, vulgarities, insights, charts, tables, re-captioned photos, home-made videos, and, since 2006, that trendiest symbol of discourse status, the tweet.

The latest technology being integrated into the discourse infrastructure is the "smart" mobile device, a cell phone which can perform the functions of computers. This development sustains the technological trend toward convergence, the capacity of a terminal to link to multiple communication channels. The transition to mobile devices means at least two things. First, obvious as a phenomenon but elusive in its implications, is the big social fact of ubiquitous and nonstop connectivity. Densification seems poised to take a quantum leap as the computer leaves the desk and lap and accompanies people from place to place. Second, mobile usage lifts U.S. adult Internet penetration off the 75 percent plateau, where it has stayed for close to a decade, and brings it closer to the universal media summit, although with variations of channel connectivity and bandwidth capacity (speed and resolution). This, too, will enhance densification.

And so, thanks to half a century of technological change, devotees of presidential politics have been resituated relative to the campaigns. In 1961, even the most enthusiastic political spectators were mainly observers of White's vivid but remote milieu of elite decision-makers. Today, they belong to a still hierarchical but vastly more permeable community in which their thoughts, dollars, and digital applause (e.g., Facebook "likes") register with the elites. Post-election books adopting the White perspective on presidential campaigns, such as *Game Change* by Mark Halperin and John Heilemann, still attract mass readerships. But —as that book and other narrative accounts make plain—yesterday's scene gazers are also today's screen tappers, contributing to the conversation about the race for the presidency in more ways than one: five, to be precise.

FIVE DIMENSIONS OF DISCOURSE DENSIFICATION

On each and every topic that people discuss, the new media—the Internet, the World Wide Web, mobile devices, and social network platforms—have increased the density of public communication along five dimensions. There are:

- more voices uttering remarks
- more remarks per voice
- more days remarks are available
- more places from which remarks can be dispatched and accessed
- more categories in which remarks are grouped.

The information-rich interfaces of digitally networked channels have infiltrated and entwined every aspect of campaigns and campaign media. Newspapers, magazines, televisions, radios, smart phones, desk and laptop computers, mail, and printed literature all sport the icons and Web addresses of the online world. Screens proliferate at events such as conventions and rallies and at conversation venues such as doorsteps, bus stops, and diners. The lighted contents of the screens truncate and divide attention spans. Private communication now requires willful self-discipline and cooperation. Campaign messages are seeded with invitations to search, subscribe, share, and speak.

The discourse is denser in part because those invitations are being accepted. In the time span of the last five presidential elections, U.S. online news consumption has grown at the expense of print and is approaching the levels of television use. This migration of news consumption can serve as a proxy indicator for the densification of discourse communication, because news so often triggers campaign discussion, and digital channels carry far more content than their predecessors and offline correlates.

The Pew Research Center data in Figure 5.1 show that local television news remains the most common news source for Americans. That is why candidate satellite tours and visits to local stations remain staples of campaigning. Television is still a one-way and regimented medium. However, local stations have websites, many of which have become quite popular in their own right—and they run longer segments of candidate interviews, available for a longer time to viewers well beyond the originating broadcast or cable market, often in an inset on the digital screen embroidered by the comments and ratings of previous viewers. Local television news, in other words, has been subsumed into the digital grid.

With the growth in online news usage documented in Figure 5.1 has come a behavioral change. For much of the twentieth century, mass media news was ingested like a meal at a single sitting (often with a real-food counterpart). But online news and discourse lend themselves to day-long snacking, and Figure 5.2 depicts its rise. Information snackers have more opportunities to contribute to the discourse than one-time diners. The less formal modes of composition associated with blogging, tweeting, and posting in social networks enhance these opportunities.

According to a March 2010 Pew report about changing news habits, more than half of American adults (56 percent) follow news all or most of the time. Three-quarters of U.S. adults are Internet users, and of these 61 percent use social networking sites such as Facebook or MySpace and 8 percent use Twitter. These news consumers are, thanks to digital media, increasingly "participatory," in that they pass along links they like (48 percent of net users), and comment, contribute content, and share with bunches of people at a time via social network platforms (37 percent of net users).[1]

Another Pew survey released one year later reported that 21 percent of net users used social networks to engage with the 2010 elections as political information consumers, sharers, and activists.[2] A third survey delved into

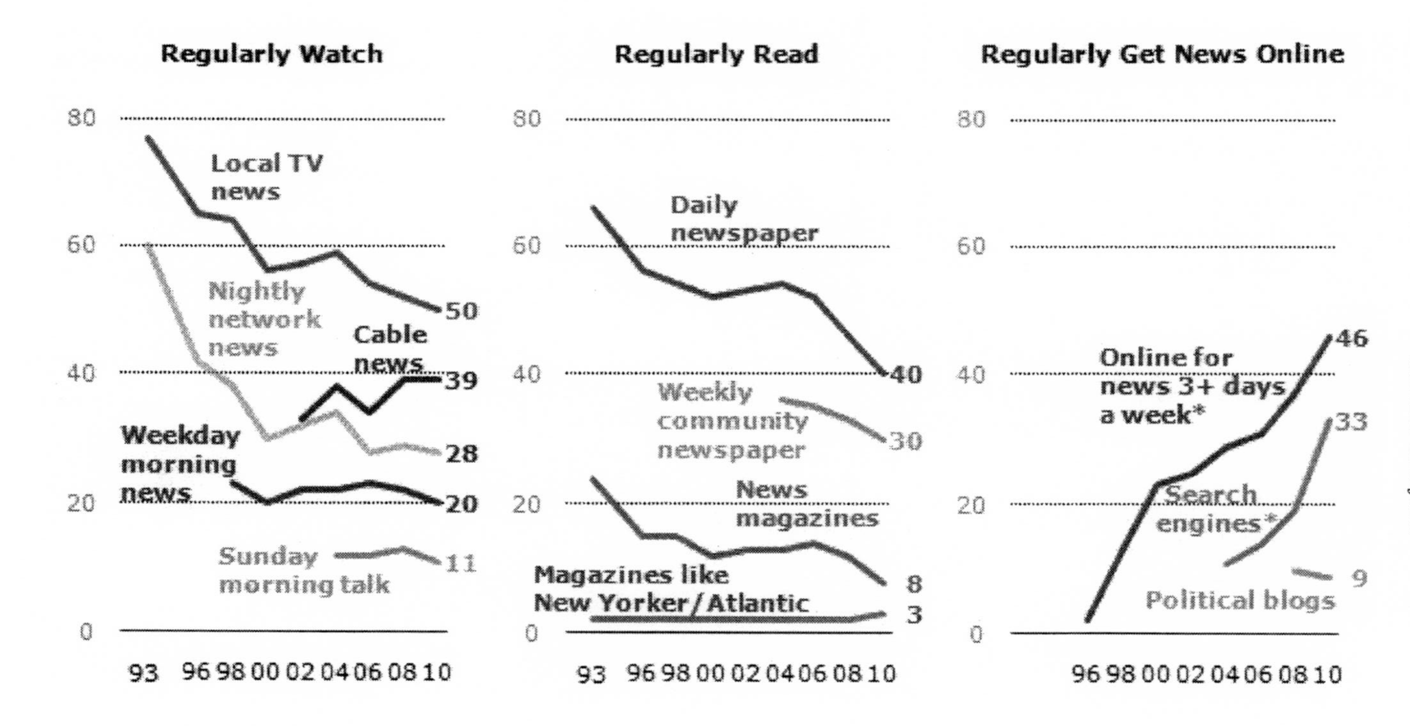

Figure 5.1. Trends in Regular News Sources

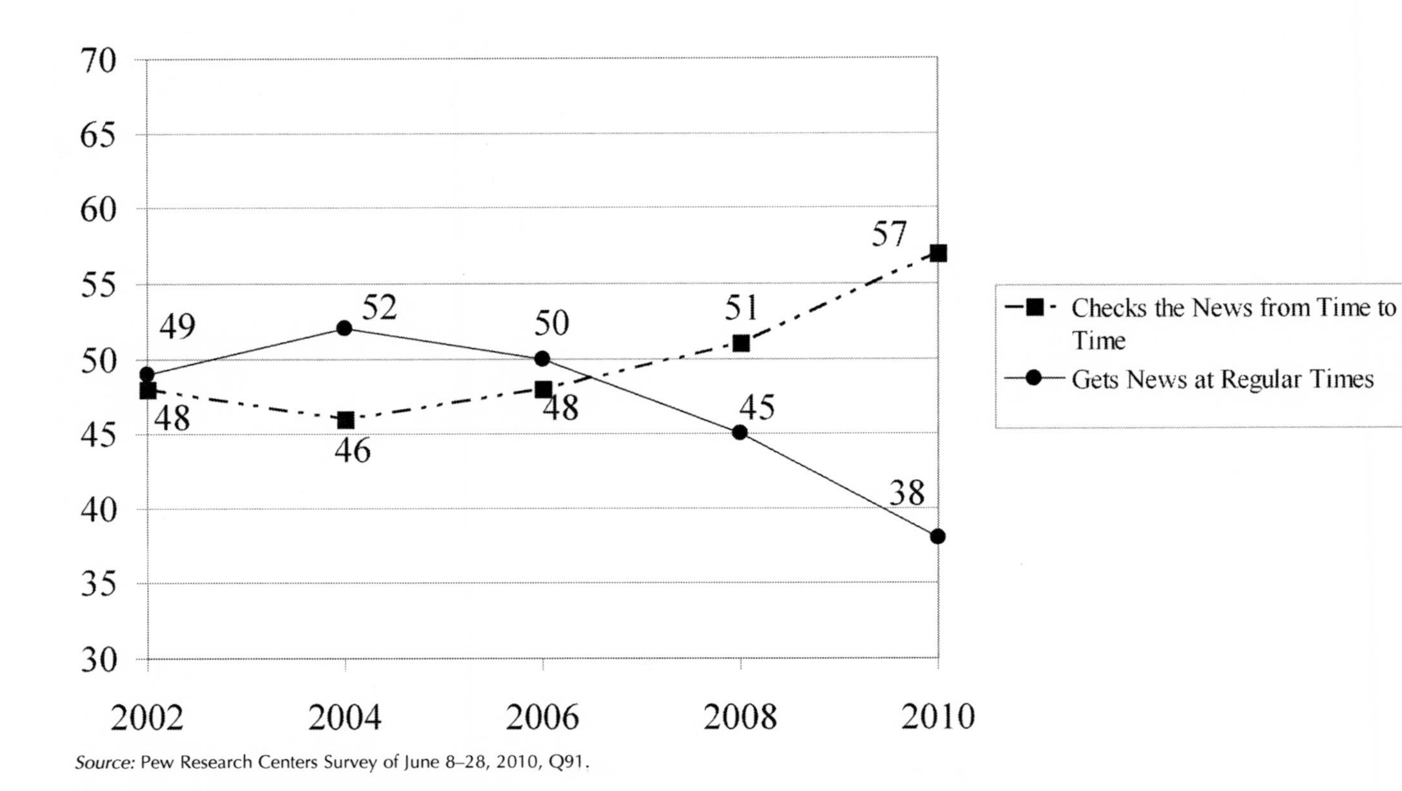

Source: Pew Research Centers Survey of June 8–28, 2010, Q91.

Figure 5.2. More Say They Graze for News

specific activities. When they turned to politics, 58 percent of the poll respondents said they looked for political news online—and 32 percent got most of their campaign news there. Moreover, 53 percent of adult Internet users did at least one of the eleven online political activities Pew measured in 2010: watching videos about the campaigns (up to 31 percent from 19 percent in 2006); looking for candidate voting record and issue position information (35 percent); fact checking campaign claims (28 percent); following a campaign in a location where they did not reside (20 percent); sending email about the campaigns to friends and colleagues (16 percent); announcing the fact that they voted and even the specifics of their vote choices (12 percent); signing up for campaign updates (8 percent); organizing or getting information about campaign meetings (7 percent); participating in an online discussion about the campaigns (6 percent); volunteering via the net (5 percent); and giving money to a campaign (4 percent).[3]

The Pew data show a sharp drop from news consumption to political participation. Not surprisingly, campaigns attempt to close that gap to their advantage: "As Americans increasingly use these sites to connect with public figures, find out about and respond to events in the news, and share their views on a range of topics, politicians and political groups on both ends of the ideological spectrum have begun using them to organize and communicate with their supporters and the public at large."[4] For example, a net-savvy campaign will produce live video streaming of pre- and post-event candidate activities backstage with a running band of texts and tweets by supporters in order to foster excitement for the event and expand the campaign's support network by drawing in people via advertising. When those drawn to the event respond to the ad and "click-through" to the campaign website, they see the participation of existing supporters and are induced to join by taking an action on behalf of the campaign. The success of initiatives like this has helped expand the first dimension of densification.

1. *More Voices.* A small but growing percentage of online discourse consumers also act as content producers and providers. There are more public speakers in the digital age, in part because to be a speaker in digital media takes less preparation, effort, and bravery than in either a classical public setting (the fear of speaking live in front of people is legendary) or a modern one (no make-up, rehearsal, and expensive equipment are required for video). As used here, the term "speaking" should be taken figuratively as well as literally, to encompass all forms of public communication on the topic of the presidential race. Forwarding a news article qualifies as digital speaking. So does rating a debate performance.

These minimal acts merit inclusion along with talking to a speaker and camera on a wired device and then posting it, not because they might influence other voters (often a dubious proposition) but because the statistics are monitored, analyzed, and when strategically appropriate publicized by campaigns as evidence of popular support.

Long-term data from the American National Election Studies project, displayed in Figures 5.3–5.6, show increases of nearly 10 percentage points in citizen participation in a quartet of campaign communication activities during the period in which digital media emerged. (Note: the spike in 1976 campaign donors was partly due to a temporary change in the tax deductibility of such expenditures.) This attests to more voices in the discourse. Does Web use *per se* inspire or cause as well as carry these voices? That is less certain. Other factors besides Web use drive increases in participation (which commenced, ironically, about the time that Robert Putnam published his admirable study of the decline in participation, *Bowling Alone*).

There is some social scientific evidence that Net use stimulates greater political participation. Karen Mossberger, Caroline J. Tolbert, and Ramona S. McNeal found that chat room denizens were more likely to vote in presidential elections, as were to lesser degrees emailers and online news consumers. They concluded that, "The necessary building blocks for citizenship in the information age are quality public education combined with universal access [to the Net]."[5]

The larger number of public speakers should not be taken as an increase in discourse diversity. Matthew Hindman has shown how a power law applies to several aspects of online political communication: that is, a few voices garner the lion's share of attention.[6] It would indeed be wrong to equate voices relegated to the comments sections with those featured in posts, and those in self-published posts with those in major news outlets. Still, all those sparsely heard voices on the long tail of the audience distribution curve are publicly accessible, politically usable, and contribute to the fact as well as the perception of discourse density. A campaign recruiter can scroll down the comments pages looking for voices that belong to potential volunteers and try to enlist them. If this is not quite the robust democratic dialogue that some envision, it is still more populated than it was previously. Aaron Smith, Kay Lehman Schlozman, Sidney Verba, and Henry Brady found evidence in 2009 that social media use may bring less wealthy and well-educated voices into the public arena.[7]

2. *More Remarks (including Messages).* From the unknown to the famous, each speaker contributes more remarks to the discourse today thanks to the (all too) easy public access afforded to our taps, keystrokes, utterances,

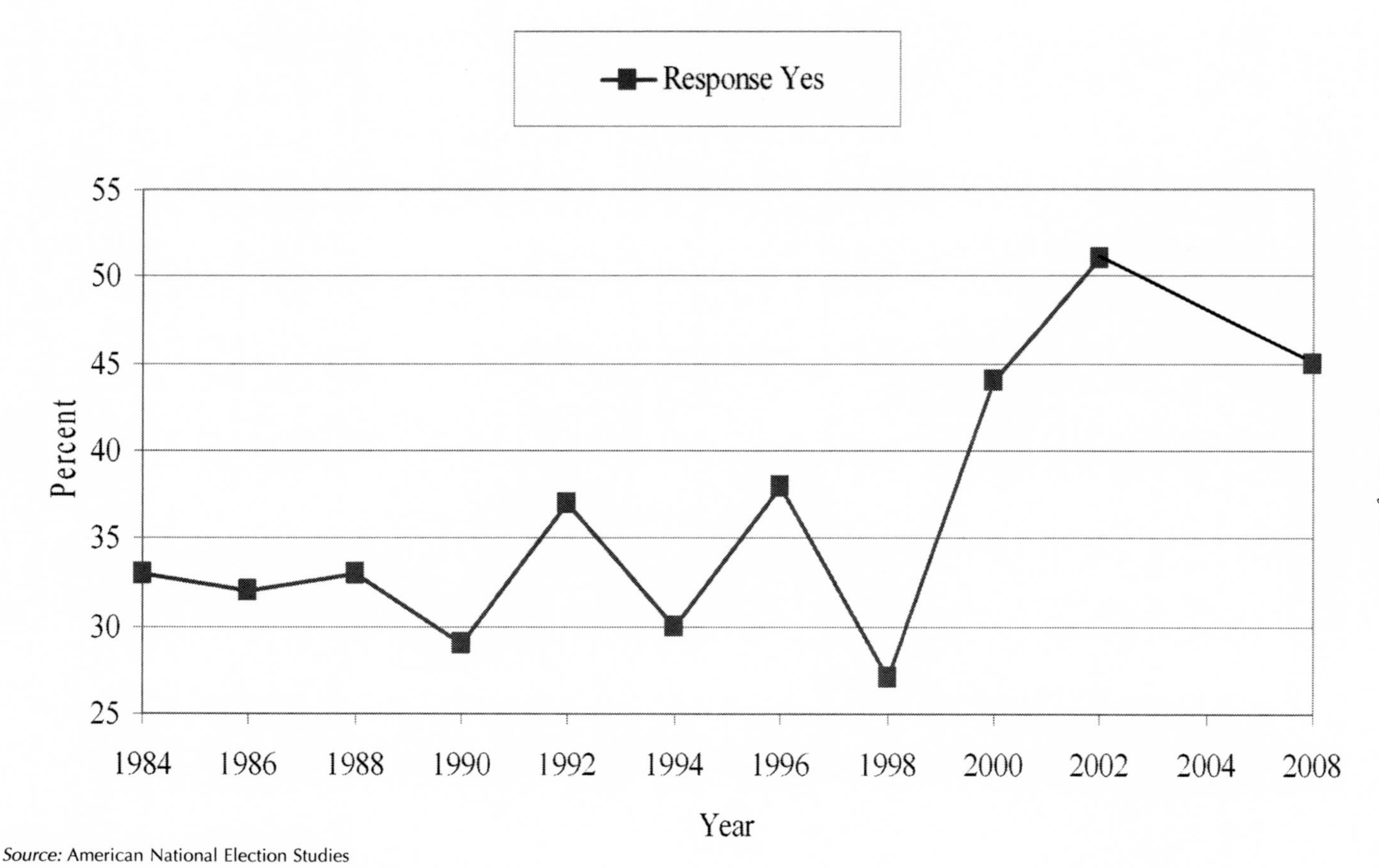

Source: American National Election Studies

Figure 5.3. Percent Contacted to Register or Vote, 1984–2008

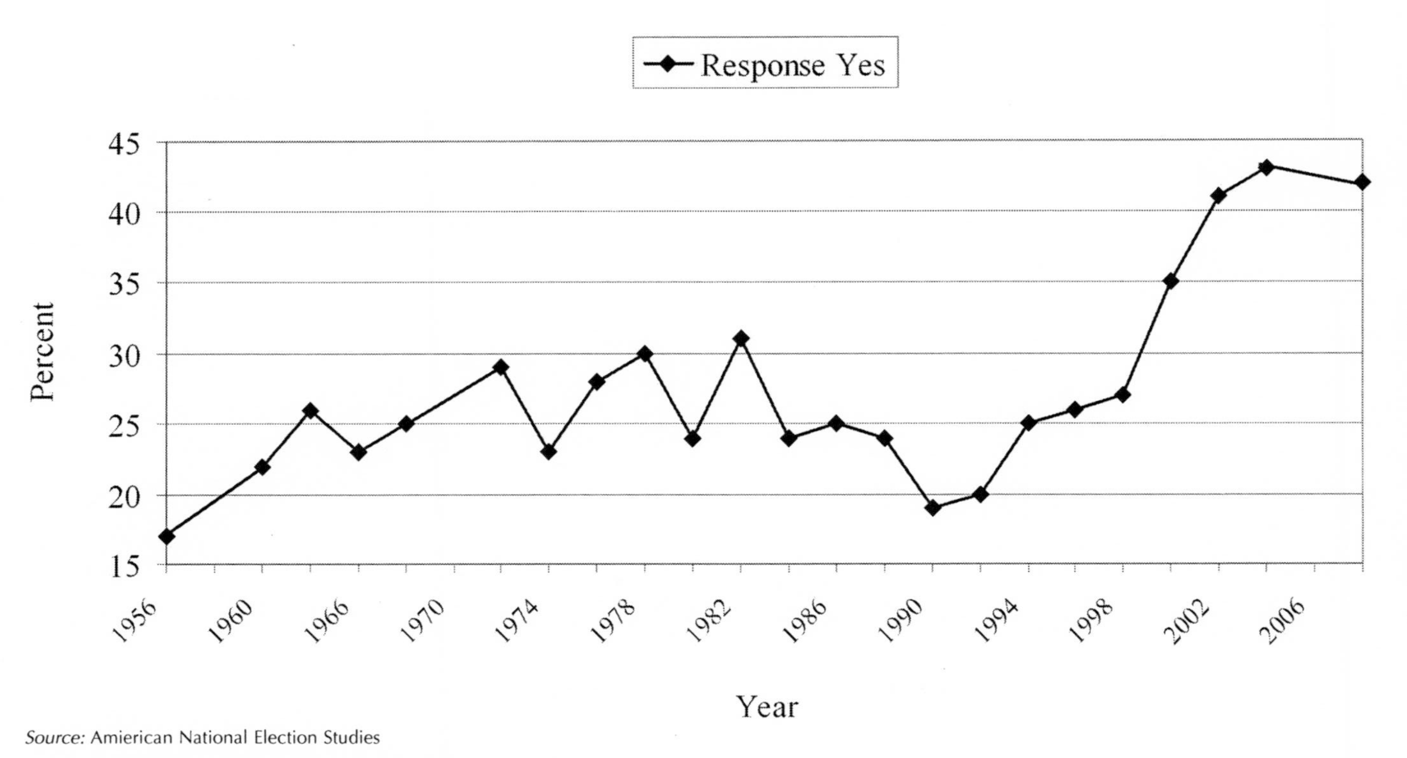

Source: Amierican National Election Studies

Figure 5.4. Percent Contacted by Either Major Party, 1956–2008

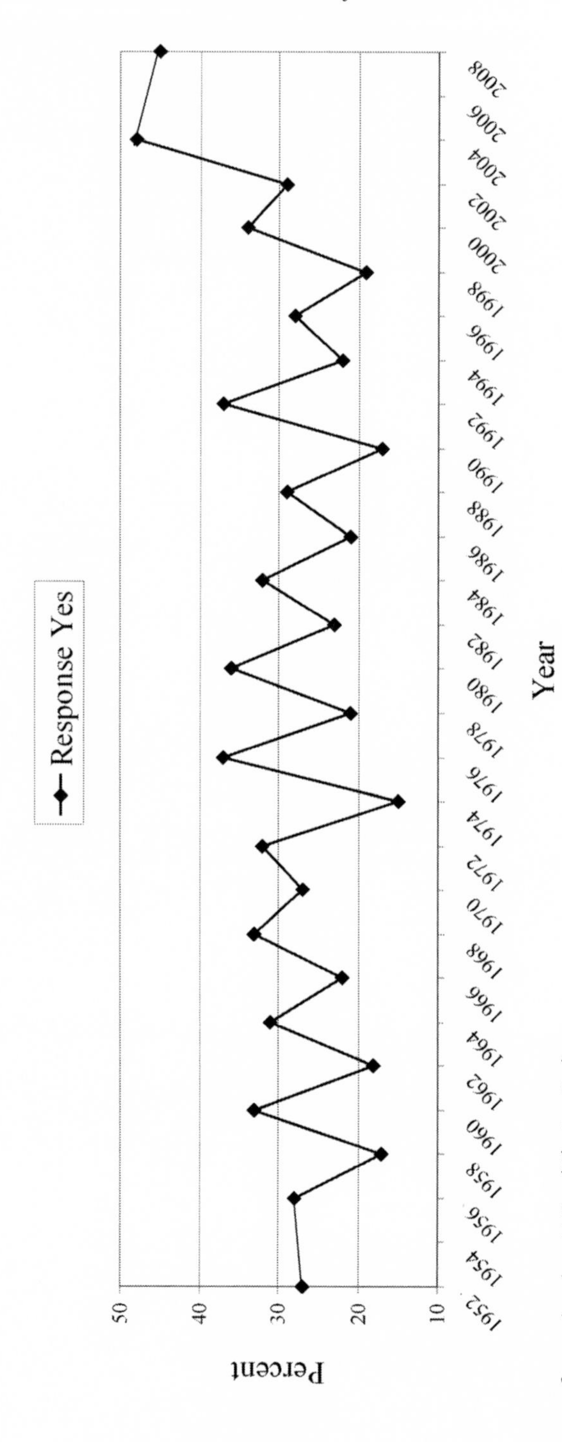

Source: American National Election Studies

Figure 5.5. Percent Who Tried to Influence How Others Vote, 1952–2008

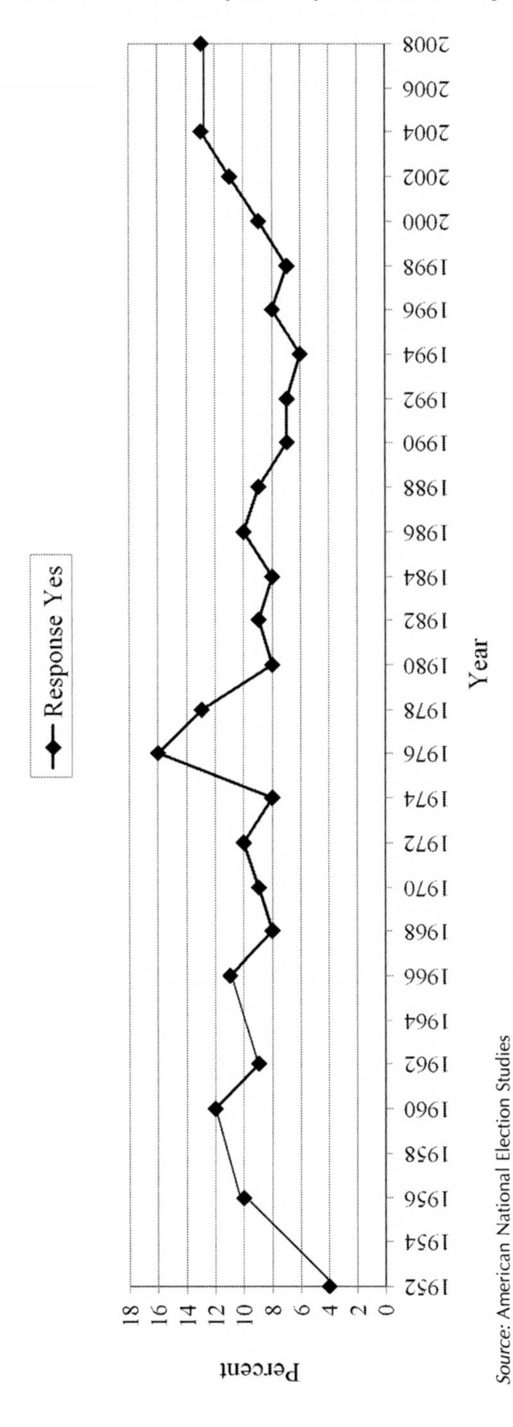

Source: American National Election Studies

Figure 5.6. Percent Who Gave Money to Help a Campaign, 1952–2008

and poses. A single stroke can send a message into the public sphere. A glance at many digital screen displays (except, ironically and powerfully, the minimalist home page of Google) confirms information growth in this dimension. The number of discrete items per screen page has mushroomed from the mass media era; one has to click "full screen" to simulate a television or theatrical viewing experience, and even then ads and bulletins will pop up. Multiple items per page is the new normal. Some of them are animated, to suggest or relay breaking news and commentary. And some of them are hypertext links to messages on other pages.

The content of a digital screen page changes much faster, too. The viewer scrolls or clicks to other pages, or the content on the page being viewed is dynamically "refreshed" by the provider. This supply and demand side changing is especially evident during live events. Multitasking while a candidate debate is occurring—monitoring the show, and the comments about the show, and checking the accuracy and consistency of statements against archived information–is becoming a routine of the politically engaged.

There are more remarks on mass media channels as well. Campaign advertising buys need to be bigger to "cut through the clutter" fostered by crowded screens and broadened consumer choices of what to put on them. The number of commercial airings deemed likely to assure that each member of a targeted population has been exposed to a broadcast message continues to rise. David Plouffe, Obama's campaign manager in 2008 (and again in 2012), summarized the approach of the 2007–08 "Campaign for America" this way:

> We put a huge premium on direct digital communication, as well as on the power of human beings talking to human beings, online, on the phone, and at the door. The principle underlying this was fairly simple: we live in a busy and fractured world in which people are bombarded with pleas for their attention. Given this, you have to try extra hard to reach them. . . .
>
> We tried to be on our target voters' network TV, cable, satellite, and on-demand; on their radios; all over the Internet; in their mailboxes; on their landlines and their cell phones, if we could; at their doorsteps; and out in their communities. Balanced communications across all mediums is critical to messaging effort today.[8]

Having just quoted a campaign professional, at this point I need to introduce an academic distinction between discourse *remarks* and campaign *messages*. The two words are often used interchangeably in ordinary language. However, for the remainder of this chapter, a "message" will refer to a subcategory of remarks in the presidential discourse: specifically, those that serve a strategic purpose in a campaign. A message often articulates the primary reason offered to an audience for its members to support a particular candidate. In crisis situations, a message aims to restore the reputation of a person and/or organization. Another type of message seeks financial contributions. Whatever the purpose, campaigns strive for consistency and coordination in message delivery.

The expanded volume and faster pace of remarks puts intense pressure on presidential campaigns to strafe their targets with messages (to continue with the military metaphor Plouffe used). Pressure is just as severe and unremitting on campaigners to stay current with the remarks of others. Campaigns must monitor what has just surfaced that may be relevant to them, and they must generate meaningful content frequently enough to stay visible on the top pages of ever-changing news feeds and blogs. The combination of watching, responding to, and initiating discourse information used to be known as "winning the day," when the main venues for the discourse were the nightly network television news broadcasts and major morning newspapers. It became famous as a primary activity of campaign war rooms. Today a campaign tries to win *discourse moments*, as manifest in sudden clumps or spikes of communication about a topic, whenever they crystallize. And they must compete for primacy in many more venues at the same time.

3. *More Places.* In the most basic sense, one's place in politics is where one lives and therefore votes. That's one reason direct mail remains valuable to campaigners, since it can be sent directly to specific households even as Americans quit landline telephones. However, one's place in the discourse is wherever one's mobile device is, which is, increasingly, strapped to the body or otherwise proximate to it regardless of one's geophysical location. Digital media put politics in perpetual motion.

The magic of telecommunication results from all the other places accessible from one's place, stationary or mobile. The negligible costs at the margin of long-distance digital communication, for the sender and the receiver, along with the capacity to transfer money as well as messages, has the potential to mitigate the disproportionate influence awarded by the existing system to residents of the early states in the nominating process (Iowa, New Hampshire, South Carolina) and battleground states in the general election. Californians can't participate in the Iowa caucuses, to be sure. But their capacity to be heard and seen by caucus attendees, even to communicate with them on an individual basis, has been greatly enhanced. "Outside money" can have an impact more readily, and communications that solicit, spend, track, and comment on outside money contribute to discourse density. So do grassroots canvassing and opinion shaping conducted long-distance, as when the Obama 2008 campaign set a Guinness Book of World Records mark for simultaneous phone calls by having attendees of a rally in a South Carolina football stadium use mobile phones to contact undecided voters in New Hampshire.[9]

Increasingly, messages are developed in an array of versions with variations to suit the attributes of places to which they are being sent. Direct mail has been tailored with personalized greetings for some time; distinct Facebook advertisements may be sent according to the location of one's terminal (IP address), geographic radius, age and birthday, likes and interests, education, and such recorded behavioral moves as joining a Facebook group, RSVP'ing to a Facebook event, downloading a Facebook app, and so forth. AOL, Yahoo, and MSN, which possess data on individuals who use their email services, permit different versions of ads to be shown to them based on their political leanings, thanks to the overlaying of the identifying information with publicly available data from voter registration files. Advertisers rely on cookies placed on remote terminals to "re-market": a technique by which messages land on the pages ad viewers are likely to visit after an initial exposure. For instance, people who see a video on a campaign website may be tagged via the cookie, and then see ads from the campaign on a political news story. In re-marketing, ads follow and find people.

These online advertising and contact techniques raise privacy issues beyond the scope of this essay. The point here is that the more types of segmentation by place in use, the more dense the discourse becomes.

4. *More Time.* The public life span of information in political discourse can be quite short. Popular sites and obscure blogs both tend to banish older messages to back pages that few people visit; Twitter and Facebook feeds march onward in double time. Even when a remark stays in a prominent location, digital snackers are wont to move elsewhere instead of staying for the end of the program or story in which the remark is embedded. While the time of exposure seems unusually brief by mass media standards, it is similar to the fate accorded to what human beings have been saying to each other since the dawn of social gatherings.

   With one big difference: digital remarks do not vanish as readily. The contents of those quickly changing and quickly exited pages are recorded, replicated, and thus potentially retrievable for extensive public consideration. This archival timelessness is a boon to opposition research and investigative journalism, whose practitioners have become adept at reaching into the past of candidates and secondary actors in the discourse drama and then releasing the evidence into the discourse as situations warrant.

Dredging up the past and the private has long been part of presidential discourse, from Sally Hemings to Swift Boats and the controversy regarding Barack Obama's birthplace. The last instance prompted the Obama 2008 campaign to create a special website dedicated to dispelling false information. Entitled fightthesmears.com, it prolonged the public exposure time for a host of dubious assertions about the candidate on the assumption that rebuttal was preferable to silence, which could be interpreted as acquiescence. The effectiveness of the gambit is debatable; some argue that repeating an accusation in order to refute it only perpetuates the accusation in the minds of many. What is not debatable is the fact of prolongation as a contributing factor to densification. As of this writing, fightthesmears.com was still accessible—three years after its debut, two and a half years after Obama's election.

5. ***More Categories.*** Digitally stored information can be indexed by multiple search terms, keywords, and hashtags. (For the uninitiated, a hashtag is the # symbol that is used to mark keywords or topics in a tweet.) It can thereby be examined in a variety of different combinations and contexts.[10] A candidate video on a YouTube channel may be grouped in one place along with others featuring the same candidate; elsewhere, it could be found with others dealing with the same issue or appearing in the same election cycle, and so forth. This unbounded and decentralized indexing—also known as *meta-language* to distinguish it from the information being indexed—stimulates and facilitates the reframing of remarks, an important technique in rhetoric.

   More categories mean more juxtapositions, more meanings. Speakers guess at these as they post remarks, providing keywords and hashtags with the hope that people interested in those topics or conversant with those phrases will then see what they have to say. Meanwhile, those in search of answers to questions or roaming for interesting information enter keywords and hashtags with the hope of reading or viewing something from a stranger that is on point. They may also add new tags. Following a topic into a segment of the discourse is a new way of making the one-to-one, one-to-some, and one-to-many connections on which public communication is based. It is advanced enough for the meta-language to have become an alluring category unto itself: Twitter, Yahoo, and other Web portals feature "trending topics," as in "what are people talking about right now."

Perhaps no website better illustrates the expanding dimensions of presidential discourse density than Wikipedia. In June 2011, the "Mitt Romney" entry was viewed more than 229,000 times, with a spike of interest on June 14, the day after Romney took part in a presidential candidate debate in New Hampshire. The entry had been revised 6,480 times since its debut on January 10, 2004, at an average rate of .42 revisions a day, by 2,043 individuals. Nearly 250 individuals were "watchers" of the entry, who had signed up to be notified automatically any time a change was made. The opening two paragraphs featured 22 hypertext links to other categories, including "CEO," "70th Governor of Massachusetts," "Mormon missionary," and "candidate for the 2012 Republican Party presidential nomination." The archive for the companion section containing discussions of possible improvements to the entry had eight sections to date. The entry was also the second highest listing on the page shown to me when I entered "Mitt Romney" into Google (after the campaign's own website).

FROM MESSAGE TO CONTENT: CITIZEN QUESTIONS, CANDIDATE ANSWERS, AND THE GROWTH OF ATTENDANT COMPLICATIONS

A five-dimensional thickening of publicly available communication about specific topics—more voices, remarks, durations, locations, and kinds—characterizes the ambient social environment of our lives. Digital media constitute the main setting for public comprehension of the making of the president. In the span of fifty years (twenty, mostly), the civic thumb has rotated downward, from the position in which it held a book or remote control, to one permitting continuous manipulation of a touch screen or keypad. Is this rotation emblematic of a revolution? Do we hold the presidential campaign process, its principal players, and its associative ideals in different regard now that there is staggeringly too much communication about them instead of tantalizingly too little? Such questions are as natural to ponder as they are difficult to answer. I will focus instead on how discourse densification affects the practice of campaign management (and the broader field of public relations) as it permeates the citizen-campaigner-mediator relationships at the core of presidential discourse.

A New Intersection for "The Man on the Street": Madison Avenue Meets YouTube

Consider a simple and symbolically rich communication format: a citizen asks a candidate a question about an issue and the candidate answers. This "man on the street" format has an outdated name, but it endures because presidential candidates need to be seen listening to and speaking with voters. It reinforces belief in popular sovereignty, a core value of a constitutional republic.[11] But density has complicated the nature of this exchange, thereby complicating the things that strategic mediators can do to work it in their favor.

As a genre of campaign television advertising, the public view of the man on the street was oversimplified for voters. In 1952, Dwight Eisenhower spent one day in a Manhattan television studio answering questions culled by an advertising team from a collection it had filmed outside Radio City Music Hall. Footage of questions posed by selected persons on the street were spliced with the general's scripted responses to create a series of forty television advertisements entitled "Eisenhower Answers America." This series took advantage of the new medium's reach into American homes—a few examples are enshrined in an online exhibit at the Museum of the Moving Image called "The Living Room Candidate"—to send the message that the great war hero was also "Ike," a son of the prairie who could speak to voter concerns in everyday language. There was no actual conversation, no body language predicated on personal interaction. The questioners were anonymous, the answers were anodyne, the backgrounds blurred and empty.

This was an early and rudimentary illustration of the process known as strategic message development. A campaign conceives a goal—branding, persuasion, delegitimation, mobilization—and moves toward it by commissioning, creating, testing, and deploying packages of information (the message) to designated ("targeted") audiences. Polling, testing, and other audience research supplies guidance and feedback to the developers. Their intuition and experience also inform the process. Strategic message development lies at the heart of the small but important vocation of campaign management as it has been practiced since it became a profession in the 1930s.[12]

In 1968, sixteen years after "Eisenhower Answers America," television was firmly at the center of the media mix. Eisenhower's former running mate was making his second run for the presidency, and his advisers created "The Man in the Arena" series on his behalf. In these half-hour television programs, Richard Nixon stood on a stage and extemporaneously fielded questions from invited citizens representing desirable demographic constituencies. The exchanges showed off his policy knowledge; viewers were supposed to identify with the impressed members of the audience, shown in cutaway shots as raptly attentive and frequently applauding. The programs embodied orderly dialogue, an important theme for the campaign at a time of national protest and countercultural ferment.

Unlike the 1952 Eisenhower ads, Nixon's messages were presented in the form of a full-scale commercial television show, with more elaborate production features: multiple cameras, a cast of characters, a set. This format, like ads with cut and pasted dialogue, continues to this day; presidential campaigns resemble film companies in some respects. There is more room for natural input and interaction in shows than in advertisements. The questions and answers in the Nixon series were long and often thoughtful; the body language may have been rehearsed but it was a live performance. Still, this was predominantly unidirectional messaging. The press and general public were excluded.[13]

Next, jump to 1992, for all intents and purposes the last presidential election without the new media. In this election cycle, a television production of the citizen-candidate exchange became a regular feature of earned as well as paid media; the candidates agreed to cede control over aspects of the event in order to gain the public credibility that comes with an independently run operation. The Commission on Presidential Debates put three candidates (President George H. W. Bush, Bill Clinton, and Ross Perot) in a Richmond, Virginia auditorium for the first "town hall meeting style debate." Journalists, not campaign advisers, mediated the questions and answers, which came from voters who had told the Gallup Organization that they were undecided. The event became a reference point for a candidate contrast of great benefit to Bill Clinton. In one memorable segment of the telecast, he walked toward a questioner to demonstrate audience empathy and intercandidate primacy.[14] This program was a co-production of campaigns and broadcast mediators. Strategists had to negotiate with journalists as well as prepare their candidates to deliver messages.

By the 2008 cycle, access to these and other advertising spots, town hall programs, and town hall-style debates was available to anyone with Internet access.[15] Lots of citizens were ready to step up their participation and they received more chances to do so in the "man in the street" format. In 2007, YouTube teamed with CNN to stage an innovative pair of television programs with digital input built into the format. Citizens sent questions for candidates that they put on video themselves and submitted for the journalists' consideration. The Democratic debate featured 39 of 2989 qualified submissions; the Republican debate used 34 of 4927. One query came from an Alzheimer's disease caregiver, who appeared on screen with the sufferer. Another originated from a refugee camp in war-torn Darfur. Other videos were whimsical, strident, and bizarre (a talking snowman). The videos were aired interspersed with live candidate responses and video statements provided by their campaigns. They, too, remain publicly available online.

This innovation reflected social reality—or, more precisely, "reality programming." Television had become a spotlighted and constrained platform for public videos featuring non-actors. Meanwhile, candidates and their campaign staffs stepped up their video production. Presidential aspirants now routinely declare their candidacies through videos which, in keeping with the aforementioned strategy, aim above all to attract viewers to the campaign website, where they may be converted into grassroots volunteers and donors. YouTube registered channels for 110 political candidates for office in 2008, and these publicity platforms attracted 220 million views that year. Half went to the Obama channel, which uploaded more than 1,800 videos, including 100 in the last week of the campaign.[16] These totals do not include the most widely viewed campaign video of the cycle, "Yes We Can," a celebrity musical tribute to Obama produced by hip-hop star Will.i.am of the Black Eyed Peas, a famous citizen, but a citizen nonetheless.

The Obama 2008 campaign developed its own video variation on the "man on the street" format. It made videos of the candidate having lunch with winners of low-dollar contributor contests. The camera eavesdropped on what appeared to be unrehearsed conversations; the candidate actually asked questions about the supporters' lives and views. Videos also hurt the campaign: most notably, those of Reverend Jeremiah Wright preaching, which were, astonishingly, unviewed by opposition researchers on all campaigns until an ABC News reporter purchased some in the lobby of the church. Obama was also caught off guard at least twice by citizen questions—as all candidates are, but not always sparking major campaign controversies. During the Democratic primary season, Mayhill Fowler, a citizen journalist for the online news site *Huffington Post*, posted a commentary on Obama's remarks at a San Francisco fund-raiser (she also released them in audio form), in which he seemed to patronize blue-collar residents of Pennsylvania. The ensuing controversy was big—and would have been bigger had Obama's comments been recorded on video. Near the end of the general election campaign, while at a meet-and-greet in Ohio answering a challenging question, Obama used the phrase "redistribute the wealth," and the resulting hubbub and McCain campaign response made a celebrity out of the questioner, Joe Wurzelbacher, a.k.a. "Joe the Plumber." In both instances, the Obama campaign message was smacked by a snowball of discourse about his intentions and beliefs. The man on the street answered back.

A SEA CHANGE IN POLITICAL MANAGEMENT

Sixty years after "Eisenhower Answers America," presidential candidates still have to at least pay lip service to the concerns of the average citizen. Today, however, the ritual sprawls well beyond the control of campaign message developers. At the same time, they now enjoy unfiltered access to audiences as though they owned and operated a set of media properties. Message developers have a huge palette of options. The engaged public has more, too. In the right circumstances, a heretofore unknown citizen's comment, edit, or question can be viewed by a huge audience along with campaign messages that prompted and responded to it, as well as the contributions (some rhetorical, some financial) of others.

When we encounter the presidential discourse today, we typically see content: campaign messages accompanied by public commentary and indexing terminology. The job of the strategic message developer has therefore expanded to become what is being called digital content management. The crucial task of targeting audiences has expanded to include the cultivation of, and response to, audience member reactions. Audiences are not just to be bombarded with messages; their vocal members are to be connected with campaign representatives in conversational exchanges, the better to recruit and mobilize supporters. Citizen involvement in presidential discourse has moved beyond simulation and control and into live on-screen interaction and supplemental modes of community outreach.

In these ways, discourse densification necessitates more diligent and more skillful political management. As online advertising expert Michael Bassik remarks: "Professionalization of online political consulting has undergone a big change in the last seven years. The Internet is no longer relegated to the computer geek in the candidate's circle; in the last five years, a new class of consultants has emerged whose entire role is to help build and manage online communities: email, content, blogger relations, advertising, fund-raising."[17]

Presidential campaigners used to focus on the acquiring and allocation of four basic campaign resources: time, money, message, and people. They would post a calendar on the wall of their headquarters and work backward from election day, assigning resources to time slots and geophysical locations. In the digital era, campaigners still do this, but they take two additional factors into consideration: public reputation and grassroots activities. These discourse-based factors can be monitored, measured, analyzed, and acted upon through the assignment of campaign resources. But because reputation and grassroots activities belong to the discourse and not the campaign, they are resources only to the extent that outsiders cooperate.

Content managers cannot define the key words for campaign messages; instead, they must identify and try to tweak the category terms into which messages are being sorted by the public. Content managers patrol virtual public spaces like Wikipedia and Facebook, and dispatch volunteers to chime into conversations about entries and posts as warranted. They test Google and other website advertisements on the fly and redirect ad purchases according to early message results. To acquiesce to the discourse response and traffic patterns that greet their campaign messages is to ignore risks and forgo benefits that could affect reputation, support, the ongoing supply of basic resources, and, thereby, electoral outcomes.

Note the job description language for this "Digital Campaign Director" position recently listed on the politics and digital technology website techpresident.com :

> Manages every aspect of online campaigning, including (but not limited to) making a campaign plan; writing content for email and Websites; directing the purchase of online advertisements for list-building and persuasion, creating channels for driving online activists to offline action, coordinating the direction of online video creation, and other responsibilities as needed. Works with campaign and department leaders on the development of online strategy, content, and technology to advance campaign goals. Analyzes and reports on metrics for their campaigns; works with other digital staff and directors to develop internal best practices. Manage relations and engage local, political . . . and issue bloggers in the campaign. Performs other duties as required to support the department and its mission.

The scope is wide; the skill set varied; the functionalities and stakeholders diverse. There is an emphasis on metrics, best practices, and mission.

CONCLUSION: JUDGING THE QUALITY OF DISCOURSE

The growing profusion of public voices, remarks, links, potentially significant moments, and categorical groupings is a social phenomenon which individuals can embrace, resist, or not even notice—the last of these being, I suspect, the case with most people under the age of 30, who have grown up mostly in the digital age and regard today's expanded set of screen options as normal. To those of us old enough to have lived through much of this development, however, it is worth remarking upon, at least for its strategic and civic consequences. Densification simultaneously simplifies the capacity to perform a public political action—which helps account for the increases shown in Figures 5.3–5.6—and complicates the action's ramifications. Digital media confer more expressive options, accompanied by instant and sometimes voluminous feedback.

Like many technologically tethered trends, this has its positive and negative features. There are several ways to evaluate the quality of a conversation about the presidential race. There's the technical proficiency angle: is the delivery infrastructure working well? The political process angle: are we talking well—substantively, inclusively, coherently, truthfully—about the most important public choices facing the nation? And the civics angle: are people being engaged, discouraged, inspired, disgusted, abusive, productive, or bored?

To help people make these evaluations, Web-appropriate standards have started to emerge in the political campaign discourse. Transparency has become a popular indicator of integrity: do we know who has paid for this remark? The number of campaign contributors is supplementing poll results and cash-on-hand as an indicator of campaign popularity and grassroots commitment. The effectiveness of bad-remark damage control indicates campaign strength and dexterity.

It is a constant and vital challenge to develop and hold to one's own evaluation standards amid all the conflicting voices and metrics. Back to David Plouffe's review of the Obama 2008 campaign he headed:

> We measured our progress exclusively with our own yardstick. That takes discipline, but discipline without attention to the right metrics is meaningless. Whether it came to fund-raising, voter registration, our local press footprint, filling volunteer shifts, or ultimately reaching our vote goals, we had clear internal benchmarks that the campaign leadership used to measure our progress or lack thereof, and that all of our staff and volunteers could use to measure their own work.[18]

Plouffe's approach is admirable. We need civic metrics, too, ones citizens can adopt for themselves as they participate. But (as he states elsewhere in his book) it is just as important to articulate a mission that the metrics purport to gauge. The inherent danger of the denser discourse triggered by digital technology may lie not in participant misunderstandings (a timeless problem) or even the possibility that people are listening only to voices and messages that simply reinforce their own preconceptions. It may lie, instead, in the tug of politics away from policy and social life which occurs when discourse participants get caught up in responding to the last political comment and planning for the next. Winning the moment should not take precedence over the things on which the moment has been predicated.

Seeking outsider approval is intrinsic to democratic campaigns, and listening to others is essential to good communication. But there is no wisdom in crowds when it comes to democracy, according to the author of the book bearing that phrase as its title, James Surowiecki. He maintains that, "Choosing candidates and making policy in a democracy are not, in that sense, cognition problems [i.e. problems with objective answers that lots of separated people can hone in on as their responses are aggregated], and so we should not expect them to yield themselves to the wisdom of the crowd."[19] Instead, Surowiecki sees the reverse: it is democratic communication which, as a discursive process, makes a crowd's constituent parts wiser, because it inculcates respect, patience, tolerance, and a search for compromise. Vibrant democracies make for wiser crowds. It is this conversational steeping which enlightens individual choices.

As one gets immersed in political discourse, it is important to wander: to surf the Web, follow a wayward thread, roll with changes of topic, tone, and speaker. Again, there is no valuable communication without listening. But in political discourse, one must come back to purpose and mission, and judge conversations by that standard. Presidential campaign discourse is supposed to be about policy and social life, the things that everyday people care about, not just the campaign as a process. The best discussants rarely miss an opportunity to pivot out of the pleasures of gossip about the candidates and guessing who will win (and they are, indeed, pleasurable) and back into their mission-governed evaluations.

Like campaigns, each policy domain has its own specialized discourse with its own centripetal preoccupations. It is the presidential discourse which has the capacity, via its ultimate dependence on a national electorate, to lift policy debates out of specialization and into fuller public consideration by citizens as well as officials, lobbyists, experts, and campaigners. Given the demands on the latter, it really falls to citizens to keep the focus on policy. They must perform as the reality check on the discourse. Mayhill Fowler and Joe Wurzelbacher, and all those who talked about their encounters with Obama, kept campaigners, consultants, and journalists honest, as their own data and conversations could not.

That is why the more citizen-generated content about policy matters there is for campaigns to deal with, the better the 2012 campaign discourse will be.

NOTES

1. Kristen Purcell, Lee Rainie, Amy Mitchell, Tom Rosenstiel, and Kenny Olmstead, "Understanding the Participatory News Consumer," Pew Internet & American Life Project, March 1, 2010.

2. Aaron Smith, "22% of Online Americans Used Social Networking or Twitter for Politics in 2010 Campaign," Pew Internet & American Life Project, January 27, 2011, 3.

3. Aaron Smith, "The Internet and Campaign 2010," Pew Internet & American Life Project, March 17, 2011, 4.

4. Aaron Smith, "22% of Online Americans," 3.

5. Karen Mossberger, Caroline J. Tolbert, and Ramona S. McNeal, *Digital Citizenship: The Internet, Society, and Participation* (Cambridge, MA: MIT Press, 2008).

6. Matthew Hindman, *The Myth of Digital Democracy* (Princeton, NJ: Princeton University Press, 2008).

7. Aaron Smith, Kay Lehman Schlozman, Sidney Verba, and Henry Brady, "The Internet and Civic Engagement," Pew Internet & American Life Project, September, 2009.

8. David Plouffe, *The Audacity To Win* (New York: Viking, 2009), 378–79.

9. Ben Smith, "'Largest Phone Bank Ever,'" *Politico*, December 9, 2007.

10. David Weinberger, *Everything Is Miscellaneous* (New York: Times Books, 2007).

11. Akhil Reed Amar, *America's Constitution: A Biography* (New York: Random House, 2005).

12. Dennis W. Johnson, *No Place For Amateurs: How Political Consultants Are Reshaping American Democracy,* 2nd ed. (New York: Routledge, 2007); and Johnson, *Campaigning in the Twenty-First Century: A Whole New Ballgame?* (New York: Routledge, 2011).

13. On 1952 and 1968, see Kathleen Hall Jamieson, *Packaging The Presidency: A History and Criticism of Presidential Campaign Advertising*, 3rd ed. (New York: Oxford University Press, 1996).

14. Mark Goodman, Mark Gring, and Brian Anderson, "The Visual Byte: Bill Clinton and His Town Hall Meeting Style," *Journal of Communication* 1 (2007).

15. "Eisenhower Answers America" ads at www.livingroomcandidate.org/commercials/1952; excerpt from a "Man in the Arena" program at www.criticalpast.com/video/65675053773; Richmond debate at http://www.c-span.org/Events/1992-Presidential-Town-Hall-Debate/11606/ .

16. YouTube statistics from Steve Grove, Political Director of YouTube, public remarks at George Washington University, December 8, 2008.

17. Interview with the author, March 14, 2011.

18. Plouffe, *Audacity.*

19. James Surowiecki, *The Wisdom of Crowds* (New York: Doubleday, 2004), 270.

Chapter 6

How Television Covers the Presidential Nomination Process

Stephen J. Farnsworth and S. Robert Lichter

Few political institutions have been criticized as frequently and as vehemently as the mass media. Politicians of all parties and all ideological stripes regularly rail against the media's role in the political process, reserving their harshest judgments for media coverage of national elections. While their complaints might be self-serving, they are often supported by scholarly studies of media performance, critiques by in-house media analysts, and even by the *mea culpas* of reporters and editors.

While media and elections scholars often focus on how journalists cover the general elections, their concerns about news content are at least as relevant to primary campaigns. Citizens depend most heavily on the media during the presidential nomination process, a time when most candidates are not well-known, when the selection process often takes place quickly, and when voters cannot use partisanship as a cue to choose among competitors from the same political party.[1]

Researchers have identified four key problems with mainstream news coverage of campaigns and elections: (1) there is not enough coverage of the campaigns; (2) the coverage is misdirected, focusing on the horse race rather than on how

Thanks to Bill Mayer and to the staffs of the Center for Media and Public Affairs and of Media Tenor, especially Dan Amundson, for their assistance with this project. Thanks also to George Mason University, which provided support for this chapter. All errors remain the authors' responsibility.

the candidates would address important issues if elected; (3) the coverage is not fairly allocated among the candidates; (4) the tone of news coverage is unfair, as reporters treat some candidates more harshly than others.[2]

To assess these issues, this chapter analyzes network television's coverage of recent presidential nomination campaigns. Although more and more citizens are frustrated with newspaper and television coverage of campaigns and are turning to online sources, in 2008 far more people relied on traditional media outlets than on cyberspace for their campaign news. Indeed, television news continues to be the most significant news outlet for voters. In a poll conducted just after the 2008 election, the Pew Research Center found that 68 percent of those surveyed named television as one of their two major sources for news about the presidential campaign, as compared to 36 percent who relied on the Internet, 33 percent who named newspapers as a leading information source, and 16 percent who turned to radio.[3] Surveys confirm that large majorities of the voting public, particularly in the high-turnout older age groups, rely on conventional media sources for most of their campaign information.[4] Moreover, a significant amount of the cable and online news now obtained in the United States originates from traditional media outlets, either via their online operations or by being referenced by bloggers and other Internet voices. Finally, examining network television allows us to make effective over-time comparisons, whereas both the Internet and cable television have become key public media sources only recently. Our study period covers the six presidential election cycles from the 1988 through the 2008 campaigns.

We examine media content through the technique of content analysis, in which specially trained coders analyze each campaign news story appearing on every evening newscast of ABC, CBS, and NBC. In order to make the process as objective and as reliable as possible, we break each news story into segments, roughly corresponding to individual sound bites, which can be coded on such dimensions as length, topic, and tone. Most of the statements that air on television news are relatively straightforward comments that can be classified reliably in terms of our coding system. For example, an unnamed voter told ABC during the 2008 campaign that presidential candidate Sen. John McCain (R-AZ) "has shown that he can work both sides of the table to help this country," a comment coded as a positive statement aimed at McCain. For all variables discussed in this chapter, intercoder reliability—the extent to which one coder agreed with a second coder looking at the same news segment—exceeded 90 percent.[5]

We examine key concerns about news content during two phases of the nomination campaign. We start with the "preseason"—the year before the primary elections, when most candidates officially declare their candidacies and start raising money and making regular treks to Iowa and New Hampshire, the homes of the first presidential caucuses and first primary, respectively. We also examine the primary campaign season itself. During a nomination process that usually lasts about ten to twelve weeks—a period considerably shorter than a single college semester—the two major parties formally select their presidential nominees.[6] In presidential election cycles prior to 2008, the competitive phase of the primary season generally lasted from January 1 until the first or second week of March of the presidential election year. In 2008, however, the timetable began earlier, as the Iowa caucuses were held on January 3 and the New Hampshire primary on January 8. Therefore, we set December 16, 2007 as the effective start of the competitive nomination phase for the 2008 cycle.

AMOUNT OF COVERAGE: PRESEASON AND PRIMARY

The 2008 campaign was the first presidential election cycle since 1952 in which neither a sitting president nor vice president was competing for a presidential nomination. As a result, the amount of news coverage of the hard-fought 2008 nominating contests was likely to be quite large. Add the first viable African-American and female presidential candidates to the mix, and you have the makings of a record-breaking primary season. And so it was, as shown in Table 6.1. For the 2008 "preseason" (January 1 through December 15, 2007), the evening newscasts of ABC, CBS, and NBC broadcast 651 stories on the upcoming Democratic and Republican presidential nomination contests. Those stories included a total of 1,336 minutes—more than 22 hours—of campaign news.

The 2007 coverage was more than three times as heavy as in 2003, when only the Democrats had a nomination contest, and more than double the coverage in 1999, the last time both parties had a competitive nomination campaign. The 2007 coverage also exceeded that of 1995 by a significant margin. In 1995 and 2003, incumbent presidents Bill Clinton (D) and George W. Bush (R) were effectively unopposed for renomination.[7] Of the three preseason campaigns besides 2007 that included nomination contests in both major parties—the preseason campaigns of 1987, 1991, and 1999—none featured nearly as many campaign stories as did the most recent contest.

Table 6.1. Amount of Coverage: Preseason Presidential Campaign News

	1987	*1991*	*1995*	*1999*	*2003*	*2007*
Number of Stories	379	211	485	294	187	651
Minutes per Day	2.1	1.1	2.3	1.2	1.1	3.8
Total Time (Minutes)	683	383	842	420	320	1336
Contesting Parties	D,R	D,R	R	D,R	D	D,R

Note: Preseason coverage includes evening network news stories for 2007 from Jan. to Dec. 15, 2007, from Jan. 1 through Dec. 31, 1991-2003; Feb. 1 through Dec. 31, 1987

In addition to the precedent-setting nature of the candidates, the media's focus on the campaign may also reflect the relatively stable international environment in 2007. Although the U.S. military continued to be engaged in Iraq and Afghanistan, coverage of those efforts was light compared to the media's initial attention to the 2003 war and subsequent occupation of Iraq.[8] The second lowest amount of preseason campaign coverage in the period covered by our study occurred in 1991, the year of the first Gulf War. The 211 stories and 383 minutes of election news airtime during 1991 represent less than half the preseason coverage of 1995.[9] The year with the third lowest amount of preseason coverage, 1999, also was marked by military action—the U.S. and NATO bombing campaign against Serbia over the occupation of Kosovo.[10] However, the downward trend in preseason election coverage (with the exception of 2007) cannot be wholly attributed to competition for the news agenda from international crises. The Iran-contra scandal, which broke in November 1986, did not push campaign news off the air during 1987. That year ranked third behind 2007 and 1995 in amount of preseason news coverage.

In most years, television really tunes in only when the nomination process is in full swing. As shown in Table 6.2, all six election cycles show a massive increase in the amount of coverage once the preseason jockeying ended and the primary season began in earnest. In the most competitive phase of the 2008 primary season for both parties, from December 16, 2007 through March 22, 2008, the networks set a new record for campaign attention. The 932 stories and 1,710 minutes (28.5 hours) on these three 30-minute newscasts were far higher than the totals for the five previous cycles.

Because the 2008 period of news content analyzed here is roughly one month longer than the previous years—the Iowa caucuses were earlier and the active nomination contest lasted longer in 2008—the best comparative measure in Table 6.2 is the number of minutes of campaign news per day. Even by this measure, 2008 was exceptional. The 17.6 minutes per day total for all three networks is more than 40 seconds a day more than the

Table 6.2. Amount of Coverage: Presidential Primary Campaign News

	1988	*1992*	*1996*	*2000*	*2004*	*2008*
Number of Stories	597	370	699	550	356	932
Minutes per Day	13.3	10.7	16.9	13.4	11.2	17.6
Total Time (Minutes)	1,126	738	1,202	882	684	1,710
Contesting Parties	D,R	D,R	R	D,R	D	D,R

Note: Primary news coverage includes evening network news stories during the most competitive phase of the nomination contest for all years: December 16, 2007 through March 22, 2008, from Jan. 1 until Super Tuesday in 1992, 1996, 2000, and 2004 (March 2, 2004; March 7, 2000; March 12, 1996 and March 10, 1992. The 1988 data is from Jan. 1 through the Illinois Primary on March 15, 1988.

16.9 minutes per day in 1996, which ranked second in amount of coverage. The 2000 and 1992 contests, both of which featured nomination competitions for both major parties, ranked third and fourth. The intense, hard-fought Obama-Clinton contest helps explain the high level of news and public interest in the 2008 campaign. Once the other Democratic contenders were effectively eliminated after the New Hampshire Primary, it was clear that the Democrats would go where no major party had gone before: nominating someone other than a white male for president.

How much network television coverage of the presidential primaries is optimal? The answer depends on the circumstances. One would expect that when both major parties have competitive nomination struggles, the coverage would be heavier than in years when only one party has a real contest. Yet we found no relationship between the number of competitive nomination campaigns and the amount of coverage. The two one-party cycles were second (1995–6) and last (2003–4) in amount of campaign news coverage during the primaries and the preseason.[11] The clearest pattern is that of a downward trend over time in the amount of coverage, with a sharp uptick in 2008. Whether that uptick is a one-time result of the precedent-setting nature of the Obama and Clinton campaigns or a renewed interest by network news in politics will only become apparent after the 2012 race has run its course.

ISSUE COVERAGE VERSUS THE HORSE RACE

Though some political scientists have recently argued otherwise, the conventional view of media coverage is that its usefulness depends on whether it focuses on matters of substance or ignores public policy in favor of campaign hoopla, ephemeral campaign trail controversies, and the horse race. Reporters frequently vow that they will improve future campaign coverage by making it more substantive, but research shows that they have rarely kept that promise.[12] With polls being released daily in the weeks before pivotal contests like New Hampshire, every day can be a poll-reporting day for correspondents who are tempted to provide horse-race journalism.[13] Table 6.3 shows that horse-race coverage has been dominant in the last three primary campaign cycles: 71 percent of the primary coverage in 2008 focused on the horse race, just slightly below the 78 percent we recorded in 2000 and 77 percent in 2004.[14] The 1988 nomination contest was the least oriented toward the daily rankings of the candidates, with 49 percent horse-race coverage. The 1992 and 1996 primaries were also far better than 2000, 2004, and 2008 in this regard.[15] Thus, even in the best of times, roughly half the campaign news provides little information to help voters learn what the

Table 6.3. Horse-Race Coverage in Presidential Primary Campaign News

	1988	*1992*	*1996*	*2000*	*2004*	*2008*
Horse-Race	49	55	56	78	77	71
Policy Issues	16	72	44	22	18	14
Contesting Parties	D,R	D,R	R	D,R	D	D,R

*Stories can include a horse-race or policy focus (or neither focus); numbers therefore do not sum to 100 percent.
Note: Primary news coverage includes evening network news stories during the most competitive phase of the nomination contest for all years: December 16, 2007 through March 22, 2008, from Jan. 1 until Super Tuesday in 1992, 1996, 2000, and 2004 (March 2, 2004; March 7, 2000; March 12, 1996 and March 10, 1992. The 1988 data is from Jan. 1 through the Illinois Primary on March 15, 1988.

candidates would do if elected. In the worst of times, issue coverage loses to horse-race journalism by a four-to-one margin.[16]

The relative absence of issue coverage is particularly troubling during the fast-moving primary campaigns. Such contests often involve several viable but little-known contenders. The differences among candidates of the same party are likely to be far more subtle than differences between candidates of opposing parties. This increases the value of news reports examining the candidates' issue positions during the early primaries. Frequently, supporters of a losing candidate, like those backing Senators Joe Biden (D-DE) and Chris Dodd (D-CT) in 2008, had only a few days to find an alternative champion after their first choice withdrew from the race following a poor showing in Iowa.[17]

American Research Group's tracking polls of likely New Hampshire primary voters demonstrate the volatility of the primary season. In 2004, for example, Howard Dean, the former Vermont governor, led in the first 16 of the 22 tracking polls the group conducted before the primary. Dean often was ahead of Sen. John Kerry of Massachusetts, the eventual nominee, by double-digit margins. Kerry was ahead only in the final six tracking polls, all conducted at least in part after his Iowa caucuses victory.[18] Surveys in New Hampshire in 1992, 2000, and 2008 also demonstrate rapidly changing multi-candidate contests.[19]

While this volatile political environment may encourage reporters to cover the horse race aggressively, they do so by shortchanging voters interested in learning where these relatively unknown governors, legislators, and activists would take the country were they to be elected.[20] Indeed, a heavy diet of horse-race coverage encourages citizens to discount issues when they evaluate candidates.[21] This agenda-setting pattern appears to be the case even in New Hampshire, where voters pride themselves on the face-to-face meetings with candidates that are alleged to dominate the state's primary. Research has demonstrated the influence of both media agenda setting and face-to-face "retail politics" for explaining a person's vote choice in the Granite State.[22]

FAIRNESS (OR NOT) IN AMOUNT AND TONE OF NEWS COVERAGE OF CANDIDATES

The media can reward or punish candidates in two different ways: by the amount of news coverage a candidate receives and by the tone of that coverage. Since most candidates are relatively unknown nationally, their greatest challenge is to build name recognition. If a candidate does not have much money, and most campaigns do not until they start doing well in the polls, news coverage (known by campaigns as "free media") is the best way to become better known.[23] Greater amounts of news coverage can increase one's name recognition, which can translate into improved poll standings and greater support from financial contributors. These factors can lead to greater media coverage, as reporters start to view the candidate as a more serious contender.[24] Indeed, the rush to raise huge sums of money during the preseason is often referred to as the "money primary."

The accelerated nomination process of recent years, accompanied by reduced amounts of campaign news coverage, can work against candidates who do not start out as front-runners.[25] Despite the rise of insurgent campaigns like those of former Governor Howard Dean (D-VT) in 2004, Sen. John McCain (R-AZ) and former Senator Bill Bradley (D-NJ) in 2000, and television commentator Pat Buchanan (R) in 1996, establishment-backed candidates with greater name recognition usually became the nominees.[26] Obama is a mixed case: though Hillary Clinton initially received more support from Democratic party leaders and office holders, Obama also had a substantial amount of elite support, including, for example, the coveted endorsement of Edward Kennedy.

Past studies of news coverage of nominations suggest that a form of journalistic triage takes place well before the first votes are cast in Iowa and New Hampshire.[27] Robinson and Sheehan in particular found that for purposes of allocating scarce media resources, candidates are categorized as "hopeless," "plausible," and "likely." The "likely" nominees, also known as front-runners, get a lot of coverage by virtue of their status as favorites. In the middle category are the "plausible" candidates, who get some coverage, but not as much as "likely" nominees. If these mid-range campaigners exceed expectations, though, they may suddenly receive a lot more media attention and even become "likely" nominees themselves. Then there are the "hopeless" candidates, who get little news coverage unless their campaigns show some signs of life—which probably won't happen since reporters are ignoring them.

The 2007 coverage of the upcoming Democratic nomination struggle was substantial, but it favored the already well-known candidates like Clinton, who was well ahead in most preseason polls. On the GOP side, the principal

Table 6.4 Tone of Preseason Presidential News Coverage by Candidate and Time

	Full Year 1999		*January-June 1999*		*July-December 1999*	
	Percent Positive	*(N)*	*Percent Positive*	*(N)*	*Percent Positive*	*(N)*
Democrats						
Al Gore	45	(78)	42	(12)	46	(66)
Bill Bradley	50	(36)	*	(4)	53	(32)
All Democratic Candidates	48	(119)	38	(16)	50	(103)
Republicans						
George W. Bush	68	(94)	88	(34)	57	(60)
John McCain	57	(30)	*	(6)	58	(24)
Elizabeth Dole	57	(21)	75	(12)	*	(9)
Pat Buchanan	*	(3)	*	(0)	*	(3)
Steve Forbes	*	(6)	*	(2)	*	(4)
All Republican Candidates	64	(155)	78	(55)	56	(100)

	Full Year 2003	
	Percent Positive	*(N)*
Democrats		
Howard Dean	67	(12)
Wesley Clark	*	(5)
John Kerry	*	(1)
John Edwards	*	(4)
Al Sharpton	*	(2)
All Democratic Candidates	65	(31)

	Full Year 2007		*January-June 2007*		*July-December 2007*	
	Percent Positive	*(N)*	*Percent Positive*	*(N)*	*Percent Positive*	*(N)*
Democrats						
Barack Obama	63	(101)	48	(27)	69	(74)
Hillary Clinton	45	(170)	56	(52)	42	(118)
John Edwards	71	(34)	80	(15)	63	(19)
Joseph Biden	*	(9)	*	(3)	*	(6)
All Democratic Candidates	54	(324)	52	(100)	55	(224)
Republicans						
John McCain	51	(49)	*	(6)	56	(43)
Rudy Giuliani	36	(121)	35	(20)	36	(101)
Mike Huckabee	53	(67)	*	(0)	52	(67)
Mitt Romney	29	(56)	38	(8)	27	(48)
Fred Thompson	30	(46)	*	(1)	29	(45)
Ron Paul	100	(10)	*	(0)	100	(10)
Sam Brownback	*	(5)	*	(3)	*	(2)
All Republican Candidates	39	(372)	38	(39)	39	(333)

* Less than 10 evaluations, too few for meaningful analysis.

Note: Based on the number of evaluations by nonpartisan sources on the ABC, CBS, and NBC evening news.

target of media coverage was preseason front-runner Rudy Giuliani, the mayor of New York City at the time of the 2001 terrorist attacks. While many candidates spent the entire year (and more) before the contests wooing donors and the citizens of Iowa and New Hampshire, reporters spent little time on-air discussing these activities for candidates who were below the top tier.[28]

Table 6.4 shows that the old Robinson and Sheehan (1983) typology of candidate viability, first used to explain differences in candidate coverage in 1980, remains an effective model for understanding news coverage dynamics. (Following in the footsteps of this pioneering work, we also limit our calculations of tone of coverage to sources not identified as partisan, making them more credible to many voters who lack clear partisan identities). In the 2008 Democratic primary preseason, when Hillary Clinton seemed to be the clear front-runner, she received substantially more coverage than any other Democratic candidate. Among the 324 tonal evaluations of all Democratic candidates, a majority (170) were directed at the former First Lady and then US Senator from New York. Plausible nominee Obama was the subject of 101 evaluations, while John Edwards, a former U.S. Senator from North Carolina and the Democratic Party's 2004 vice presidential nominee, finished third. All the other Democratic candidates were in single digits.

The story was much the same for the GOP candidates, with Giuliani, who led in the early polls, getting much of the attention. Of the 372 tonal evaluations during 2007 for the Republican candidates, roughly one-third (121) focused on the former New York City mayor. Former Arkansas Governor Mike Huckabee, a favorite of the Christian conservative voters who are highly influential in GOP nomination politics, placed second with 67 tonal evaluations. Former Massachusetts Governor Mitt Romney, another plausible nominee who also polled well in the early going, ranked third with 56 tonal evaluations, followed by McCain and Fred Thompson, a former senator from Tennessee and an actor best known for his role in the television drama *Law & Order*.

Turning to the tone of preseason coverage, we see first of all that the Democratic candidates fared far better than the Republican field in 2007, with 54 percent positive coverage versus 39 percent positive coverage, respectively. Although he received less coverage than his two major rivals, Edwards had the most positive news reports, with positive evaluations 71 percent of the time. Obama was in the middle, and front-runner Clinton had the most negative notices of the three leading Democratic candidates.

For the Republicans, the most positive evaluations were also reserved for the lagging candidates. Huckabee, with 53 percent positive coverage, and McCain, with 51 percent positive coverage, both outpaced Giuliani, whose heavy coverage was also heavily negative (only 36 percent positive evaluations).

As discussed above, there was far less coverage of the candidates during 2003 than in other preseason campaign periods that we studied. In 2003 only

Howard Dean received enough evaluations to allow us to measure the tone of his coverage in Table 6.4 (and his twelve evaluations for the full year are barely above our ten-evaluation minimum). Most of Dean's substantive evaluations, and his most positive coverage, came in December 2003, after he received the endorsement of former Vice President Al Gore, the party's nominee four years earlier.[29]

In the 1999 preseason, the last time both parties had contested nominations before 2007, the same compensatory patterns emerged. Early favorites Gore and Bush both had more than twice as many substantive evaluations as any of their rivals. Both these preseason favorites were doing well both in the preference polls and with their party's donors. In a September 1999 Gallup poll, for example, Bush was favored by 62 percent of Republican Party identifiers, while Gore had the support of 63 percent of Democratic identifiers.[30]

Table 6.4 also demonstrates the extent to which the reporters distinguish the "plausible" from the "hopeless" candidates when it comes to evaluating candidates during the preseason.[31] Obama's advantage over Edwards in the preference polls (though both trailed Clinton) was roughly replicated by his clear advantage in the number of substantive nonpartisan evaluations and the tone of that coverage.[32] Polls in late 2007 showed a five-person race on the GOP side, and the candidates not on that list were largely ignored.[33] As in previous elections, the front-runners in 2007 suffered from more intense media scrutiny, while candidates behind in the polls sometimes obtained "compensatory coverage," reporting that was more positive in tone than that of the front-runner.[34]

Finally, Table 6.4 shows that news coverage accelerates as the election year approaches. More than two-thirds of the evaluations of Democratic and Republican candidates took place during the final six months of 2007. In effect, much of the testing of the campaign waters and early organizing takes place away from the television cameras, even for the front-runners. It is a chance for a nascent presidential campaign to get organized before reporters decide whether to talk about it on the evening news.

Primary Season News: The Democratic Candidates

Once Obama emerged as the key rival to Hillary Clinton and then as the likely Democratic nominee, both the volume and the tone of his coverage increased. Obama's coverage during the entire, exceptionally long 2008 primary season (measured here as the period from December 16, 2007 through Hillary Clinton's withdrawal from the race on June 7, 2008) was 64 percent positive. As shown in Table 6.5, that figure is slightly behind the tone of coverage for John Edwards, who dropped out relatively early in 2008.

But Obama fared considerably better in the media than Hillary Clinton, who received 45 percent positive coverage during that same lengthy campaign period. Reporters who had hyped Hillary Clinton's "likely" nomination in 2007 were forced to explain why that prediction did not come to pass. Former front-runners often face harsh media attention when their campaigns fail to meet journalistic expectations. Even so, her coverage was only slightly more negative than positive during the 2008 primary season.

Table 6.5. Primary Election News: The Democratic Candidates 1992–2008

	Tone of Coverage (percent positive)[a]	*Number of Stories*[b]
1992		
Bill Clinton	37	292
Paul Tsongas	56	105
Bob Kerrey	52	31
Tom Harkin	52	28
Jerry Brown	82	108
All Democratic Candidates	*50*	
2000		
Bill Bradley	62	107
Al Gore	40	110
All Democratic Candidates	*50*	
2004		
John Kerry	81	160
Howard Dean	48	86
John Edwards	96	62
Wesley Clark	63	33
All Democratic Candidates	*75*	
2008		
Barack Obama	64	926
Hillary Clinton	45	698
John Edwards	67	78
Joe Biden	100	7
All Democratic Candidates	*56*	

[a] From January 1 through the eve of Super Tuesday Primaries on March 2, 2004; March 7, 2000; and March 10, 1992. 2008 data cover from Dec. 16, 2007 through the end of the primaries on June 7, 2008.
[b] Based on the number of evaluations by nonpartisan sources on the ABC, CBS, and NBC evening news. Only candidates with 10 or more evaluations are reported individually.
Note: Based on the number of stories extensively discussing one or more candidates on the ABC, CBS, and NBC evening news. Extensive discussions were any discussion of a candidate lasting more than 20 seconds.

Although there was far less coverage of the Democratic nomination campaign in 2004, the coverage that year was more positive in tone. John Edwards, who finished second to John Kerry in 2004, fared particularly well, with an astonishing 96 percent positive news coverage; Kerry received 81 percent positive press; and former general Wesley Clark's coverage was 63 percent positive. The tone of Kerry's coverage during the primary period was more than twice as positive as that of the two previous Democratic nominees examined here (Gore in 2000 and Bill Clinton in 1992) and exceeded the Obama coverage in 2008. Journalists who had largely discounted Kerry in the 2003 preseason subsequently explained his sudden rise to the top of the Democratic field by broadcasting a steady stream of positive assessments from political operatives, academics, and ordinary voters.[35]

The outlier in 2004 was clearly Howard Dean, the only one of the four major candidates that year to suffer from mostly negative primary season coverage. The easiest way for reporters to explain why Dean did so much worse than expected was to pile on the negative assessments after the votes were counted.[36] Much of that negativity related to the aftershocks of the famous "Dean scream" after he finished third in Iowa—just eight days before the New Hampshire primary.[37] Dean's exhortations to his supporters, endlessly retelevised, were thought by some to illustrate a temperament that made him unsuitable for the high-pressure job of being president. In his defense, Dean claimed that the media created an inaccurate image of that moment because of the noise-canceling microphone used onstage.[38]

As the 2004 race illustrates, nominees routinely get the most attention from the media, but the tone of their coverage is generally less positive than that of their leading rivals. Bill Clinton, the 1992 Democratic nominee, had by far the largest amount of media attention that year. Former Sen. Paul Tsongas (D-MA), who won the New Hampshire primary but slumped in the contests that followed, received more positive treatment from journalists but less attention.[39] In fact, all four of Clinton's major rivals were treated more positively than was Clinton: former California Governor Jerry Brown, Sen. Bob Kerrey (D-NE), Sen. Tom Harkin (D-IA), and Tsongas all enjoyed far more positive press than the eventual 1992 nominee.[40] The tone of Bill Clinton's nonpartisan evaluations was only 37 percent positive (i.e. 63 percent negative), the worst of any of the Democratic candidates examined in Table 6.5. The rule of thumb is that reporters are roughest when they think their coverage matters and gentlest when they think it doesn't.

Compensatory coverage also seemed to be the norm for the Democrats in 2000, when the sitting vice president received 40 percent positive evaluations on his way to the nomination. Long-shot candidate Bill Bradley received 62 percent positive evaluations, but it did him little good, for he lost every caucus and primary that year.[37]

Primary Season News: The Republican Candidates

On the Republican side, as shown in Table 6.6, the most positive evaluations were received by former Arkansas Governor Mike Huckabee. Former Massachusetts Governor Mitt Romney and eventual nominee John McCain

Table 6.6. Primary Election News: The Republican Candidates 1992–2008

	Tone of Coverage[a] *(percent positive)*	*Number of Stories*[b]
1992		
George H. W. Bush	24	279
Pat Buchanan	34	110
All Republican Candidates	27	
1996		
Pat Buchanan	43	283
Steve Forbes	36	249
Bob Dole	44	386
Lamar Alexander	39	173
Richard Lugar	88	28
Phil Gramm	67	90
Bob Dornan	0	12
All Republican Candidates	*43*	
2000		
John McCain	63	244
George W. Bush	53	251
All Republican Candidates	*59*	
2008		
John McCain	43	511
Mike Huckabee	58	158
Mitt Romney	44	171
Rudy Giuliani	16	70
All Republican Candidates	*48*	

[a] Through the eve of Super Tuesday Primaries on March 7, 2000; March 12, 1996 and March 10, 1992. 2008 data cover from Dec. 16, 2007 through the end of the primaries on June 7, 2008.
[b] Based on the number of evaluations by nonpartisan sources on the ABC, CBS, and NBC evening news. Only candidates with 10 or more evaluations are reported individually.
Note: Based on the number of stories extensively discussing one or more candidates on the ABC, CBS, and NBC evening news. Extensive discussions were any discussion of a candidate lasting more than 20 seconds.

received almost identical and slightly negative coverage. The harshest news coverage was reserved for the candidate who failed to meet the media's projected odds: the fast-falling campaign of Rudy Giuliani. His coverage, only 16 percent positive during the campaign season, is one of the worst measured over the past four competitive GOP nomination contests. Only Congressman Bob Dornan (R-CA), an unsuccessful candidate in 1996, received more negative assessments.

In 2000, the GOP's most recent competitive nomination struggle before 2008, John McCain clearly benefited from his spectacular rise against the favored George W. Bush. McCain had more positive evaluations than Bush during the primary period, in sharp contrast to the Texas governor's coverage advantages during the preseason. For a front-runner, though, Bush was not treated particularly badly during the nomination phase—his 2000 evaluations (53 percent positive) were more positive than Bob Dole received on his way to becoming the 1996 nominee (44 percent positive) or than George H.W. Bush got in 1992 (24 percent positive).

In 1996, television commentator Pat Buchanan, like McCain in 2000, defeated Bob Dole, the party's front-runner and eventual nominee, in New Hampshire. Along with that upset came a great deal of media attention. Of all the Republican candidates that year, Buchanan had the largest number of evaluations and coverage roughly as positive as Dole received. Steve Forbes, a wealthy publisher who has never held elective office, received substantially more negative treatment on television, much of it because he pumped tens of millions of dollars of his own money into his campaign.[42]

There was very little media coverage of the party's other competitors in 1996, including just a handful of stories on Sen. Richard Lugar (R-IN), and Rep. Bob Dornan (R-CA). These candidates were all designated "hopeless" under the media triage system. Some could at least console themselves with their largely favorable evaluations when the media did focus on them. Leading congressional figures, like Sen. Richard Lugar (R-IN), chairman of the Senate Foreign Relations Committee, and Sen. Phil Gramm (R-TX), who led the Senate Banking Committee, were treated quite well. Dornan, a less influential member of Congress, was treated extraordinarily negatively (0 percent positive coverage) when he wasn't being ignored. The lack of attention these lesser candidates received corresponded to the lack of public support for their campaigns.[43]

CHANGES IN TONE DURING THE PRIMARY SEASON

There are distinct trends in the amount of attention devoted to individual candidates, as well as in the tone of coverage, over the course of the brief

Table 6.7 Tone of Primary Season Campaign News Coverage by Candidate and Time

	Total		*Pre-Iowa* *Jan. 1-24*		*Iowa to NH* *Jan. 25-31*		*NH to Super Tuesday* *Feb. 1-March 6*	
	Percent	*(N)*	*Percent*	*(N)*	*Percent*	*(N)*	*Percent*	*(N)*
2000 Democrats								
Al Gore	42	(36)	55	(11)	31	(13)	42	(12)
Bill Bradley	62	(39)	69	(13)	33	(12)	62	(14)
All Democrats	52	(75)	63	(24)	32	(25)	62	(26)
2000 Republicans								
George W. Bush	53	(105)	60	(15)	*	(5)	51	(85)
John McCain	64	(135)	*	(5)	58	(12)	65	(118)
All Republicans	59	(240)	55	(20)	65	(17)	59	(203)

	Total		*Pre-Iowa* *Jan. 1-18*		*Iowa to NH* *Jan. 19-26*		*NH to Super Tuesday* *Jan. 27-March 1*	
	Percent	(N)	Percent	(N)	Percent	(N)	Percent	(N)
2004 Democrats								
Howard Dean	48	(52)	52	(25)	33	(15)	58	(12)
John Kerry	81	(84)	77	(14)	89	(28)	71	(42)
John Edwards	96	(45)	100	(22)	*	(9)	93	(14)
Wesley Clark	63	(16)	*	(0)	69	(13)	*	(3)
All Democrats	74	(197)	78	(64)	74	(77)	72	(71)

	Total		*Pre-NH* *Dec. 16-Jan. 7*		*NH to So. Carolina* *Jan. 8-25*		*SC to Super Tuesday* *Jan. 26-Feb. 5*	
	Percent	*(N)*	*Percent*	*(N)*	*Percent*	*(N)*	*Percent*	*(N)*
2008 Democrats								
Barack Obama	88	(138)	90	(49)	74	(38)	96	(51)
Hillary Clinton	53	(98)	61	(33)	46	(48)	59	(17)
John Edwards	67	(12)	*	(9)	*	(3)	*	(0)
Joseph Biden	*	(1)	*	(1)	*	(0)	*	(0)
All Democrats	66	(294)	77	(98)	53	(110)	72	(86)
2008 Republicans								
John McCain	48	(122)	97	(35)	47	(19)	24	(68)
Mike Huckabee	60	(63)	54	(35)	70	(27)	*	(1)
Mitt Romney	51	(51)	41	(27)	67	(9)	60	(15)
Rudy Giuliani	16	(19)	13	(15)	*	(3)	*	(1)
Ron Paul	*	(7)	*	(2)	*	(5)	*	(0)
Fred Thompson	*	(2)	*	(1)	*	(1)	*	(0)
All Republicans	48	(277)	55	(123)	62	(66)	28	(88)

* Less than 10 evaluations, too few for meaningful analysis.

Note: Based on the number of evaluations of major candidates by nonpartisan sources on the ABC, CBS, and NBC evening news.

primary season. For purposes of Table 6.7, we have divided the primary season into three periods. For 2008, the periods run from December 16, 2007 through the New Hampshire primary (January 8, 2008); from New Hampshire through the South Carolina primary (January 25); and from South Carolina through Super Tuesday (February 5).[44] In most other years, the periods run from the start of the season through Iowa; from Iowa to New Hampshire; and from New Hampshire to Super Tuesday. (For precise details, see Table 6.7.)

In 2008 Obama, Clinton, McCain, and Romney were the only candidates with enough evaluations to establish measures of tone for all three periods.[45] The tone for Obama was consistently very upbeat: 90 percent positive before the New Hampshire Primary, 74 percent positive between that primary and the one in South Carolina, and 96 percent positive after Obama's win in the South Carolina contest. Clinton's coverage lagged behind Obama's but was still relatively positive leading up to the New Hampshire primary that temporarily revived her fortunes.[46] On the Republican side, McCain's coverage was also very positive leading up to the 2008 New Hampshire primary, a state where he decisively beat George W. Bush eight years earlier. After McCain's 2008 New Hampshire victory established him as the front-runner, both Huckabee and Romney enjoyed more positive coverage than McCain. Perhaps journalists treated Romney and Huckabee well because of a vested interest in keeping the nomination process interesting. After all, once the nominee is determined, these national reporters must leave the excitement of the campaign trail to go back to covering the daily slog of legislation mired in Capitol Hill committees.[47]

Throughout these recent nomination struggles, television seemed unable to focus on more than two or three candidates at a time. In 2008, this limitation particularly hurt John Edwards, who did not receive nearly the amount of media attention enjoyed by Clinton and Obama. Although Edwards finished second to Obama in Iowa (and ahead of Hillary Clinton), he received no real bump in media attention. Of course, given his extramarital affair and the eventual scandal it caused, Democrats might consider themselves fortunate Edwards did not get more media attention.[48]

The volume of network news evaluations of the Democratic candidates in 2000 was far more consistent across the primary period than it was in 2004 or 2008. Bill Bradley and Al Gore received roughly equal numbers of evaluations in all three primary campaign periods. But there were considerable differences in tone, with Bradley treated far more positively before Iowa and after New Hampshire than he was during the week between the two earliest contests. Although Gore's coverage was consistently more negative than Bradley's, the middle period also contained the most negative Gore evaluations. Bradley's generous coverage in the final primary period appears to be another example of compensatory coverage for a trailing candidate.

Reporters spent much more time evaluating the Republican candidates that year. The 240 evaluations of McCain and Bush during the 2000 primary season were three times the number of evaluations provided the two Democratic candidates. Indeed, reporters also seem to have trouble dealing with more than one party nomination at a time—and McCain's solid victory over Bush in New Hampshire in 2000 made that contest far more interesting to reporters that winter.[49] McCain's decision to concentrate on New Hampshire and not campaign in Iowa limited his coverage in the weeks before the first test of 2000. There were very few evaluations of McCain before Iowa, few evaluations of either Bush or McCain before New Hampshire, and many, many evaluations of both men following McCain's upset victory in the Granite State.

Part of the explanation for the media's gentle treatment of the Arizona senator throughout the primary season stems from McCain's aggressive courting of the media, a crucial component of his political style throughout his career.[50] McCain was unusually accessible to the media for a presidential candidate during the 2000 primaries, and that accessibility translated into greater amounts of coverage for his underdog campaign.[51] Reporters are often kind to candidates who are willing to talk to them, particularly in the unscripted way typical of the Arizona senator holding court on his campaign bus that year.[52] In addition, McCain's five years as a North Vietnamese prisoner during the Vietnam War also probably reduced the criticism the Navy veteran faced from reporters.

Another part of the explanation for McCain's positive treatment in 2000 can be found in the results from New Hampshire—he did the unexpected and beat Bush by a surprisingly large margin. Better-than-expected performances draw reporters to campaigns like flies to honey. But good relations with reporters and a win in New Hampshire were not enough for McCain to overcome Bush's advantages in fund-raising, elite endorsements, and the support Bush received from many key GOP constituencies.[53]

Conclusion

Our findings contain several lessons for presidential candidates concerning their nomination campaign coverage. First, television does little to reverse a painful reality of modern presidential nominations: if a candidate does not start out as a front-runner, he or she is probably not going to be the nominee.

Candidates at or near the top in fund-raising and in the early polls receive the bulk of media and public attention. That makes the early front-runners nearly unstoppable. While they do not generally get the most positive coverage, the coverage likely nominees receive is usually not that much worse than their main rivals.

If you can't be the front-runner, the best advice for a presidential aspirant is to be like Barack Obama. Outsider candidates who energize the party's base get very favorable coverage, particularly when they dethrone a presumptive nominee, as Obama did in 2008. The nature of Obama's historic campaign as the first African-American major-party nominee created a favorable media climate that lasted well beyond the nomination stage, through the general election and even into his first years in office.[54]

More generally, the Obama example offers this key piece of campaign and media advice for non-front-runners: Do better than expected in the early contests. Huckabee and Obama in Iowa in 2008, Kerry in Iowa and New Hampshire in 2004, and McCain in New Hampshire in 2000 all surged far beyond their preseason expectations, and each received very positive coverage from reporters trying to explain the rise of candidates they had previously ignored. While the kind media coverage did not win the nomination for either Huckabee in 2008 or McCain in 2000, positive news reports may have been a tie-breaker in the closely fought Obama-Clinton struggle of 2008.

While the nomination process itself has favored current or former governors (who often find it easier to spend significant amounts of time in Iowa and New Hampshire), the media coverage tends to be kinder to senators. Perhaps the Washington-based reporters who cover the campaigns know the Washington-based senators better than the governors who toil in the relative obscurity (as seen from inside the Washington Beltway) of Montpelier, Little Rock, or Austin.

As shown in Table 6.5, four of the five most positively treated Democratic candidates since 1992 were senators—Edwards and Obama in 2008 and Edwards and Kerry in 2004. A similar pattern is found in Table 6.6, where the three most positively treated Republican candidates—Lugar and Gramm in 1996 and McCain in 2000—were also senators. If media tone determined nominations, senators would win most of the time. But nominations usually go to governors, not to the Washington insiders who get treated so well by their fellow Washington insiders reporting on the evening news.

Candidates pushing a pet cause should expect to be ignored by the news media, unless they are very wealthy. In 1996 Steve Forbes promoted his flat tax proposal through an expensive barrage of television ads.[55] Forbes' willingness to spend tens of millions of dollars of his own money made him a serious contender and generated news coverage and improved poll numbers. But the coverage was often negative, as reporters frequently focused on the billionaire publisher's attempts to buy the GOP nomination, and Forbes' campaign faded in the face of Dole's string of primary successes.

A popular message offered by a viable candidate can help generate media coverage, as it did for Obama, whose campaign was focused on the mantra of "change."[56] Four years earlier, Dean's harsh criticism of the Bush administration's war in Iraq likewise propelled him to the front ranks of the Democrats, at a time when U.S. problems in Iraq were intensifying.[57] Dean's focus on the Iraq war also offered an important way for the former governor to separate himself from four key 2004 rivals—Kerry, Edwards, Lieberman, and Gephardt—who all voted for military action and continued to trip over the subject of Iraq during the campaign.[58]

After their 2004 general election defeat, Democrats debated many plans to limit the importance of Iowa and New Hampshire in 2008. They sought to reduce the influence of those two states by adding South Carolina, which has a relatively large African-American population, and Nevada, with an above-average Latino population, to the list of early caucus and primary states. But this change, like other campaign calendar redesigns of the past, did little to curb the influence of the first primary and the first caucus. If anything, the pressure toward front-loading the nomination process over the past several decades has increased the influence of those two small and demographically unrepresentative states. Further campaign season compression may take place in 2012, as states continue to jostle for a position as early in the process as possible. One other likely consequence of the concentrated nomination calendar for 2012 will be to increase the influence of the news media. Candidates will have less time to campaign in any one state and will be forced to rely even more on "wholesale" media-oriented politics and campaign contributions to finance large advertising appeals.

While we cannot predict whether the increased amount of preseason and primary campaign season coverage of 2008 will be replicated in 2012, the mass media's tendency to focus its attention primarily on the most popular candidates seems likely to continue regardless of the precise number of candidates on the Republican side in 2012. Despite some grumbling by liberals who expected more, Obama is likely to face no serious opposition on his way to renomination. His fund-raising prowess alone should be sufficient to deter all but the most reckless would-be Democratic challengers.[60]

With a sizable field of contenders in 2012, Republican candidates will be competing all the more aggressively for limited mainstream media coverage. Previous multi-candidate fields encouraged the use of media triage to allocate air time, which leads to the now-familiar pattern of focusing on front-runners and major contenders with the largest poll numbers and the greatest fund-raising success. Candidates who are further back in the field will be tempted to try to repeat the outsider strategy employed with great success by Obama in 2008 and with some initial success by Howard Dean in 2004. The former Vermont governor's fortunes rose dramatically during the last half of 2003 thanks to an aggressive online strategy for fund-raising and building his support base. By the turn of 2004, Dean seemed to be the likely nominee, until he stumbled in Iowa and New Hampshire.[61]

The lesson non-front-runners may take from all this is, if you can't beat the traditional media, campaign through the new media. The online news environment, without the tight time restrictions of network news, seems far more accessible to secondary candidates, particularly those farthest back in the pack.[62] This online-focused approach should be especially effective at reaching and mobilizing young adults, who are more comfortable than their elders with computers. While young adults tend to be more Democratic than Republican in their loyalties, the GOP needs these young activists to increase its chances of success in November 2012.[63]

This time, however, an outsider-oriented candidate seeking to follow Obama's example will not have the same head start online. Front-runners, serious challengers, and dark horses will all try to use the Internet aggressively to compensate for limited network television attention, to raise money, and to expand their support base. The question is whether anyone on the Republican side can duplicate Obama's online success, now that several candidates are courting voters early and aggressively in cyberspace. Indeed, one of the more interesting competitions in 2011 and 2012 may take place among the media outlets seeking to capture the attention of the voting public during the next round of America's volatile presidential nomination campaigns.

NOTES

1. Andrew E. Busch, "The Reemergence of the Iowa Caucuses: A New Trend, An Aberration, or a Useful Reminder?" in *The Making of the Presidential Candidates 2008*, ed. William G. Mayer (Lanham, MD: Rowman & Littlefield, 2008); James W. Ceaser, *Presidential Selection: Theory and Development* (Princeton, NJ: Princeton University Press, 1979); Marty Cohen, David Karol, Hans Noel, and John Zaller, "The Invisible Primary in Presidential Nominations, 1980–2004," in *The Making of the Presidential Candidates 2008*, ed. William G. Mayer (Lanham, MD: Rowman & Littlefield, 2008); Stephen J. Farnsworth and S. Robert Lichter, "The 2004 New Hampshire Democratic Primary and Network News," *Harvard International Journal of Press/Politics* 11 (2006): 53–63; James I. Lengle, *Representation and Presidential*

Primaries: The Democratic Party in the Post-Reform Era (Westport, CT: Greenwood, 1981); William G. Mayer, "The Basic Dynamics of the Contemporary Nomination Process: An Expanded View," in *The Making of the Presidential Candidates 2004*, ed. William G. Mayer (Lanham, MD: Rowman & Littlefield, 2004); Nelson Polsby, *Consequences of Party Reform* (Oxford, UK: Oxford University Press, 1983); Tom Rosenstiel, *Strange Bedfellows: How Television and the Presidential Candidates Changed American Politics, 1992* (New York: Hyperion, 1994).

2. See, among many other works, Kiku Adatto, "Sound Bite Democracy," Research Paper, Kennedy School of Government, Harvard University, June 1990; Lance W. Bennett, *News: The Politics of Illusion* (New York: Pearson/Longman, 2009); Joseph N. Cappella and Kathleen Hall Jamieson, *Spiral of Cynicism: The Press and the Public Good* (New York: Oxford University Press, 1997); Timothy E. Cook, *Governing With the News: The News Media as a Political Institution* (Chicago, IL: University of Chicago Press, 2005); Kenneth Dautrich and Thomas H. Hartley, *How The News Media Fail American Voters: Causes, Consequences and Remedies* (New York: Columbia University Press, 1999); Richard Davis and Diana Owen, *New Media and American Politics* (New York: Oxford University Press, 1998); Stephen J. Farnsworth and S. Robert Lichter, *The Nightly News Nightmare: Media Coverage of U.S. Presidential Elections, 1988–2008* (Lanham, MD: Rowman & Littlefield, 2011); Doris A. Graber, *Mass Media and American Politics* (Washington, DC: CQ Press, 2009); Shanto Iyengar, *Is Anyone Responsible? How Television Frames Political Issues* (Chicago, IL: University of Chicago Press, 1991); Matthew Robert Kerbel, *Edited for Television: CNN, ABC, and American Presidential Elections* (Boulder, CO: Westview, 1998); Regina G. Lawrence, "Defining Events: Problem Definition in the Media Arena," in *Politics, Discourse, and American Society: New Agendas*, ed. Roderick P. Hart and Bartholomew H. Sparrow (Lanham, MD: Rowman & Littlefield, 2001); S. Robert Lichter and Richard E. Noyes, *Good Intentions Make Bad News: Why Americans Hate Campaign Journalism* (Lanham, MD: Rowman & Littlefield, 1995); Diana Owen, *Media Messages in American Presidential Elections* (Westport, CT: Greenwood Press, 1991); Diana Owen, "Media Mayhem: Performance of the Press in Election 2000," in *Overtime: The Election 2000 Thriller*, ed. Larry Sabato (New York: Longman, 2002); Diana Owen, "The Campaign and the Media," in *The American Elections of 2008*, ed. Janet Box-Steffensmeier and Steven E. Schier (Lanham, MD: Rowman & Littlefield, 2009); Thomas E. Patterson, *Out of Order* (New York: Vintage, 1994); Michael J. Robinson and Margaret A. Sheehan, *Over the Wire and on TV* (New York: Russell Sage Foundation, 1983); Larry J. Sabato, Mark Stencel, and S. Robert Lichter, *Peep Show: Media and Politics in an Age of Scandal* (Lanham, MD: Rowman & Littlefield, 2000); and Philip Seib, *Going Live: Getting the News Right in a Real-Time, Online World* (Lanham, MD: Rowman & Littlefield, 2001).

3. Pew Research Center for the People and the Press. "High Marks for the Campaign, A High Bar for Obama," report issued November 13, 2008, www.people-press.org (accessed November 13, 2008).

4. David T. Z. Mindich, *Tuned Out: Why Americans Under 40 Don't Follow the News* (New York: Oxford University Press, 2005); and Pew, "High Marks for the Campaign."

5. For further information on our coding system, consult Farnsworth and Lichter, *Nightly News Nightmare*, chap. 1 and appendix A.

6. In most recent nomination struggles, the nominees have effectively clinched the nomination during a group of primaries known as "Super Tuesday," which in recent election cycles has taken place during February or early March. The 2008 Democratic contest was the first time a presidential nomination contest lasted beyond Super Tuesday since 1988, when eventual Democratic nominee Michael Dukakis did not emerge as the clear nominee until the New York primary on April 19, 1988. While the modern primary-dominant nomination system (put in place after the divisive Democratic convention of 1968) does not always produce a quick winner, it has been over three decades since either party has opened a convention uncertain about who will be selected as its nominee. See James W. Ceaser, Andrew E. Busch, and John J. Pitney, Jr., *Epic Journey: The 2008 Election and American Politics* (Lanham, MD: Rowman & Littlefield, 2009), William G. Mayer and Andrew E. Busch, *The Front-Loading Problem in Presidential Nominations* (Washington, DC: Brookings Institution, 2004); Mayer, "Basic Dynamics of the Contemporary Nomination Process"; and Polsby, *Consequences of Party Reform.*

7. To state this more precisely, no sitting or former governor, Member of Congress, or member of a presidential cabinet, nor any other candidate polling in the double digits in any nationally recognized poll, challenged these two presidents for renomination.

8. Stephen J. Farnsworth and S. Robert Lichter, *The Mediated Presidency: Television News and Presidential Governance* (Lanham, MD: Rowman & Littlefield, 2006), 90–91.

9. Foreign news coverage in 1991, a year marked by the first Persian Gulf War as well as the collapse of the Soviet Union, represented 34 percent of all network news coverage, second only to the 43 percent of news coverage relating to international matters in 2003, the year a U.S.-led coalition invaded and then occupied Iraq. See Farnsworth and Lichter, *Mediated Presidency*, 90–91.

10. Farnsworth and Lichter, *Mediated Presidency*, 99.

11. Overall, 33 percent of stories on the network evening newscasts during 2004 dealt with foreign policy matters, according to the Center for Media and Public Affairs.

12. Jonathan Alter, "Go Ahead, Blame the Media," *Newsweek*, Nov. 2, 1992; Austin Ranney, *Channels of Power* (New York: Basic Books, 1983); Timothy J. Russert, "For '92, The Networks Have to Do Better," *New York Times*, March 4, 1990; Farnsworth and Lichter, *Nightly News Nightmare*; Kerbel, *Edited for Television*; Owen, "Media Mayhem."

13. The fact that the polls can be very volatile during the primary season does not seem to discourage media coverage of the horse race. See Andrew E. Smith, "The Perils of Polling in New Hampshire," in *The Making of the Presidential Candidates*

2004, ed. William G. Mayer (Lanham, MD: Rowman & Littlefield, 2004); Farnsworth and Lichter, "2004 New Hampshire Democratic Primary."

14. Farnsworth and Lichter, *Nightly News Nightmare*, 50.

15. Farnsworth and Lichter, *Nightly News Nightmare*, 50.

16. This observation relates only to primary season news coverage. We did not code for horse-race coverage during the preseason.

17. Both Dodd and Biden, who eventually became vice president, withdrew from the nomination contest following their failure to finish in the top three in the Iowa caucuses on January 3. The New Hampshire Primary was held on January 8, five days later.

18. Farnsworth and Lichter, "2004 New Hampshire Democratic Primary," 57.

19. For the Democrats in 2008, Hillary Clinton led Obama before her third-place showing in Iowa, Obama then surged and overtook Clinton in New Hampshire surveys in the days that followed, but Clinton ended up winning the Granite State primary narrowly. For the Republicans, McCain, who defeated eventual nominee George W. Bush in the 2000 New Hampshire Primary, was a far more consistent favorite of the state's GOP primary voters from late 2007 through the day of the primary. Ceaser, Busch, and Pitney, *Epic Journey*.

20. Evidence suggests that despite citizen complaints about the lack of substance in campaign coverage, there is nevertheless a thriving market for horse-race news content. Shanto Iyengar, Helmut Norpoth, and Kyu S. Hahn, "Consumer Demand for Election News: The Horserace sells." *Journal of Politics* 66 (2004): 157–75.

21. Thomas E. Patterson, *The Mass Media Election: How Americans Choose Their President* (New York: Praeger, 1980); Patterson, *Out of Order*.

22. For network news effects on New Hampshire voters in recent primaries, see Farnsworth and Lichter, "The 2000 New Hampshire Democratic Primary." For discussions of retail politics and whether it remains a key part of the New Hampshire primary, see Tami Buhr, "What Voters Know about the Candidates and How They Learn It: The 1996 New Hampshire Republican Primary as a Case Study," in *In Pursuit of the White House 2000: How We Choose Our Presidential Nominees*, ed. William G. Mayer (New York: Chatham House/Seven Bridges, 2001); Dayton Duncan, *Grass Roots: One Year in the Life of the New Hampshire Presidential Primary* (New York: Viking, 1991); and Dante J. Scala, *Stormy Weather: The New Hampshire Primary and Presidential Politics* (New York: Palgrave Macmillan, 2003).

23. Mayer, "Basic Dynamics."

24. Mayer, "Basic Dynamics."

25. Mayer and Busch, *Front-Loading Problem in Presidential Nominations*.

26. Barry Burden, "The Nominations: Technology, Money, and Transferable Momentum," in *The Elections of 2004*, ed. Michael Nelson (Washington, DC: CQ Press, 2005).

27. The "triage" model of distinguishing candidates for purposes of allocating media coverage was presented by Robinson and Sheehan, *Over the Wire*, 75–82.

28. Ceaser, Busch, and Pitney, *Epic Journey*.

29. "Dean Trails in Race for Positive Press," news release, Center for Media and Public Affairs, January 16, 2004, available at www.cmpa.com (accessed on January 6, 2006).

30. William G. Mayer, "The Presidential Nominations," in *The Elections of 2000: Reports and Interpretations*, ed. Gerald M. Pomper (Chatham, NJ: Chatham House, 2001), 18–21.

31. Robinson and. Sheehan, *Over the Wire*.

32. In the last *USA Today*/Gallup poll taken during 2007, Hillary Clinton was favored by 45 percent of those Democrats expressing a preference, as compared to 27 percent for Obama and 15 percent for Edwards. Howard L. Reiter, "The Nominating Process," in *Winning the Presidency 2008*, ed. William J. Crotty. (Boulder, CO: Paradigm, 2009).

33. In the last *USA Today*/Gallup poll taken during 2007, Giuliani was favored by 27 percent of those Republicans expressing a preference, as compared to 16 percent for Huckabee and 14 percent each for McCain, Romney, and Thompson. Reiter, "Nominating Process."

34. Robinson and Sheehan, *Over the Wire*.

35. The most positive media treatment of all can sometimes be delivered to candidates who do better than expected, observed Robinson and Sheehan in *Over the Wire*. Patterson, in *Out of Order*, observed this same pattern of media favoritism to the surprisingly successful. Given his come-from-way-behind nomination victory in 2004, Kerry certainly qualifies as a candidate who did far better than expected. See Burden, "Nominations." The same thing occurred in 2008, when Obama defeated the well-funded Clinton family political operation on his way to the White House.

36. "By the time Gore endorsed him in mid-December [2003], Dean seemed unbeatable. If momentum exists in contemporary presidential nomination campaigns, Dean had it." Burden, "Nominations," 26.

37. Burden, "Nominations"; Farnsworth and Lichter, *Nightly News Nightmare*; Joe Trippi, *The Revolution Will Not Be Televised: Democracy, the Internet, and the Overthrow of Everything* (New York: HarperCollins, 2004).

38. John Eggerton, "Howard Dean: Scream Never Happened." *Broadcasting & Cable,* June 14, 2004.

39. Stephen J. Farnsworth and S. Robert Lichter, "No Small Town Poll: Public Attention to Network Coverage of the 1992 New Hampshire Primary," *Harvard International Journal of Press/Politics* 4 (1999): 51–61.

40. Ross K. Baker, "Sorting Out and Suiting Up: The Presidential Nominations," in *The Election of 1992: Reports and Interpretations*, ed. Gerald M. Pomper (Chatham, NJ: Chatham House, 1993); James Ceaser and Andrew Busch, *Upside Down and Inside Out: The 1992 Elections and American Politics* (Lanham, MD: Rowman & Littlefield, 1993).

41. Although the 2000 New Hampshire primary was relatively close (Gore won by a 50 percent to 46 percent margin), the vice president received at least 54 percent of the vote in every other primary during the time that Bradley remained an active candidate. Mayer, "Presidential Nominations," 21–28.

42. Anthony Corrado, "Financing the 1996 Elections," in *The Elections of 1996: Reports and Interpretations*, ed. Gerald M. Pomper (Chatham, NJ: Chatham House, 1997).

43. Lugar, Gramm, and Dornan all failed to break into double digits in the WMUR/ Dartmouth College polls of New Hampshire voters leading up to the 1996 campaign season. In fact, Gramm didn't even make it to the primary, withdrawing early as a result of his losses in the Louisiana and Iowa caucuses. William G. Mayer, "The Presidential Nominations," in *The Elections of 1996: Reports and Interpretations* (Chatham, NJ: Chatham House, 1997), 42–46.

44. On February 5, 2008, the so-called Super Duper Tuesday involved primaries in sixteen states and caucuses in eight others, by far the largest single-day list of contests in primary history. Obama's strong showing on that day might have ended the contest had not the Clinton political operation been as committed and as well-financed as it was. See Arthur C. Paulson, "The Invisible Primary Becomes Visible," in *Winning the Presidency 2008*, ed. William J. Crotty (Boulder, CO: Paradigm, 2009); and Ceaser, Busch, and Pitney, *Epic Journey*. In 2004, nine states held Democratic presidential primaries on Super Tuesday (March 2), including some of the nation's largest: California, New York, Ohio, Georgia, Massachusetts, and Maryland. Burden, "Nominations," 31. Eleven states held Democratic primaries on Super Tuesday four years earlier, March 7, 2000, including all of the major states listed earlier for Super Tuesday 2004. Mayer, "Presidential Nominations," 32.

45. Our content analysis system did not record the specific nomination event referred to in individual reports. But a review of the taped newscasts indicates that most of the campaign news stories before Iowa were about Iowa, most of the stories between the first caucuses and the first primary were about New Hampshire, and most of the stories after New Hampshire were about the next set of nomination contests leading up to Super Tuesday.

46. Indeed, many recent nominees in competitive nomination struggles lost at least one of the two pivotal contests: Barack Obama in 2008 lost New Hampshire, John McCain in 2008 lost Iowa, George W. Bush in 2000 lost New Hampshire, Bob Dole in 1996 lost New Hampshire, and Bill Clinton in 1992 lost both Iowa and New Hampshire.

47. This potential journalistic motivation is discussed in several campaign studies, including Tom Rosenstiel, *Strange Bedfellows;* and David Shribman, "Only a Lunatic Would Do This Kind of Work," in *The Making of the Presidential Candidates 2004*, ed. William G. Mayer (Lanham, MD: Rowman & Littlefield, 2004).

48. Kim Severson, "Edwards Lies Low, but That Won't Last," *New York Times*, March 1, 2011.

49. McCain upset Bush by a 49 percent to 30 percent margin in New Hampshire, while Bradley's hoped-for upset of Gore failed by a 50 percent to 46 percent margin. Mayer, "Presidential Nominations," 32–36.

50. James Ceaser and Andrew Busch, *The Perfect Tie: The True Story of the 2000 Presidential Election* (Lanham, MD: Rowman & Littlefield, 2001); Elizabeth Drew, *Citizen McCain* (New York: Simon & Schuster, 2002); and Mayer, "Presidential Nominations."

51. For a comparison of the media strategies of the candidates, see Scala, *Stormy Weather*, especially chap. 7.

52. Scala, *Stormy Weather*, chap. 7.

53. Mayer, "Presidential Nominations."

54. Farnsworth and Lichter, *Nightly News Nightmare*; Stephen J. Farnsworth and S. Robert Lichter, "Network News Coverage of New Presidents, 1981–2009," paper delivered at the annual meeting of American Political Science Association, Washington, DC, September 2010.

55. Darrell M. West, *Air Wars: Television Advertising in Election Campaigns, 1952–2004* (Washington, DC: CQ Press, 2005).

56. Ceaser, Busch, and Pitney, *Long Journey*.

57. Michael Dimock, "Bush and Public Opinion," in *Considering the Bush Presidency*, ed. Gary Gregg II and Mark J. Rozell (New York: Oxford, 2004); James W. Ceaser and Andrew E. Busch, *Red over Blue* (Lanham, MD: Rowman & Littlefield, 2005); Douglas Kellner, *From 9/11 to Terror War: The Dangers of the Bush Legacy* (Lanham, MD: Rowman & Littlefield, 2003); Dana Milbank and Walter Pincus, "Cheney Defends U.S. Actions in Bid to Revive Public Support," *Washington Post*, September 15, 2003; Farnsworth and Lichter, *Mediated Presidency*.

58. Nina Easton, et al., "On the Trail of Kerry's Failed Dream," *Boston Globe*, Sunday Magazine, November 14, 2004; Burden, "Nominations."

59. Several influential Republicans have decided to pass on running in 2012, including Mississippi Gov. Haley Barbour, Indiana Gov. Mitch Daniels, and Mike Huckabee, a prominent 2008 candidate and former governor of Arkansas. Others committed early to running, including Mitt Romney and Tim Pawlenty, former governor of Minnesota. Still others remained on the sidelines longer than most candidates in previous election cycles. See, among others, Dan Balz, "Texas' Rick Perry Weighing a 2012 Candidacy," *Washington Post*, June 8, 2011; Richard Perez-Pena, "Christie Keeps Saying No to a Presidential Race, but Republicans Keep Calling," *New York Times*, May 17, 2011; Jim Rutenberg and Kate Zernike, "Palin, Amid Criticism, Stays in Electronic Comfort Zone," *New York Times*, January 10, 2011.

60. Strategic politicians prefer to run when their chances of nomination are greatest, which often means not campaigning against an incumbent president or vice president. See Marc J. Hetherington and William J. Keefe, *Parties, Politics, and Public Policy in America* (Washington: CQ Press, 2007); and Nelson W. Polsby and Aaron Wildavsky, *Presidential Elections: Strategies and Structures of American Politics* (Lanham, MD: Rowman & Littlefield, 2004).

61. Burden, "Nominations."

62. Farnsworth and Lichter, *Nightly News Nightmare*; Owen, "Campaign and the Media"; and Trippi, *Revolution Will Not Be Televised*.

63. Paul Abramson, John H. Aldrich, and David W. Rhode, *Change and Continuity in the 2008 Elections* (Washington, DC: CQ Press, 2010).

64. Stephen E. Frantzich, "E-politics and the 2008 Campaign," in *Winning the Presidency 2008*, ed. William J. Crotty (Boulder, CO: Paradigm, 2009); and Owen, "Campaign and the Media." At the start of 2004, Dean was ahead in the polls in both New Hampshire and Iowa. Had those contests been roughly two weeks earlier, Dean probably would have emerged victorious in both, and that would have made it nearly impossible for other candidates to have caught him in the fast-moving nomination process. Burden, "Nominations."

Chapter 7

Theory Meets Practice: The Presidential Selection Process in the First Federal Election, 1788–89

William G. Mayer

In an article published in the previous volume in this series, I examined how and why the Framers of the Constitution devised the complex procedure set forth in Article II, Section 1 for electing the president of the United States.[1] This chapter continues the story, by describing how that process actually worked when it was put into practice in the first presidential election.

To summarize the denouement of that earlier article: When the Constitutional Convention adjourned *sine die* on September 17, 1787, the election of the president had been entrusted, at least initially, to a group of presidential "electors," the group we know today as the electoral college, though that term is never actually used in the Constitution. Each state was given the same number of electors as it had members in the new Congress—i.e., the number of representatives plus the number of senators. How the electors would be chosen was left to the discretion of the state legislatures.

The electors would meet in their respective states and vote for two presidential candidates. The votes would later be counted before a joint session of Congress, and the candidate with the largest number of votes would be elected president—if that candidate received a vote from a majority of the electors. The second-place finisher would become vice president. If no one received a majority vote, or if two candidates tied for the lead, the final decision would be made by the House of Representatives, with each state casting one vote.

Perhaps the most striking feature of this constitutional text is how little apparent relationship it bears to the way we have conducted presidential elections for the last 170 years or so. I still remember the time when, as a college undergraduate, I first undertook a close, careful reading of the text of the Constitution. Having followed American politics for a number of years, and having sat through my share of grade-school and high-school civics classes, many features of that document were unsurprising: there was a bicameral legislature, a unitary executive, an amending procedure, a detailed list of powers granted to the new national government, etc. But what was one to make of the elaborate process described in Article II for selecting the nation's chief executive? It seemed nothing like the presidential elections I had been observing over the previous decade.

To be sure, analysts of contemporary American politics often claim that this or that aspect of our system of government functions in a very different manner than was intended or anticipated by the men who wrote the Constitution. The extensive range of powers exercised by the national government and the frequency and breadth of judicial review are two features commonly singled out in this regard. Yet there *were* advocates of a strong national government among the Framers; and many Framers *did* foresee that the federal courts would have the power—indeed, the duty—to declare laws null and void if they violated the provisions of the Constitution. By contrast, I am not aware of *any* person from the founding era who suggested that the presidential selection process would or should evolve into anything like the system we know today.

So how did we wind up with the contemporary presidential selection process? The short answer is that, as the provisions of Article II, Section 1 were put into operation, Americans of the founding period were required to "fill in the blanks": to decide how a process that the Constitution described only in the most general terms would actually work in practice. In some cases, the blank spaces were deliberate. The Constitution, as we have already noted, did not specify how the presidential electors were to be chosen, leaving that matter instead to the determination of the state legislatures. Now the state legislatures had to decide how to use that discretion. In other cases, the blanks were less obvious. The Constitution said nothing about how the electors were to make their decisions, though (as we will see shortly) the Framers probably expected them to be independent, uninstructed decision-makers. But enforcing such an assumption in a democratic political system would prove enormously difficult. Above all, there were the clashing intentions of the men who wrote the Constitution, who were desperately anxious to insulate the presidential selection process from faction, intrigue, and all forms of outside influence, and the politicians who had to live under it, whose overriding concern was precisely to influence the process so as to ensure the election of their favored candidates.

The bottom line is that, almost from the moment that the Constitution went into effect, the presidential selection process began to operate in ways that the Framers clearly had not expected or intended. And if one wishes to examine the clash between theory and practice, there is no better vantage point than the presidential election of 1788-89. (As the subsequent narrative will show, all of the formal stages in the first presidential election took place in 1789, but much of the organizing, legal wrangling, and what might reasonably be described as nomination activity occurred in the latter half of 1788.) The first presidential election is often dismissed with the observation that Washington was the obvious, consensus choice and that the whole exercise was therefore just a formality. In fact, however, the story is a good deal more complicated. While in some respects the first election provided an easy tryout for the new presidential selection system, in other respects it revealed quite clearly the process's major flaws and the ways that candidates and other political leaders could manipulate it. Just as the first Congress and the early Supreme Court are sometimes regarded, along with the Framers of the Constitution, as the "co-creators" of the American system of government, so, too, that title may reasonably be applied to the men who organized and participated in the first federal elections.

WHAT THE FRAMERS EXPECTED: A RECAP

As a baseline for the analysis that follows, it is worth returning briefly to the work of the Framers. I have already described the legal framework they established in Article II for the election of the president. But how exactly was this system supposed to work? Four specific questions deserve our attention.

1. *How would the presidential electors be chosen?* As I argued in my 2008 article, this is one case where we should take the Framers at their word.[2] Given the option of having the electors appointed by the state legislature or having them selected by popular vote—proposals of both types were considered at one point or another—the delegates to the Constitutional Convention finally decided to leave the decision to the determination of the state legislature precisely because they did not have a strong preference on the issue. Had they really hoped or intended that the electors would be chosen directly by the people, as some modern historians have argued,[3] they could easily have mandated that, just as they had already done with respect to the House of Representatives. While there were some statements made during the ratification debates that the electors would be selected by popular vote, these were balanced by an equal number of comments which merely said that the state legislatures had that option.
2. *How would the electors make their decisions?* In particular, would they be independent decision-makers or would they be explicitly instructed

by whoever chose them to vote for a specific pair of candidates? Though this issue was not extensively discussed during the Convention or the ratification debates, the evidence that does exist strongly implies the former: that the electors would be free agents, able to exercise their own, independent judgment when deciding how to cast their votes. One of the few contemporary documents that provides some insight into how the electors would comport themselves is Alexander Hamilton's well-known analysis of the presidential selection system in Federalist 68. In appointing the "Chief Magistrate of the United States," Hamilton asserted,

> It was equally desirable that the immediate election should be made by men most capable of analyzing the qualities adapted to the station and acting under circumstances favorable to deliberation, and to a judicious combination of all the reasons and inducements which were proper to govern their choice. A small number of persons, selected by their fellow-citizens from the general mass, will be most likely to possess the information and discernment requisite to so complicated an investigation.[4]

Clearly, Hamilton believed—and thought his audience believed—that the electors would be making their own decisions. If the electors were merely to serve as messenger boys for the voters or the state legislators, they would not be "analyzing the qualities adapted to the station," nor would it matter whether they possessed "information and discernment" or were "acting under circumstances favorable to deliberation." Hamilton's comments make sense only if the electors were doing more than just repeating the names of candidates who had already been selected by someone else.

Another piece of evidence bearing out the same conclusion appears in James Madison's journal of the Constitutional Convention. In mid-July, the Convention delegates briefly appeared to decide that the president would be "chosen by Electors appointed for that purpose by the legislatures of the states," with the electors from all over the country meeting in one, central location to cast their votes. Several days later, however, this plan was abandoned, in large part because, as delegate William Houstoun of Georgia argued, it was improbable "that capable men would undertake the service of Electors from the more distant States." Again, if the electors were not expected to be independent decision-makers, Houstoun's argument would lose most of its force, for it would scarcely matter whether the electors were especially capable individuals.[5]

3. *How would the huge number of potential presidential candidates be narrowed down to a manageable number of alternatives?* Put another way, how would presidential nominations be accomplished? To the extent

that the Framers thought about nominations as a distinct and significant stage in the presidential selection process—most probably did not—they would likely have answered these questions in two ways. Most delegates at the Constitutional Convention thought of the electoral college itself as a nominating mechanism. In most years, that is to say, the electoral votes would be so scattered among a host of state and regional favorites that no candidate would receive a vote from a majority of the electors. The final selection would then be made by the House of Representatives, voting by state, with the important stipulation that the House's choices would be limited to the top five finishers in the electoral voting. Two Convention delegates, James Madison and Roger Sherman, explicitly referred to this arrangement as one in which the large states, which were expected to dominate the electoral voting, would be given the "nomination" of the presidential candidates.[6] Though this sort of contingent election has, in fact, occurred only twice in American history, the majority of Convention delegates who addressed the issue expected it to happen on a regular basis. George Mason of Virginia said it would happen "nineteen times in twenty."[7]

But a number of delegates suggested another possibility: what might be called *nomination by natural consensus.* As the country became more integrated, the argument went, as its citizens became less parochial, thinking about presidential possibilities would gradually come to center on a small number of individuals of outstanding merit and national reputation. As Abraham Baldwin of Georgia put it, "The increasing intercourse among the people of the States, would render important characters less & less unknown," with the result that contingent elections would become "less & less likely." James Wilson of Pennsylvania concurred: "Continental characters will multiply as we more & more coalesce, so as to enable the electors in every part of the Union to know & judge of them."[8] The model for this sort of consensus was, of course, George Washington, who, as the delegates all knew, was all but certain to become the first president.[9]

Two other features of the original presidential selection process helped increase the chances that the electoral college would reach a consensus. First, the presidential electors were likely to be a relatively elite group and therefore presumably better informed than ordinary voters about the qualifications of the various candidates, especially those candidates who lived in a different state. Second, the fact that each elector had two presidential votes, as we will see shortly, held out the prospect that an elector could cast one vote for a home-state favorite and then give the second to a person of more national stature and appeal.[10]

Whatever disagreement existed about the proper or expected way of conducting presidential nominations, there was no dispute about what the

Framers hoped to avoid: *political parties.*[11] Throughout the Convention's extended deliberations about how to select the new chief executive, the delegates were obsessed with the need to insulate the selection process from a cluster of problems they generally described as cabal, faction, and intrigue.[12] Though these terms were never explicitly defined nor used with any obvious precision, it is unlikely that there were any significant "party-like" activities of which the delegates would have approved. To take one particularly revealing example: Both Elbridge Gerry and George Mason opposed electing the president by popular vote because, as Gerry observed, "The ignorance of the people would put it in the power of some one set of men dispersed through the Union & acting in Concert to delude them into any appointment." The group both men cited as an illustration was the Society of the Cincinnati, a nationwide organization of Revolutionary War officers and their descendents. Though Gerry and Mason both professed great "respect" for the Society, they nonetheless stressed the "danger & impropriety of throwing such a power into their hands."[13] If the Cincinnati were beyond the pale, it is difficult to imagine any organized group whose electioneering activities would have been considered acceptable.

4. *How was the dual-vote system supposed to work?* Here, too, the historical record is distressingly thin. The idea of giving presidential electors more than one vote was first broached at the Constitutional Convention on July 25, where it was seen as one more way to alleviate the anxieties of the smaller states. Particularly if the president were elected by popular vote, the small-state defenders had complained, most people would just vote for someone from their own state, so that only large-state residents could get elected president. "As a cure for this difficulty," Hugh Williamson of North Carolina suggested "that each man should vote for 3 candidates. One of these he observed would be probably of his own State, the other 2. of some other States; and as probably of a small as a large one." Gouverneur Morris immediately proposed a slight amendment: "that each man shall vote for two persons one of whom at least should not be of his own State."[14] There was a brief allusion to this proposal the next day—and then no further mention of the subject until September 4, when the so-called Committee of Eleven, which had been created to deal with unresolved issues, incorporated Morris's proposal into its plan for electing the president.

At least one expectation of the dual-vote system, then, was that one of the two votes would be given to a local favorite and that an elector's second choice might actually be a person of greater stature and ability. Or as James Madison put it, "The second best man in this case would probably be the first, in fact."[15] Did the Framers foresee the many ways that the dual-vote system could be manipulated by crafty politicians or how it might malfunction to produce largely undesired outcomes? They did anticipate one such possibility: that the electors would cast one vote for their real favorite and then (to quote Madison again) "throw away [their] second [vote] on some obscure Citizen of another State, in order to ensure the object of [their] first choice." This, indeed, seems to have been the principal reason they created the vice presidency—to make the second vote count for something and thus encourage the electors to take it seriously.[16] Unfortunately, as the men of the founding generation would soon discover, there were lots of other ways that the system could malfunction that had not been anticipated or adequately guarded against.

FIRST STIRRINGS

The first presidential election was held under a highly compressed calendar.[17] Under the terms of Article VII, the Constitution was to go into effect when ratified by nine states. This critical threshold was passed on June 21, 1788, when the New Hampshire state convention voted in favor of ratification, though the Articles of Confederation Congress, then meeting in New York City, didn't receive word of this milestone until four days later. On July 2, the delegates appointed a committee to draft an election ordinance for "putting the said Constitution into operation."[18]

But the Confederation Congress was in no great hurry to write its own death notice. In mid-July, it suspended consideration of the entire subject for two weeks in order to see whether New York state would ratify the Constitution. The Congress then kicked away another month and a half arguing about one issue: where the new government should begin operations. (Philadelphia; Lancaster, Pennsylvania; Baltimore; New York; Wilmington, Delaware; and Annapolis, Maryland were all considered and rejected before the Congress finally decided to leave the national government, at least temporarily, in New York.) Not until September 13 did the Congress finally pass the election ordinance and send it on to the eleven states that had thus far ratified the Constitution.

That ordinance required the states to choose their electors on January 7, 1789. The electors would meet in their respective states and cast their votes on February 4. The votes would then be counted at a joint session of the new Congress, which was scheduled to convene in New York City on March 4. The new nation's large geographical expanse and primitive communications system notwithstanding, this timetable gave the states just four months to:

Box 7.1

CONNECTICUT: Selected by the state legislature

DELAWARE: Popularly elected by district

GEORGIA: Selected by the state legislature MARYLAND: Popularly elected by statewide vote, with the stipulation that five electors had to come from the Western Shore and three from the Eastern Shore

MASSACHUSETTS: Mixed method. Popular elections were held within each of the state's congressional districts; the state legislature then chose the elector from the top two finishers in each district. State legislature also chose two at-large electors.

NEW HAMPSHIRE: Mixed method. A statewide popular election was held, in which all eligible voters were allowed to vote for five persons. Any person receiving a vote from a majority of the voters automatically became an elector. If five persons were not elected in this way, the remainder were selected by the state legislature from among the top finishers in the popular vote.

NEW JERSEY: Selected by the governor and privy council

PENNSYLVANIA: Popularly elected by statewide vote

SOUTH CAROLINA: Selected by the state legislature

VIRGINIA: Popularly elected by district

Table 7.1. Methods of Choosing Presidential Electors in the First Presidential Election

Summary of Selection Methods	*No. of States*
Selected by state legislature	3
Popularly elected by statewide vote	2
Popularly elected by district	2
Mixed method	2
Selected by governor and privy council	1

Note: New York had also ratified the Constitution by this time, but the two houses of its state legislature were unable to agree upon a method for appointing presidential electors.
Source: Compiled from the actual election statutes, as reported in Merrill Jensen, Robert A. Becker, Gordon DenBoer, and Lucy Trumbull Brown, eds., *The Documentary History of the First Federal Elections*, 4 vols. (Madison, WI: University of Wisconsin Press, 1976–1984).

receive notification of the election ordinance, call the state legislature into session, pass the requisite state laws (none already had a statute covering elections of this type), and then do whatever was necessary (e.g., hold an election) to select their presidential electors.

The Constitution, as has already been noted, allowed the states to appoint their presidential electors "in such Manner as the Legislature thereof may direct." Table 7.1 lists the method that each state finally settled on for choosing its electors in 1789. Much as one might have expected, the states chose to exercise their discretion in a wide variety of ways. The only pattern is that there is no pattern. Three states had the state legislature appoint their electors, two states chose their electors by a statewide popular vote, two states used popular vote by district, one state assigned the task to the governor and his privy council, and two employed mixed methods, in which a popular vote in effect nominated the candidates for elector and the state legislature then made the final selection. As for James Madison's often-quoted statement that "the election of Presidential Electors by district . . . was mostly, if not exclusively, in view when the Constitution was framed and adopted," one can only conclude that the governors and state legislators of the immediate post-ratification period were never informed of this consensus.[19] Of the ten states that participated in the first presidential election, only two used district-based elections to choose their electors.[20]

THE PRESIDENTIAL CONTENDERS

Who were the major presidential candidates in the 1789 election? At a time when it was thought inappropriate for candidates openly to seek high office, there were no formal announcements or official campaign organizations, but that does not mean that there was no discussion of such matters. To the contrary, throughout the preelection period, there was a rich dialogue about the presidential and vice presidential possibilities carried on in private correspondence and the contemporary media. And thanks to recent historical research, we can, to a remarkable extent, quantify just which candidates were talked about.

Beginning in 1966, the First Federal Elections project at the University of Wisconsin attempted to collect all extant public and private documents pertaining to the elections that launched American national government under the Constitution. In Table 7.2, I have taken this project's complete set of documents with respect to the election of the president and vice president—primarily newspaper articles and private letters—and counted up the number of times that various men were *mentioned* as a candidate for the

Table 7.2. Candidates Mentioned for President in the First Federal Election, 1788–89

	Mentions		*Tone (in Percentages)*		
Candidate	*Number*	*Percent*	*Positive*	*Neutral*	*Negative*
George Washington	318	88	78	22	0.3
Patrick Henry	24	7	0	0	100
John Hancock	9	2	0	56	44
Other	11	3	0	91	9

Source: Based on a content analysis of all extant documents pertaining to the first presidential election, primarily newspaper articles and private letters, written or published between January 1, 1788 and February 4, 1789. For the full set of documents, see Gordon DenBoer et al., The Documentary History of the First Federal Elections, 4 vols. (Madison, WI: University of Wisconsin Press, 1976–1984), 4:22–161. For further details, see the appendix to this chapter.

presidency. I have also coded the "tone" of each mention: i.e., whether the article or letter's basic evaluative stance toward the candidate was positive, negative, or neutral. (For further details on how these data were analyzed, see the appendix to this chapter.)

As these data demonstrate, discussion of the upcoming presidential election was dominated by the commanding figure of George Washington. At least in the first election, there really was a widespread, unforced consensus about the best person to serve as the nation's chief executive. Whenever a newspaper article or private letter mentioned a specific person as a possible, likely, or desirable candidate for the presidency, 88 percent of the time that candidate was General Washington. These "mentions," moreover, were overwhelmingly positive. There were a fair number of letters and newspaper articles that simply observed that Washington was likely to be elected president, without pronouncing judgment on that fact. But whenever a writer expressed an opinion about Washington's suitability for the position, the opinion was almost invariably favorable. Indeed, of all the thousands of documents collected in the First Federal Elections project, there is, so far as I have been able to determine, exactly *one* that openly opposed Washington's election.[21]

Yet even these figures do not entirely capture how much Washington's availability for the presidency meant to his contemporaries. Washington was not just mentioned as the best person to fill this job; upon his election, many insisted, hung the very existence of the new government, maybe even the nation. Failing to elect Washington, said one newspaper correspondent, "would be so unfortunate an incident, as to cast a shade over our dawning prospects—and perhaps occasion a breach in the glorious chain of union, of which he is the most important link." "If he is not it [i.e., the president]," said another observer, "there is no new Constitution." A third person declared, "for the great chair [the presidency] are the Candidates G. W: or God-Almighty."[22]

This remarkable unity suffered just two minor disturbances. The first of these two "boomlets" concerned John Hancock, then the governor of Massachusetts.[23] Hancock had once been perhaps the single most prominent leader of the resistance to British rule in America, an eminence reflected in his selection as president of the Second Continental Congress in 1775. By 1788, his star had been eclipsed by many others', yet his name was still sufficiently well-known that proponents of the Constitution were reportedly able to enlist his support at the Massachusetts ratifying convention by holding out the prospect that, if Virginia failed to ratify the Constitution and Washington was therefore ineligible for the office, Hancock would be the most likely person to be elected president.

As it turned out, Virginia did narrowly ratify, yet Hancock apparently still held out some hope of becoming president, in one of two ways. One possibility was that Washington would decline the office. (Through the entire period being considered here, Washington lived at Mount Vernon in apparent retirement from public life, and refused to say whether he would serve as president if elected to the position.) Alternatively, Hancock might get elected by accident. An important feature of the original presidential selection mechanism, as we have seen, is that it required each elector to cast two undifferentiated votes for president, rather than one vote for president and one for vice president. If enough electors cast one of their votes for Hancock, because they hoped to make him vice president, and a significant number also decided not to vote for Washington, Hancock might wind up with a higher total vote than Washington and thus sneak in ahead of the former general.

However he hoped to grab the brass ring, in August and September of 1788 Hancock actually undertook a series of public appearances in neighboring states that may reasonably be regarded as the first presidential campaign. As one Massachusetts Federalist reported to another, "This man [Hancock] thinks himself equal to the first place—and it is said disdains the second. . . . He is now on a journey to New Hampshire probably with a view of rendering himself conspicuous there for the attainment of this end—it is said, he projects an excursion to R.Island & Connecticut with the same views."[24] According to a pamphlet published in early 1789, Hancock had also sent "a trusty hand . . . off to the southern States, to solicit votes in his favour."[25]

A few of Hancock's contemporaries worried about the possibility that he might get elected president by mistake. Otherwise, his candidacy seems to have been principally an object of ridicule and embarrassment. By contrast, the reputed presidential candidacy of Patrick Henry was taken more seriously—at least by its opponents. In the month before the electors were chosen, many newspapers and private letters contained alarmed reports that Henry, the former governor of Virginia and a leading opponent of the Constitution, had emerged as the Antifederalist candidate for president. As one Philadelphia newspaper informed its readers—attributing the report to "a correspondent"[26]—"the anti-federal party in the states of Pennsylvania, New-York, Virginia, &c. have *secretly* combined to oppose the election of general Washington to the president's chair, and to fill it with a man better calculated to serve *their purposes* . . . The person pitched upon is—PATRICK HENRY!"[27]

It is difficult to say just how substantial this effort was—or, indeed, whether it was ever anything more than a figment of the Federalist imagination. While there are numerous references to Henry's pursuit of the office in contemporary *Federalist* writings,[28] there is, so far as I have been able to determine, no evidence in Henry's surviving papers that he participated in or sanctioned this "candidacy," or that any of his associates or political allies were actively soliciting votes on his behalf.[29] Henry's biographers are similarly dismissive of the affair.[30] Several of the sources that first reported Henry's quest for the presidency later claimed it had been abandoned,[31] and in the end he received not a single electoral vote, even though he himself was one of the electors in Virginia. Perhaps the principal significance of the Henry candidacy, as we will see, was the response it provoked from his political opponents. The spectre that Henry might take votes from the hallowed Washington—and might even accidentally elevate some other person to the presidency—was one of several factors that spurred Federalists to make sure that every presidential elector was a proven supporter of the Constitution.

THE VICE PRESIDENTIAL CANDIDATES

Table 7.3 provides similar data about the persons mentioned as vice presidential candidates in the thirteen months preceding the first federal election. Perhaps the first point to make about these results is that they do, indeed, concern candidates for the *vice presidency*. According to a strict reading of Article II, Section 1, each presidential elector was supposed to cast two votes for *president*, with no distinction between them. But there is no evidence that the participants in or observers of the first election actually thought about the electors' votes this way. Instead, virtually everything that was written made clear that the writer saw or favored Washington as a candidate for president and everybody else as a candidate for vice president.[32] As we will see, this was just one of a number of ways in which Article II's vaunted dual-vote provision defied its authors' expectations from the very beginning.

The other obvious conclusion to draw from Table 7.3 is that the Americans of 1788-89 were not especially united in their assessment of the vice presidential prospects. The single most often-mentioned candidate was John Adams, who had just returned from a three-year stint as the U.S. minister to Great Britain; but Adams's position with respect to the vice presidential selection was nothing like George Washington's hold on the presidency. Particularly when the data are disaggregated by time period, it becomes clear that Adams had to share the vice presidential spotlight at various times with two other major contenders: John Hancock and George Clinton.

Table 7.3. Candidates Mentioned for Vice President in the First Federal Election, 1788–89

		Mentions	
Time Period	*Candidate*	*Number*	*Percent*
January–July 1788	John Hancock	57	77
	John Adams	14	19
	Other	3	4
August–September 1788	John Adams	14	36
	John Hancock	10	26
	Benjamin Franklin	5	13
	John Jay	3	8
	John Rutledge	2	5
	Other	5	13
October–November 1788	John Adams	61	36
	John Hancock	51	30
	Henry Knox	25	15
	George Clinton	3	2
	John Jay	3	2
	Other	24	14
December 1788–January 7, 1789	John Adams	78	44
	George Clinton	58	33
	John Hancock	18	10
	Henry Knox	7	4
	Other	17	10
January 8–February 4, 1789	John Adams	46	58
	George Clinton	25	31
	John Hancock	3	4
	John Jay	3	4
	John Rutledge	2	2
TOTALS	John Adams	213	40
	John Hancock	139	26
	George Clinton	86	16
	Henry Knox	35	6
	John Jay	10	2
	John Rutledge	6	1
	Benjamin Franklin	5	1
	Other	44	8

Source: Based on a content analysis of all extant documents pertaining to the first presidential election, primarily newspaper articles and private letters, written or published between January 1, 1788 and February 4, 1789. For the full set of documents, see Gordon DenBoer et al., *The Documentary History of the First Federal Elections*, 4 vols. (Madison, WI: University of Wisconsin Press, 1976–1984), 4:22–161. For further details, see the appendix to this chapter.

What the data in Table 7.3 do not reveal, but a more detailed reading of the documents does, is that the choice between Adams and Clinton took on, in many respects, the character of a partisan competition. While it would be an exaggeration to suggest that the first presidential election was contested by full-blown political parties, we can say that party-like activities were present in American national politics even in 1788–89.

Why and how did this sort of activity develop? To start with the most basic point: However much one might insist that the presidential electors were "judicious" men of "information and discernment" and would make their decisions "under circumstances favorable to deliberation," intensely political decisions such as the selection of a U.S. president simply cannot be made in an independent, nonpartisan, "expert" manner. The electors' decisions inevitably depended on the kinds of people chosen for that position, and the values, perceptions, opinions, and ideologies they brought to the task.

What is generally called the first American party system, almost all students of this period agree, did not come into being until the 1790s.[33] Yet, well before this, American politics was often divided along fault lines that, while they may not have possessed the durability and structure of political parties, nevertheless provided some measure of guidance and direction to both leaders and ordinary voters.[34] In the case of the first presidential election, the most important line of division was the one that remained from the ratification battle: the opposition between Federalists and Antifederalists. As numerous documents from this period reveal, this was the principal way that contemporary elites "kept score" for the 1788-89 election: by toting up the number of Federalists and Antifederalists elected, both as presidential electors and as members of the first Congress.

Though the Federalists had succeeded in getting eleven states to ratify the Constitution, the fight was far from over. The focus had simply shifted to the question of amendments. In five states, including Massachusetts, Virginia, and New York, the ratification resolution had contained a list of suggested amendments. In two other states, a dissenting minority at the state convention had also compiled a set of proposed amendments. Though many Federalists (in particular, James Madison) had by this time acknowledged the need for amendments, there remained a sizable gulf between what the Federalists and the Antifederalists had in mind. The amendments that had been submitted by the various state conventions were of two general types: the first were items for a proposed Bill of Rights; the second type would have substantially reduced the powers of the new national government.[35] The Federalist strategy, it would soon become clear, was to concede the first type of amendment—but not the second.[36]

It thus mattered a great deal whether the new government was stocked with Federalists or Antifederalists. This statement applied with particular force to Congress, which, of course, had the power to propose amendments by a two-thirds vote of both houses. Yet even though the executive branch had no formal role in the amendment process, both camps apparently concluded that their cause would be aided by filling that branch with sympathetic people. As the Philadelphia *Federal Gazette* expressed this position, "It is necessary that every friend of his country should vote for senators and representatives who are firmly federal, and for such only. It is no less necessary that men of similar principles should be chosen as electors of a president and vice-president of the United States." A contributor to the *Maryland Gazette* was equally emphatic: "As the electors are to do only a single piece of business, in which integrity and foederalism are only requisite, abilities being out of the question, therefore, in my opinion, no man ought to be trusted in that station, who has not been an uniform friend to the new government. . . . Notwithstanding the lalruels [laurels] and respectability of [Jeremiah Chase and Charles Ridgely, two prominent Maryland Antifederalists], no man, whatever possessed of a single spark of foederalism, will be for delegating either of them to chuse the president and vice-president."[37]

While the Antifederalists were reluctant to challenge Washington for the presidency, they showed no hesitation about seeking to elect an Antifederal vice president. The vice presidency was, of course, a much less important office than the presidency. But the full extent of its impotence seems not to have been widely appreciated until after the government was up and running. (The Antifederalists had often described the vice presidency during the ratification debates as a "great" or "important" office.)[38] And even if the office itself was weak, there was always the possibility that Washington would die in office—or maybe resign after the new government was launched and no longer seemed to need him.[39]

As early American political leaders started to focus their attention on the vice presidency, another distinctive feature of that office came into play. In order to be elected president, a candidate had to receive a vote from a majority of the electors. Thus, if a party split its electoral votes among a sizable number of candidates, this might (temporarily) prevent any one of them from being elected president—but it probably would not help elect someone from a different party. The more likely outcome was that no candidate would achieve the necessary majority and a contingent election would then be held in the House of Representatives. But no such threshold existed for the vice presidency. That office fell to whoever finished second in the electors' voting, no matter how many votes he received. If all or almost all of the electors cast one vote for Washington, and the rest were scattered among a large crop of local favorites, a person might be elected vice president with as few as 25 or 30 votes. In short, the outcome of the vice presidential selection might depend on which party or party-like group was most successful in uniting its votes behind one candidate.

Federalist writings from the preelection period indicate that they considered a fair number of people as prospects for the vice presidency. In October and November 1788, there was a brief flurry of interest in Henry Knox, former chief artillery officer of the Continental Army and Secretary of War under the Articles of Confederation (see Table 7.3). John Jay also received some attention.[40] But the two major contenders for Federalist support were John Adams and John Hancock. The Federalists did not, of course, have anything like a nominating mechanism or a formal party structure available to them to help assess the comparative merits of these individuals and reach agreement on a single candidate. But they clearly did engage in an extensive if informal process of communication and deliberation, both in the major Federalist newspapers of the period and in the private correspondence of group leaders. As this process proceeded, the Federalists increasingly reached a negative verdict on Hancock and a more positive decision with respect to Adams.

As Table 7.3 shows, in the six months preceding New York's ratification of the Constitution, the most frequently-mentioned vice presidential prospect was actually Hancock. From the moment that the vice presidency was seriously thought about, there seems to have been a widespread assumption that, in a country whose national unity was still quite fragile, the president and vice president should come from different regions of the country. Since Washington was from the South, that meant that the vice president should be a resident of the North. (Of all the vice presidential prospects listed in Table 7.3, the only southerner is John Rutledge of South Carolina and he could hardly be described as a leading contender for the job.) Given his background, Hancock was an obvious possibility.

Hancock continued to receive almost as many mentions as Adams from August through November 1788—and then, rather suddenly, he fell out of contention. A number of factors seem to have worked against Hancock's vice presidential fortunes. To begin with, there were recurrent reports that Hancock had no interest in playing second fiddle to Washington (or anyone else) and would refuse the position if elected to it. (One of Hancock's chief supporters insisted that the allegation was merely a rumor spread by the governor's political enemies, but it achieved wide circulation nonetheless.)[41] Hancock also suffered from chronic health problems that, according to many observers, precluded him from serving effectively in the new government. As one Massachusetts politician reported to George Washington in early January 1789, Hancock "could not act if he was elected[.] his want of health is such as to prevent his attending to the duties of so important a station[.] he has not been abroad [i.e., out of his house] but a very few times for the two months past and is now confined to his Chamber . . ."[42] Indeed, Hancock had been elected president of the Confederation Congress in November 1785 but was unable to serve because of health problems, eventually resigning the post in May 1786. Finally, many staunch Federalists doubted Hancock's commitment to the new Constitution. He had, after all, been a last-minute convert at the Massachusetts ratifying convention and seemed more willing than Adams to endorse immediate amendments. One Massachusetts Federalist wrote to Alexander Hamilton, "Mr. Hancock has been very explicit in patronising the doctrine [of] amendments. The other gentleman [Adams] is for postponing the conduct of that business untill it shall be understood from experience."[43]

At least among the Federalists, that left John Adams as the leading candidate. In addition to the fact that he wasn't a southerner, Adams had been an early advocate for independence, had extensive diplomatic experience, and was widely regarded as a man of great intelligence and integrity. An interesting example of how the Federalists were convinced to support Adams involves Alexander Hamilton. On October 9, 1788, Hamilton, then living in New York City, wrote a letter to Massachusetts Federalist Theodore Sedgwick. After first noting that John Adams "will have the votes of this state," though some might also go to John Hancock, Hamilton added, "The only hesitation in my mind with regard to Mr. Adams has arisen within a day or two; from a suggestion by a particular Gentleman that he is unfriendly in his sentiments to General Washington." Hamilton ended his letter by asking Sedgwick what he thought about Benjamin Lincoln and Henry Knox, both former generals (and Massachusetts residents), as vice presidential possibilities.[44]

Sedgwick wrote back seven days later, lauding Adams as "a man of unconquerable intrepidity & of incorruptible integrity" and adding that it was "too late" to start a push for Lincoln or Knox. On November 2, Sedgwick sent another letter to Hamilton, in which he declared, "I am very certain that the suggestion that he [Adams] is unfriendly to general Washington is entirely unfounded." It was also in this letter than he made the statement quoted two paragraphs earlier, saying that while Hancock favored immediate amendments, Adams was for postponing them. By November 9, Hamilton reported to Sedgwick that he had "upon the whole concluded that [Adams] ought to be supported—My measures will be taken accordingly." On November 23, Hamilton communicated the same sentiment to James Madison (who would soon head back home to Virginia), adding that Adams already appeared likely to receive votes from the electors in Massachusetts, New Hampshire, and Connecticut.[45]

Meanwhile, Lincoln and Knox, both of whom knew Washington from their military service, carried this process of consultation an important step further, by informing Washington himself that, "Mr John Adams will probably have the plurality of votes for vice President," and thus implicitly seeking Washington's reaction to this eventuality. Washington responded in guarded tones, but stated that, "having taken it for granted, that the person selected for that important place would be a true Foederalist . . . whosoever shall be found to enjoy the confidence of the States so far as to be elected Vice President, cannot be disagreeable to me, in that office." In early January 1789, Washington went further, offering what might reasonably be taken as a mild endorsement of Adams's candidacy: "From different channels of information, it seems probable to me . . . that Mr. John Adams would, be chosen Vice President.—He will doubtless make a very good one."[46]

Though much of the Federalist correspondence was concerned with finding a suitably qualified candidate for the vice presidency, in other cases the writers were simply concerned with promoting agreement among themselves—what modern-day political scientists might call a "coordination problem." Put another way, many Federalists wanted information about which vice presidential candidate other states were likely to support so they, too, could vote for him and thus ensure that an Antifederalist didn't win the office. In mid-December 1788, for example, Virginia Federalist and presidential elector candidate Edward Carrington wrote to James Madison, "A push is to be made for making [New York Antifederalist George] Clinton the vice president. . . . If you can give me any information as to the Characters most likely to unite the votes to the Eastward [i.e., the northeastern states], it will perhaps be for the public good that you should communicate it." In January 1789, Robert Smith of Maryland posed a similar question to Tench Coxe, a well-connected Pennsylvania Federalist: "I have the Honour to be in this State one of the Electors of the President and vice President. I therefore, much [desire to] know for whom the States, whose Politicks you are acquainted with, intend to vote. Your information may have an influence upon the Electors of Maryland."[47] The *Federal Gazette* of Philadelphia took a somewhat different tack. Believing that Adams was the leading Federalist candidate, it simply urged all Federalists to unite behind him.

> We hear from Virginia, that the anti-federalists intend to vote for General Washington, as president, but that Governor Clinton will have all their votes for vice-president of the United States. This will make it more necessary for the other states to unite in the honorable John Adams. It will require *forty-one* votes to place him in the vice-president's chair. It is to be hoped, that not a single vote will be lost, by any other federal character being put in nomination.[48]

Meanwhile, the Antifederalists were also thinking about the vice presidency. In their case, the process of intraparty coordination was even more explicit. In the fall of 1788, opponents of the Constitution in New York state consulted with their counterparts in Virginia, and agreed to support New York governor George Clinton for vice president. On or around November 13, a group calling itself the New York City Federal Republican Committee sent out the following letter to Antifederalists in other states:

> The federal Republicans in this state are of opinion, that it is of great importance in the election of vice president, that the choice fall on a person who will be zealously engaged in promoting such amendments to the new Constitution as will render the Liberties of the Country secure under it—
>
> For this purpose they have consulted some Gentlemen in Virginia, who are united in sentiment with us, and are informed that they have it in view in that State, to vote for Governor Clinton of this State for that office—We have reason to beleive that the Electors of this State will generally give their votes in his favor—
>
> It is highly probable, if your State would unite with Virginia and ours, that Governer Clinton will be elected—We need not make any observations to shew, the influence that the Vice President will have in the administration of the new Government . . . If you should concur with us in opinion, you will take such measures to communicate the matter to the Electers of your State as your prudence may direct.[49]

Like Patrick Henry, with whom he was often linked, Clinton had been a leading opponent of the new Constitution. Indeed, both Clinton and Henry were so strongly critical of the new charter of government that they were not content to remedy its defects through piecemeal amendments. Instead, each man pushed his state's legislature to pass a resolution asking Congress to call a second constitutional convention to redo the work of the first.

THE VIEW FROM THE STATES

In these ways, both Federalists and Antifederalists gradually achieved some measure of agreement on the vice presidential question. But deciding upon a preferred candidate was only the first step. The next challenge was to get as many group members as possible selected as presidential electors.

In states where the electors were chosen by the state legislature, or in New Jersey where the governor and his council did the job, it is likely that any efforts to get Federalists or Antifederalists to agree on a common set of presidential elector candidates took place in small, private gatherings, without a lot of advance preparation. Unfortunately, we can only speculate on this point, since the surviving historical record in all such states is quite thin. In Connecticut, New Jersey, South Carolina, and Georgia, we know little more than the time and place of the official selection meeting and the names of the persons finally chosen as electors. Whether these were the only candidates proposed, who voted for and against them, whether the meeting was harmonious or contentious—all such information was never recorded in the official journals, or in private diaries and letters or contemporary news accounts.

Fortunately for our purposes, the path is better marked in states that chose their electors through some form of popular vote. In the following pages, I examine how the election of presidential electors was conducted in all four of the states that chose their electors entirely by popular vote: Maryland, Pennsylvania, Delaware, and Virginia. As we will see, the extent of partisan division and activity varied significantly from state to state.

Maryland. By all available measures, Maryland was a strongly Federalist state. Its state convention had ratified the Constitution by a vote of 63-11, and there were solid Federalist majorities in both the state Senate and House of Delegates. But the Antifederalists refused to quit the field, and that in turn meant that the Federalists also had to stay mobilized.

The Maryland state legislature had decided to choose the state's eight presidential electors by statewide popular vote; but in a nod to local jealousies, the law also required that five of the eight electors be residents of the Western Shore and that the other three be residents of the Eastern Shore.[50] Three features of this law are particularly worth noting. First, the law required the voters to vote for eight separate persons. There was nothing in the law that allowed a government agency or outside group to form unified *slates* of candidates, so that voters could support eight electors by casting just one vote. Second, Maryland, like all other American states at this time, did not have an official ballot printed by the government that listed all of the candidates who had submitted the requisite number of petitions or gone through some kind of formal nomination process.[51] The voters themselves had to know the names of the candidates they wished to vote for—or someone else had to provide them with a list. Third, in order to be elected, a person only needed to be one of the top five finishers among the candidates who lived on the Western Shore or the top three finishers from the Eastern Shore. There was, in other words, no requirement that candidates receive a majority or some other minimum percentage of the vote.

Though the effect probably wasn't deliberate, these arrangements all but compelled any group that cared about the outcome of the Maryland election to engage in extensive statewide organization and coordination. A group such as the Federalists, who believed that a majority of the voters were sympathetic to their viewpoint, could not simply sit back and let the weight of numbers work its magic. In order to vote effectively, a voter who favored the Federalist cause (or any other cause) needed a great deal of detailed political knowledge: the names of the individual elector candidates, any information that might be thought relevant to how the electors would perform their duties (e.g., whether they were Federalist or Antifederalist), and whether they lived on the Eastern or Western shore (a voter who voted for four candidates living on the Eastern Shore effectively threw away one of his votes). Based on everything we have learned from modern-day sample surveys about levels of political information within the mass public, it is most unlikely that the typical voter of the late eighteenth century would have possessed this knowledge on his own.[52] Some other entity needed to help supply it for him. The law also put a premium on intragroup unity. A group that could unify its votes behind a single set of eight candidates would have a decisive advantage over a less organized rival that scattered its votes across a larger number of candidates.

To meet these challenges, both the Federalists and Antifederalists started their electioneering efforts by nominating a statewide slate of elector candidates. (Though I will not discuss them here, each side also nominated a full set of candidates for the U.S. House of Representatives.) In both cases, that task was performed by the group's members in the state legislature—what would later be called a legislative caucus. One day after Christmas 1788, an article in the *Maryland Journal* described the Federalist effort:

> The following Arrangement comes from a Number of respectable Federal Characters in our Legislature, who were anxious to secure, at this important Crisis, a GENUINE FEDERAL REPRESENTATION.—Finding it impracticable to communicate with each District on the Subject, they have, from the best Information, put in nomination those Gentlemen who were believed to be most acceptable in their respective Districts.—This Ticket is therefore, with all possible Deference, recommended—and it is confidently expected it will meet the warm Support of the FEDERAL INTEREST throughout the state.[53]

The full set of Federalist candidates for presidential elector and the House of Representatives was then listed. The Federalists were apparently somewhat more successful than the Antifederalists in reaching agreement. In four different newspaper articles and a separate broadside in which the Federalist slate is reported, the roster of names is always the same; but there are minor discrepancies in the various lists of Antifederalist candidates reported in contemporary sources. In an apparent effort to blur the differences between the two groups, most of the Antifederalist slates included two men who had also been nominated by the Federalists.[54]

Once the nominations were made, the next step was to communicate the names to local political leaders and from them to the voters. In part, as I have already indicated, this was done by getting the rival slates published in local newspapers. In addition, the Federalists appointed a committee of sympathetic Baltimore merchants to "communicate the Ticket, and their intentions respecting it, to as many gentlemen in the different Counties" as time would allow, "directing us at the same time to request their aid and influence in its support."[55] Other documents from this period show that both Federalists and Antifederalists engaged in the sorts of activities familiar to any student of later partisan campaigns. Mass meetings were held to express support for the tickets. According to one letter, "two thowsand Coppies" of the ticket were printed and distributed by one local Federalist organization. Another such organization appointed "a numerous committee of active influencial and respectable persons . . . for the purpose of riding through the country and bringing in votes."[56]

The acid test for this sort of activity, of course, is whether it had any noticeable effect on the voting. Table 7.4 reports the vote totals for all presidential elector candidates—and it is no exaggeration to say that the vote was almost wholly determined by the Federalist and Antifederalist nomination decisions. The two candidates who were fortunate enough to be listed on both the Federalist and Antifederalist tickets each received about 7600 votes. The six candidates who were listed only on the Federalist ticket all received between 5300 and 5700 votes. Four candidates who were apparently listed on all of the various Antifederalist tickets received between 2100 and 2200 votes, while those candidates whose names were included on some but not all of the Antifederalist tickets received lesser numbers of votes (depending, presumably, on how many tickets their names were listed on and how widely these tickets were distributed). Though I have not tried to fit these data to a formal statistical model, they clearly could not have come about by the random, uncoordinated decisions of thousands of individual voters. Even in 1788-89, somebody in Maryland was doing exactly the sorts of things that, just a few decades later, would be considered quintessential party functions.

Pennsylvania. The election law passed by the Pennsylvania Assembly was similar in most respects to the one adopted in Maryland. The state's ten members in the electoral college were to be elected by statewide popular vote, with each voter allowed to "deliver in writing on one ticket or piece of paper the names of ten persons to be voted for as Electors."[57] The eight Pennsylvania members of the House of Representatives were also elected statewide (i.e., the state was not divided into districts). There was, however, one key difference between the two states that may have had a significant impact on the conduct of the first presidential election in Pennsylvania. In Maryland, the congressional and presidential elections were held on the same

Table 7.4. Results of the Maryland Presidential Elector Voting, by Placement on the Federalist and AntiFederalist Tickets

	Votes Received
Candidates Listed on Both the Federalist and Antifederalist Tickets	
John Rogers	7665
George Plater	7573
Candidates Listed on the Federalist Ticket Only	
William Tilghman	5746
Alexander C. Hanson	5596
Philip Thomas	5456
Robert Smith	5455
William Richardson	5402
William Matthews	5291
Candidates Listed on All of the Antifederalist Tickets	
Jeremiah T. Chase	2278
John Seney	2209
Charles Ridgely	2199
James Shaw	2130
Candidates Listed on Only Some of the Antifederalist Tickets	
Henry Waggaman	1669
Lawrence O'Neale	1241
Thomas Johnson	718
Moses Rawlings	157

Source: Based on tickets and votes reported in Gordon DenBoer and Lucy Trumbull Brown, eds., *Documentary History of the First Federal Elections 1788–1790,* vol. 2 (Madison, WI: University of Wisconsin Press, 1984), 158–229.

day. In Pennsylvania, by contrast, the state's House members were elected on November 26, 1788, while its presidential electors were chosen on January 7, 1789. As we will see, this meant that most of the state's political energy and attention were focused on the House elections; the presidential balloting turned out to be distinctly anticlimactic.

The House of Representatives elections in Pennsylvania were, by all indications, hotly contested. Just as in Maryland, the structure of the election system compelled both sides to begin their electioneering efforts by nominating a statewide slate of House candidates. In Pennsylvania, however, perhaps because of their greater familiarity with partisan procedures,[58] the candidates were nominated by *state conventions*.

On July 3, 1788, an Antifederalist meeting in Cumberland County sent out a circular letter "to such societies in each county as have already been formed for political purposes, and to such as shall be formed in any county where none is yet formed," to appoint delegates to a "general conference of the state."[59] The principal purpose of the conference was to "devise such amendments [to the U.S. Constitution], and such mode of obtaining them, as in the wisdom of the delegates shall be judged most satisfactory and expedient." But, the circular letter then noted:

> A law will no doubt be soon enacted by the General Assembly for electing eight members to represent this state in the new Congress. It will therefore be expedient to have proper persons put in nomination by the delegates in conference, being the most likely method of directing the views of the electors [i.e., the voters] to the same object and of obtaining the desired end.[60]

The Antifederalist Convention met in Harrisburg in early September, agreed on a set of twelve amendments to the Constitution, and urged the Pennsylvania state legislature to petition the first Congress to call a second constitutional convention. They apparently also nominated a full ticket of candidates for the first House of Representatives, though the names of the candidates were not made public until early November.[61]

The Federalist state convention, which was held in Lancaster, did not take place until November 3. Not wanting any amendments to the Constitution, the convention organizers declared their purpose to be that of "deliberating on the mode of procuring gentlemen to represent this state in the House of Representatives in the new government and to fix on proper persons to elect the President and Vice President."[62] Full slates for both offices were duly chosen, then announced to the public five days later.

An additional complication soon arose, however. Pennsylvania's German citizens apparently felt that neither the Harrisburg nor the Lancaster tickets had given sufficient representation to the members of their ethnic group, who reportedly constituted about one third of the state's inhabitants. Hence, on November 13, a broadside announced the formation of a German Antifederalist ticket and a German Federalist ticket. The German Antifederalist ticket included seven men from the original Antifederalist ticket (i.e., the one reputedly named in Harrisburg), plus one additional German candidate who had originally been included on the Lancaster ticket (i.e., he was actually a Federalist). In similar fashion, the German Federalist ticket included six men who had been nominated at the Federalist convention and two German candidates from the Antifederalist ticket.[63]

There followed a short but spirited campaign. As in Maryland, it was these quasi-partisan tickets that almost wholly determined the outcome of the voting. The six Federalists whose names appeared on both the regular Federalist ticket and the German Federalist ticket were all elected, receiving an average of about 8250 votes each. The two Antifederalists whose names had been added to the German Federalist ticket were also elected, with an average vote of 7460. The two remaining Federalists, who were not included on the German Federalist ticket, each received about 7090 votes, while the six remaining Antifederalists won, on average, about 6380 votes. In short, the Federalists won a narrow but convincing victory, winning six House seats to the Antifederalists' two—and probably would have won all eight had they included a few more Germans on their original ticket. If one compares the vote for the five candidates who were listed on the Lancaster and German Federalist tickets with the five men who were listed on both the Harrisburg and German Antifederalist tickets (which probably provides the fairest basis for comparison), the Federalists beat the Antifederalists by an average vote of 8160 to 6481, or 56 percent to 44 percent.[64]

The Pennsylvania Federalists celebrated their victory and then quickly turned their attention to the election that would choose the state's presidential electors. Among the forces that energized them was the claim that the Antifederalists had formed a plan to elect Patrick Henry and George Clinton as president and vice president, in place of Washington and Adams. The Antifederalists, by contrast, apparently decided not to contest the presidential election. Perhaps they never really did have a plan to challenge Washington and/or Adams. Alternatively, they may have decided that if they couldn't put across their ticket for the House of Representatives, running against George Washington was entirely hopeless. An Antifederalist slate of elector candidates was published in one state newspaper, but there is no evidence of any concerted effort to support it. "There was an election held yesterday for Electors," two Pennsylvania Antifederalists reported in a letter written on January 8, "but our party left it to the others and did not vote." The result was an overwhelming victory for the Federalists, whose ten elector nominees each received about 6300 votes, as compared to an average of just 440 votes for the Antifederalist candidates.[65]

Delaware. Of the four states being examined here, Delaware's conduct in the first presidential election is the easiest to summarize. Throughout the ratification "battle" over the Constitution, the Antifederalists were nowhere in evidence in Delaware. The Delaware state convention approved the Constitution by a 30-0 vote, thus becoming the first state to ratify it. Even the resolution in the state legislature that authorized the ratifying convention was passed with nary a dissenting vote.

The Antifederalists continued their disappearing act during the first federal elections. Three supporters of the Constitution were chosen to be presidential electors; and so far as one can tell from the surviving records, they faced no opposition. There is also no evidence of anything that smacks of partisanship or nomination activity, such exertions only being necessary when an opposition is present.[66]

Virginia. It is difficult to say with any assurance just what sorts of organizing and electioneering activity took place in Virginia during the first federal election.

We know that a bitter, hard-fought struggle over ratification of the Constitution took place in that state, with the Federalists finally, narrowly prevailing by a vote of 89 to 79. The antipathy between Federalists and Antifederalists continued at the next meeting of the Virginia General Assembly, which convened in October 1788. With the Antifederalists having a small but dependable majority, the Assembly managed in just two months to: pass a resolution calling for a second constitutional convention; elect two Antifederalists to the U.S. Senate, rejecting the candidacy of James Madison in the process; divide the state into congressional districts in a way that was reportedly designed to make sure that Madison couldn't get elected to the House of Representatives; and pass a "disabling act" that prohibited all officials in the new federal government from simultaneously holding state offices.

Against that background, it is hard to imagine that the 1789 elections in Virginia were a calm and harmonious affair. Yet, for a variety of reasons, the historical record is surprisingly scant. In part, this reflects the fact that Virginia did not have the kind of vigorous local press that existed in states like Maryland and Pennsylvania to report and comment upon the election. Equally important was the state legislature's decision to conduct both the presidential and congressional elections on a *districted* basis. With each voter needing to cast just one vote for Congress and one vote for a presidential elector, the Federalists and Antifederalists had less need for a single group to organize and coordinate their activities on a statewide basis.

Use of the district system also meant that there was no provision in the law for collecting and tabulating the vote at some central location. As a result, we know shockingly little about how the votes were cast in Virginia. In the elections that chose the state's twelve presidential electors, we know the name of the winning candidate in each district; but we have literally no numerical results in three districts, only fragmentary results in four districts, reasonably complete results in three districts, and complete returns in just two of the districts.

Did the Federalists and Antifederalists nominate a single candidate for the electoral college in each district and thus ensure that their votes would not be divided and diluted? James Duncanson, a Federalist but not a major leader of that group, wrote a letter to another Federalist in which he claimed that the opposition had, in fact, prepared such a ticket:

> The Gentlemen of the Assembly, I mean the Anti party of them, also made out a list of the 10 Members for Congress, & 12 Electors, who they wished to be chosen in this State, every Man of whom were violent Antifederalists, this List they carryed home with them from Richmond to their respective Counties, to support the Interest of those men they had agreed upon, with all their powers, so that from the time of the Assembly rising, untill the Elections came on, go

> into what Company you would, you heard nothing but debate & altercation, about the approaching Election, some for federal, & others for Antifederal Members . . . [67]

This is, however, the only mention of an Antifederalist slate in all of the surviving documents. (There is no mention at all of a comparable Federalist slate.) Was Duncanson merely reporting a rumor? If there was, in fact, such a slate, it is striking how little attention it received from prospective candidates, group leaders, and other political observers.

The weight of the available evidence suggests that while neither the Federalists nor the Antifederalists nominated an official (or semi-official) statewide ticket, their leaders and supporters in a number of districts did work in a more decentralized way to unite their votes behind a single candidate and persuade other Federalist or Antifederalist aspirants to drop out of the race. In early January 1789, for example, Arthur Lee, whom one contemporary observer described as "violently" Antifederal, distributed a broadside announcing his candidacy for Congress in a district in eastern Virginia. Yet in mid-January, a correspondent informed James Madison that Lee "has declined pursuing his election," apparently because he was anxious not to divide the Antifederalist vote. Meanwhile, a Federalist named Henry Lee bowed out of the same race for similar reasons.[68]

How extensive these sorts of quasi-nomination activities were is difficult to say. In early December 1788, Henry Lee had predicted to James Madison that, "It is probable that each party will fix on one man [in each district], & that the election will decide the will of the people."[69] Yet both Madison and George Washington would later express the fear that, as Madison put it, "the federal candidates are too likely to stand in the way of one another."[70] The key question, of course, is how united or divided the actual votes were; but as I have already noted, the popular vote in Virginia has been very incompletely preserved. Of the five presidential elector districts for which we have at least reasonably complete returns, three appear to have been two-person races that pitted a Federalist against an Antifederalist. In the two other cases, the votes were divided among a larger number of candidates.[71] But there is some reason to think that these last two cases were both "one-party" districts: i.e., one was overwhelmingly Antifederalist, the other safely Federalist. Perhaps in this sort of circumstance, intragroup unity was seen as a less pressing concern. It should be noted finally that, whether or not there were officially-designated Federalist or Antifederalist candidates in each of the Virginia elector districts, contemporary observers apparently had no difficulty assigning the winning candidates to one camp or the other and thus concluding that the state's delegation to the electoral college consisted of eight Federalists and three Antifederalists.[72]

PUTTING JOHN ADAMS IN HIS PLACE

As the preceding narrative should suggest, the Antifederalists fared poorly in the 1789 presidential election. Federalists won eight of eleven elector slots in Virginia and swept the board in Maryland, Pennsylvania, and Delaware. Equally damaging to the Antifederalists' prospects was what happened—more precisely, what didn't happen—in New York. The two houses of the New York state legislature were unable to agree on a suitable method for choosing the state's presidential electors, so New York did not take part in the first presidential election. If there was any state that would have looked favorably on George Clinton's vice presidential candidacy, presumably it was his home state. As it was, he would get not a single electoral vote from that source. Though it is more difficult to "keep score" in states where the state legislature chose the electors, there is no contemporary evidence that any of these states chose Antifederalist electors.

But no sooner had the presidential electors been chosen than the Federalists' attention turned to a second potential problem. Under the dual-vote system detailed in Article II of the Constitution, as we have already noted, it was possible for a person whom everybody hoped to see elected as vice president to wind up as president instead. Such concerns were first raised with respect to John Hancock; now the object of the Federalists' fears was John Adams.

From the vantage point of the Twenty-First Century, it is tempting to claim that these fears were greatly exaggerated and that, especially given the Antifederalists' inability to get their supporters elected or appointed to the electoral college, there was very little chance that any substantial number of electors would decide not to vote for George Washington. But history always seems clearer in retrospect. In 1789, the electoral vote procedure was new and still untried. Moreover, because of the country's poor transportation and communication systems, many of the election results reported earlier in this chapter were not yet available when the Federalist leaders were laying their plans. (In Pennsylvania, for example, the results of the January 7 popular vote were not officially tabulated and proclaimed until February 3—one day before the electors were supposed to meet and cast their ballots.) Given the widespread perception that Washington was not just the best candidate for the presidency but absolutely essential for the success of the new government, it is hard not to feel that the Federalists' concerns were reasonable.

There is a well-known letter that Alexander Hamilton wrote to James Wilson on January 25, 1789, in which he first laid out his worries about John Adams and suggested corrective action.[73]

> Every body is aware of that defect in the constitution [said Hamilton] which renders it possible that the man intended for Vice President may in fact turn up

> President. Every body sees that unanimity in Adams as Vice President and a few votes insidiously withheld from Washington might substitute the former to the latter. And every body must perceive that there is something to fear from the machinations of Antifoederal malignity.

Hamilton then went through a detailed examination of the electoral votes likely to be cast in the ten participating states.

> Here then is a *chance* of unanimity in Adams. . . . Suppose personal caprice or hostility to the new system should occasion half a dozen votes only to be withheld from Washington—what may not happen? Grant there is little danger. If any, ought it to be run? . . .
>
> Hence I conclude it will be prudent to throw away a few votes say 7 or 8; giving these to persons not otherwise thought of. Under this impression I have proposed to friends in Connecticut to throw away two[,] to others in Jersey to throw away an equal number & I submit to you whether it will not be well to lose three or four in Pensylvania. . . . it is much to be desired that Adams may have the plurality of suffrages for Vice President; but if risk is to be run on one side or the other can we hesitate where it ought to be preferred?[74]

Given Hamilton's later prominence in establishing the new government and creating the Federalist Party, this letter is almost invariably quoted in historical accounts of the first presidential election, usually accompanied by the suggestion that Hamilton single-handedly organized a devious conspiracy to diminish John Adams.[75]

This "standard account" is, I believe, inaccurate in two major respects. First, there was nothing particularly devious or inappropriate about Hamilton's behavior, at least in 1788-89. (His behavior toward Adams in subsequent years is another matter entirely.) In early November 1788, as we have already seen, Hamilton had concluded that Adams "ought to be supported." There is no evidence in his subsequent correspondence that he changed his mind or ever worked to advance the fortunes of another vice presidential candidate. But as Hamilton forthrightly argued in his letter to James Wilson, getting Washington elected president was far more important than what happened to the vice presidency.

Second, the "conspiracy" to hold down Adams's electoral vote (if that is the proper word for it) was a good deal more than a one-man operation. When the full historical record is examined, it soon becomes clear that a quite large number of Federalists were communicating with their friends and acquaintances in other states during the pre-election period, deliberately seeking out the kinds of information that would allow them to cast their vice presidential vote (i.e., their second presidential vote) in the most effective manner. Initially, as we have already seen, much of this correspondence was designed to promote agreement on a single vice presidential candidate, in order to make sure that an Antifederalist did not win that office. As the date of the electoral college balloting approached, however, a different issue began to seem more pressing. What if the Federalists had done their job too well, achieving such unity around John Adams that his vote surpassed that of George Washington and he was accidentally elected president?

Alexander Hamilton was far from being the only one to have this thought. By the time Hamilton sent his letter to James Wilson, at least eight other people had raised the same concern, in letters and, in one case, in a newspaper article.[76] Indeed, if there is any one person who seems to be at the center of all this activity, it is not Hamilton but a less well-known Federalist named Tench Coxe, who was very active throughout the pre-election period and maintained an extensive correspondence with Federalists all over the country.

Whoever directed it, the campaign to hold down John Adams's electoral vote was successful. It is virtually certain that this effort cost Adams

- 2 electoral votes in Connecticut
- 2 electoral votes in Pennsylvania
- 6 electoral votes in Maryland
- and at least 2 electoral votes in New Jersey.[77]

It is also possible, though the evidence is less conclusive, that the campaign cost him

- 3 electoral votes in Delaware
- 5 electoral votes in Georgia
- and 3 more electoral votes in New Jersey.[78]

The actual electoral vote for the 1789 presidential election is shown in Table 7.5. Just as Hamilton had anticipated, cutting a few votes away from Adams here and there had no effect on the final outcome. Adams was easily

Table 7.5. Electoral Vote in the 1789 Presidential Election

	Number of Electoral Votes
George Washington	69
John Adams	34
John Jay	9
Robert H. Harrison	6
John Rutledge	6
John Hancock	4
George Clinton	3
Samuel Huntington	2
John Milton	2
James Armstrong	1
Benjamin Lincoln	1
Edward Telfair	1

Note: Though a total of 72 presidential electors were elected or appointed in 1789, two of the electors in Maryland and one in Virginia did not attend the meeting of the electors in their respective states.

elected vice president. The Massachusetts stalwart received 34 electoral votes; his nearest competitor, John Jay, received just 9. Adams, however, saw these results from a different perspective. One of Adams's least attractive qualities, as he himself often conceded, was his vanity; and he was, by all accounts, humiliated by his failure to receive a vote from a majority of the electors. Years later, he would learn about Hamilton's role in the 1789 election. It would be one of several factors that would eventually open up a large and politically consequential breach between the two Federalist leaders.

THEORY V. PRACTICE: A SUMMARY

How well did the presidential election process envisioned by the Framers hold up in its first encounter with the realities of American politics? Let us return to the four questions about the Framers' expectations posed at the beginning of this article.

1. *How would the presidential electors be chosen?* This was one aspect of the presidential selection process that—at least in the short term—did turn out the way the Framers intended. The Framers, I have argued, did not have a strong preference as to whether the presidential electors should be chosen by the state legislature or by popular vote, and therefore deliberately left this matter to the determination of the legislatures, no doubt recognizing that the legislatures were likely to use this discretion in a variety of ways. Which is exactly what happened. Not until the 1820s would almost every state adopt the same system: selection by statewide popular vote.
2. *How would the electors make their decisions?* At one level, the states genuinely did their best to live up to Alexander Hamilton's vision of how the electoral college would operate: they chose a remarkable group of men to serve as presidential electors, easily fulfilling Hamilton's hope that the electors would be persons of "information and discernment." The 72 people appointed or elected as presidential electors in 1789 included: 7 current or former governors (and 7 more men who would later hold that position); 20 people who had served in the Continental or Confederation Congress (including two past presidents of that body and 6 signers of the Declaration of Independence); 49 men who had served in one or both houses of their state legislature; 8 generals in the Continental Army (and many others who had held top positions in their state militias); and 2 future U.S. Supreme Court justices, 2 people who would turn down appointments to the U.S. Supreme Court, and 10 men who had served on their state's highest court. The group also knew something about the Constitution:

3 had been members of the Constitutional Convention, 38 had attended their state's ratifying convention, 14 had had a hand in writing their state's constitution.[79] That the states would pick such a distinguished set of individuals is, of course, further evidence that they expected the electors to be real decision-makers, not just a rubber-stamp.

But was all this political talent and experience actually put to use? Did the electors themselves decide which candidates to vote for—or were they just registering a decision that had already been made by someone else? Most of the evidence suggests the former. Relatively few documents from the 1788-89 campaign contained any kind of clear pledge that, if such-and-such a group of people were chosen as electors, they *would* vote for Washington or Adams or Clinton. In states such as Maryland and Pennsylvania, where there was an active, public campaign, the two sides were usually referred to as the Federalist and Antifederalist tickets or with such rubrics as "friends of the Constitution" and "those who are sincere in wishing for amendments." They were notably not identified by the names of the candidates they were likely to vote for—probably because their votes were not, in fact, committed in advance, particularly as to the vice presidency. A good example is the announcement of the Federalist ticket in Maryland quoted a number of pages earlier. Today, any self-respecting political consultant who had George Washington as his presidential candidate would make that fact the centerpiece of the whole campaign. In this instance, however, the candidates for elector and representative were merely described as the "Federal" ticket. Washington's name was literally never mentioned.[80]

Yet there were some noteworthy exceptions. The circular letter sent out by the New York City Federal Republican Committee, as we have seen, made clear that any Antifederalist electors selected in New York or Virginia would give their second vote not just to some unnamed advocate of immediate constitutional amendments, but specifically to George Clinton. An article in the *Federal Gazette* urged a vote for the Federalist slate of presidential electors in Pennsylvania with the following words:

> It is to be hoped (says a correspondent) that the citizens of Philadelphia will exert themselves in a particular manner, in supporting the ticket for the federal electors at the ensuing election. The gentlemen who compose it are worthy men, decided federalists, and warm friends to General Washington.

As to the vice presidency, however, the correspondent would only say:

> It becomes us . . . to oppose George Clinton as vice-president of the United States. . . . Let an Adams, a Rutledge, a Huntington, or some other patriot of equally respectable federal character, be chosen the second officer in the United States.[81]

In other words, no specific vice presidential candidate was endorsed, that decision presumably being left to the discretion of the electors.

The indefinite nature of the commitments made by the 1789 presidential electors was also observable when they finally cast their ballots on February 4, 1789. Today, the meeting of the electoral college, which takes place on the first Monday after the second Wednesday in December, is a pure formality—indeed, most Americans probably have no idea it occurs. The only surprise is that about once every other election, some "faithless elector" votes for someone other than the party nominee under whose banner he or she was elected, but such stray votes have never affected—have never come close to affecting—the final outcome of a presidential election. In 1789, by contrast, a sense of real uncertainty hung over the electors' work. Though Washington was no doubt a heavy favorite to win the election, no one knew for sure how many votes he would get or how the second presidential votes would be distributed or how many Federalist and Antifederalist electors there were in some of the states.

In general, the participants in the first presidential election were struggling to reconcile two conflicting inclinations, one of which argued that the presidential electors were supposed to be independent decision-makers, while the second insisted that they couldn't be completely independent, that in fact many of them were selected precisely because they were likely to vote for certain candidates rather than others. It would take another couple election cycles before Americans would finally discard the first proposition entirely and decide that they were actually quite content with a rubber-stamp electoral college—that they didn't want presidential electors making decisions on their own.

3. *How would the huge number of potential presidential candidates be narrowed down to a manageable number of alternatives?* To start with the most obvious point, the electoral college itself did not function as a nominating mechanism—in 1789 or in any other American presidential election except perhaps 1824. There was, instead, a clear, unforced, national consensus that George Washington was the ideal person to serve as the first president. This sort of consensus also helps explain the emergence of John Adams and George Clinton as vice presidential candidates, though in both cases that consensus was given a significant push by an extensive process of consultation and collaboration among political elites.

   As for political parties, most historians believe—and I agree—that it would be a mistake to regard the Federalist and Antifederalist coalitions that contested the first federal election as parties in the modern sense of that term—thought it is worth noting that the two groups were often described as "parties" by contemporary observers and participants.[82] Yet the gap between these two groups and the Federalist and Republican parties that emerged less than a decade later is probably smaller than many analysts recognize. The Federalists and Antifederalists might easily have evolved into political parties had the issue that divided them—the status of the new Constitution—proved to be an enduring one. As it was, the ratification of the Constitution by all thirteen original states and the adoption of the Bill of Rights effectively settled that question and allowed Americans to turn their attention to a different issue: what kinds of policies should the new government adopt? It was disagreements over this second question that soon led to the emergence of the first American party system.

4. *How was the dual-vote system supposed to work?* The Framers of the U.S. Constitution, I have argued in an earlier article, deserve respectful attention, not a slavish adherence. They were mortal. And there is no more vivid proof of their mortality than the dual-vote provision that was incorporated into Article II's presidential selection procedure. That provision literally never worked the way it was intended to work and created a host of problems that had not been anticipated. And though the founders were understandably reluctant to acknowledge it in public, many of them recognized that the dual-vote provision was a mistake before the first election had concluded. In a letter written on January 2, 1789, before the presidential electors had even been chosen, William Tilghman of Maryland observed, "The constitution is *defective*, in not obliging the Electors to vote for a president & vice president, distinctly." Less than a month later, Alexander Hamilton said almost exactly the same thing: "Every body is aware of that *defect* in the constitution which renders it possible that the man intended for Vice President may in fact turn up President."[83]

   One of the principal flaws in the dual-vote system was that it was designed to deal with what turned out to be a non-existent problem. The presidential electors proved to be much less parochial than the members of the Constitutional Convention had expected. Instead of squandering their first vote on a home-state favorite, the electors overwhelmingly cast both of their votes for candidates of national stature: Washington and Adams, but also John Jay, George Clinton, and John Hancock all merit this appellation.[84] Of the 138 electoral votes cast in 1789, a maximum of 18 were cast for home-state candidates who had no real pretension to national office—and many of these 18, as we have seen, were thrown away only in order to make sure that John Adams wasn't inadvertently elected president. Over the next three election cycles, the dual-vote provision would be a persistent source of trouble until finally, in 1803–04, the Twelfth Amendment abolished it and substituted a more conventional system in which separate votes were cast for president and vice president.

APPENDIX
Details on the Content Analysis Reported in Tables 7.2 and 7.3

Source Material: This analysis uses the complete set of documents collected in the *Documentary History of the First Federal Elections* with respect to the election of the president and vice president. These documents can be found in volume 4, chapter XIV, pp. 22–161, and cover the period from January 1, 1788 through February 4, 1789, the day the electors cast their votes. Of the documents analyzed, 47 percent were newspaper articles, 52 percent were private letters, and 2 percent were "other" (two broadsides and an entry in a private journal). The only items I have not included are a series of letters *from* George Washington, which are famously elusive as to whether he was or was not a candidate for the presidency (i.e., whether he would accept the job if elected to it). However, since almost all of these letters are written in response to correspondence that other political leaders had sent *to* Washington, the former general's status as a major center of communication about the upcoming election is reflected in the analysis.

Basic Unit of Analysis: The basic unit for this analysis is a "mention," defined as any instance in which a person is specifically referred to as a candidate for either the presidency or the vice presidency or both. While a mention must clearly refer to a specific individual, it need not refer to him by name. George Washington, in particular, is often referred to with such titles as "the Savior of our country" and "the great American Fabius." Similarly, Massachusetts political leaders sometimes called John Hancock "the governor" or "Mr. H." Each article or letter that refers to a candidate is counted as a single mention, even if that source devotes numerous sentences or paragraphs to that candidate. An article can, however, mention numerous candidates. A newspaper story that urges electors to vote for George Washington and John Adams rather than Patrick Henry and George Clinton is coded as one mention each for four distinct candidates.

Tone is defined as an article or letter's basic evaluative stance toward each of the candidates mentioned: that is, whether the article's assessment of the candidate, taken as a whole, is positive, negative, or neutral. Articles that have an approximately equal amount of positive and negative material are coded as neutral.

Treatment of Reprints: In the absence of copyright laws, it was common practice during this period for newspapers in one city to reprint articles that had originally appeared in a paper in a different city. Since the purpose of this analysis is to measure the content of the national discussion about presidential and vice presidential candidates, I count each reprint as a distinct mention. (I am able to do this, I should point out, only because the *Documentary History* does a superb job of itemizing reprints.) Thus, an article about Washington and Adams that was printed in five newspapers is counted as five mentions for each candidate. As a justification for this procedure, consider the following analogy. Suppose someone were doing a content analysis of newspaper coverage of a recent presidential campaign in five contemporary newspapers. If a single Associated Press story were printed in each of these five papers, should it be counted as one story or five? So far as I can determine, the invariable practice of contemporary media analysts would be to treat it as five separate stories. I follow a similar rule with respect to the newspaper stories of 1788–89.

NOTES

1. See William G. Mayer, "What the Founders Intended: Another Look at the Origins of the American Presidential Selection Process," in *The Making of the Presidential Candidates 2008*, ed. William G. Mayer (Lanham, MD: Rowman & Littlefield, 2008), 203–34.

2. See Mayer, "What the Founders Intended," 220–24.

3. See, in particular, Richard P. McCormick, *The Presidential Game: The Origins of American Presidential Politics* (New York: Oxford University Press, 1982), 25.

4. Federalist No. 68, in Alexander Hamilton, James Madison, and John Jay, *The Federalist Papers*, ed. Clinton Rossiter (New York: New American Library, 1961 [1788]), 412.

5. For Houstoun's objection, see Max Farrand, ed., *The Records of the Federal Convention of 1787*, 4 vols. (New Haven, CT: Yale University Press, 1937), 2:95, 99. Similar arguments were made by Caleb Strong and Hugh Williamson; see Farrand, *Records*, 2:100. Note that in the final version of the Constitution, this problem is remedied by having the electors meet "in their respective States" rather than in a single location.

6. Madison's comment is in Farrand, *Records*, 2:500; Sherman's at 2:513. In a similar vein is Rufus King's comment that the large states would have a disproportionate influence in "bringing forward the candidates." See Farrand, *Records*, 2:514.

7. Farrand, *Records*, 2:500. Other members of the Constitutional Convention who expressed the belief that in most years no candidate would win a majority in the electoral college include Charles Pinckney (2:501); John Rutledge (2:511); James Wilson (2:522); and Alexander Hamilton (2:524–25).

8. Both quotations can be found at Farrand, *Records*, 2:501.

9. For Washington's influence on the Convention's thinking about the presidency, see, in particular, the comments of Pierce Butler in his letter to Weeden Butler, May 5, 1788, in Farrand, *Records*, 3:302.

10. The argument that the dual–vote system would make contingent elections less likely was made by Gouverneur Morris in Farrand, *Records*, 2:512.

11. On the founders' attitude toward political parties, the classic discussion is Richard Hofstadter, *The Idea of a Party System: The Rise of Legitimate Opposition in the United States, 1780–1840* (Berkeley, CA: University of California Press, 1969), esp. chaps. 1 and 2.

12. For a fuller discussion, see Mayer, "What the Founders Intended," 216–18. The word "party" is used less frequently in the records of the Constitutional Convention, though when it does appear, it is almost always used pejoratively. See Farrand, *Records*, 1:82–83; 2:68; 2:100; and 2:104. Both Richard Hofstadter and Jackson Turner Main have argued that while contemporary dictionaries sometimes provided slightly different definitions for "party" and "faction," many Americans of this time period used the terms interchangeably. See Hofstadter, *Idea of a Party System*, 10–11; and Main, *Political Parties before the Constitution* (Chapel Hill, NC: University of North Carolina Press, 1973), xviii.

13. See Farrand, *Records*, 2:114, 119.

14. Both quotes are from Farrand, *Records*, 2:113.

15. Farrand, *Records*, 2:114.

16. See, in particular, the comment of Hugh Williamson in Farrand, *Records*, 2:537.

17. As will soon become clear, my analysis of the first presidential election draws heavily upon the remarkable collection of primary source materials in Merrill Jensen, Robert A. Becker, Gordon DenBoer, and Lucy Trumbull Brown, eds., *The Documentary History of the First Federal Elections*, 4 vols. (Madison, WI: University of Wisconsin Press, 1976–1984), hereinafter cited as *DHFFE*. The secondary literature on this election is somewhat thinner than that concerning many of the other elections in this period, but see Edward Stanwood, *A History of the Presidency from 1788 to 1897* (Boston, MA: Houghton Mifflin, 1926), chap 2; Marcus Cunliffe, "Elections of 1789 and 1792," in *History of American Presidential Elections 1789–1968*, ed. Arthur M. Schlesinger, Jr. (New York: Chelsea House, 1985), 1:3–19; McCormick, *Presidential Game*, 27–40; William Nisbet Chambers, *Political Parties in a New Nation: The American Experience, 1776–1809* (New York: Oxford University Press, 1963), 29–33; and Norman K. Risjord, *Chesapeake Politics 1781–1800* (New York: Columbia University Press, 1978), chap. 11.

18. For full (and generally uninteresting) details about how the Confederation Congress debated and finally passed its election ordinance, see *DHFFE*, 1:9–143.

19. See Madison's letter to George Hay, August 23, 1823, in Farrand, *Records*, 3:459.

20. Richard McCormick has argued that many states used state legislatures to choose their electors in 1789 because the compressed timetable did not leave them sufficient time to organize and hold a popular election. See McCormick, *Presidential*

Game, 31. But states were no more inclined to use elections (statewide or district-based) in 1792, when such time pressures were no longer a factor.

21. The exception is Cato, *Delaware Gazette*, January 10, 1789, in *DHFFE*, 4:135–38.

22. These quotations are taken from, respectively, Federalist, *Massachusetts Centinel*, August 20, 1788, *DHFFE*, 4:56; Victor Marie DuPont letter to Pierre Samuel DuPont, November 28, 1788 (4:98); and Baron von Steuben letter to William North, December 12, 1788 (4:111).

23. For accounts of Hancock's campaign for the presidency—or was it for the vice presidency?—see Herbert S. Allan, *John Hancock: Patriot in Purple* (New York: The Beechhurst Press, 1953), 334–39; William M. Fowler, Jr., *The Baron of Beacon Hill: A Biography of John Hancock* (Boston, MA: Houghton Mifflin, 1980), 274–75; and Harlow Giles Unger, *John Hancock: Merchant King and American Patriot* (New York: John Wiley & Sons, 2000), 320–22.

24. Christopher Gore letter to Theodore Sedgwick, August 17, 1788, *DHFFE*, 4:53.

25. Laco, Pamphlet No. VII, March, 1789, in *DHFFE*, 4:196–97.

26. In assessing this report, it is important to note that in 1788–89, a "correspondent" was not a reporter in the modern sense of the term (the occupation of newspaper reporter had yet to be invented), but simply someone who had corresponded with (i.e., written a letter to) the paper's editor/printer.

27. *Federal Gazette*, December 13, 1788, in *DHFFE*, 4:112.

28. Note, in particular, that the tone of the letters and articles about the Henry candidacy analyzed in Table 7.2 is 100 percent negative. That is to say, *all* of the documents referring to Henry's purported quest to be president were written by people who opposed it.

29. As virtually every historian who has studied him agrees, the documentary record for Patrick Henry is exceptionally thin. Richard R. Beeman, for example, begins his biography of Henry by noting "the dismal state of the historical records relating to Henry's life." See Beeman, *Patrick Henry: A Biography* (New York: McGraw–Hill, 1974), xii. Such records as have survived, however, including the writings of other Virginia politicians and contemporary Virginia newspapers, also fail to show any signs of an active campaign on Henry's behalf. See *DHFFE*, especially 2:247–423.

30. Robert Douthat Meade, for example, concludes that "there is no proof that Henry was ever approached on the subject of the presidential nomination." See Meade, *Patrick Henry: Practical Revolutionary* (Philadelphia, PA: J.B. Lippincott, 1969), 385. Henry Mayer similarly finds that Henry returned home to Prince Edward County after the Virginia legislature passed the state election law and elected its first two senators, and "played only a minor role in launching the new government. . . . The political gossips had whispered that the Antis would support a Henry–Clinton ticket as a means of subversion, but Henry would neither seek national office nor challenge the invincible Washington." See Mayer, *A Son of Thunder: Patrick Henry and the American Republic* (Charlottesville, VA: University Press of Virginia, 1991), 453. Richard Beeman never mentions the episode at all. Beeman, *Patrick Henry*, 165–70.

31. See, in particular, *Federal Gazette*, December 23, 1788, *DHFFE*, 4:118; and *Federal Gazette*, January 14, 1789, *DHFFE*, 4:141.

32. The only person discussed for both offices was John Hancock, though even he was usually seen (at least by others) as a candidate for the vice presidency.

33. There is some disagreement about exactly when during the 1790s political parties can be said to have come into existence—undoubtedly it was a gradual process—but virtually everyone who has written on the subject places it sometime during this decade. See, among others, Chambers, *Political Parties*; John F. Hoadley, *Origins of American Political Parties, 1789–1803* (Lexington, KY: University Press of Kentucky, 1986); Everett Carll Ladd, Jr., *American Political Parties: Social Change and Political Response* (New York: Norton, 1970), 79–83; and Noble E. Cunningham, Jr., *The Jeffersonian Republicans: The Formation of Party Organization, 1789–1801* (Chapel Hill, NC: University of North Carolina Press, 1957).

34. For a general assessment of the state of parties or party–like groups before 1789, see Main, *Political Parties*. For a useful attempt to clarify how Main's "parties" compare with those that followed, see William Nisbet Chambers, review of *Political Parties before the Constitution*, by Jackson Turner Main, in *Reviews in American History* 1 (December 1973): 499–504.

35. For data on this point, see Mayer, "What the Founders Intended," 226.

36. For a similar reading of the different positions with respect to constitutional amendments in late 1788, see James Madison letter to Thomas Jefferson, December 8, 1788, in *DHFFE*, 4:109.

37. See *Federal Gazette*, January 3, 1789 (4:128, emphasis in original); and A Marylander, *Maryland Gazette*, January 2, 1789, in *DHFFE*, 4:126 (emphasis in original). For an example from the Antifederalist side, see "New York City Federal Republican Committee to Antifederalists in Other States," c. November 13, 1789 (4:91), which is quoted at length later in this chapter.

38. See "Essays by a Farmer," in *The Complete Anti–Federalist*, ed. Herbert J. Storing, 7 vols. (Chicago: University of Chicago Press, 1981), 5:44; Richard Henry Lee letter to Edmund Randolph, October 16, 1787, *Complete Anti–Federalist*, 5:111; and Luther Martin, "The Genuine Information Delivered to the Legislature of the State of Maryland Relative to the Proceedings of the General Convention Held at Philadelphia," *Complete Anti–Federalist*, 2:66. For similar comments written during the 1788–89 campaign, see *Herald of Freedom*, October 30, 1788, in *DHFFE*, 4:85; New York City Federal Republican Committee to Antifederalists in Other States, c. November 13, 1788 (4:91); and Delawarensis, *Delaware Gazette*, January 31, 1789 (4:158).

Another indication of the overestimation of the vice presidency's significance is the fact that John Adams, a man with a robust sense of his own importance, was willing to serve in the position. See, in particular, his letter to his daughter, Abigail Smith, July 16, 1788, in *DHFFE*, 4:43. It was not until he had actually served as vice president that he famously called it "the most insignificant office that ever the invention of man contrived or his imagination conceived." See his letter of December 19, 1793, in *The Works of John Adams*, 10 vols., ed. Charles Francis Adams (Boston, MA: Little, Brown, 1856), 1:460.

39. In a letter to Alexander Hamilton on October 3, 1788, Washington suggested that he might "lend whatever assistance" he could to get the government going and

then retire "at a convenient and an early period." *DHFFE*, 4:74. James Madison apparently raised the same possibility in a conversation with Washington held at approximately the same time, though Madison did not record the event in writing until four years later. See "Memorandum on a Discussion of the President's Retirement," May 5, 1792, in *The Papers of James Madison*, ed. Robert A. Rutland et al., 17 vols. (Charlottesville, VA: University Press of Virginia, 1983), 14:301.

40. Another northerner who almost certainly would have received a great deal of attention was Benjamin Franklin, had he not been 83 years old and in declining health when the new government commenced operations.

41. The supporter referred to is James Sullivan; see his letter to George Thacher, October 8, 1788, in *DHFFE*, 4:75–76. See also A.B., *Independent Chronicle*, December 4, 1788 (4:107–08). For contemporary documents that appear to credit the rumor, see, among others, Benjamin Lincoln letter to Theodore Sedgwick, August 6, 1788 (4:49); Christopher Gore letter to Rufus King, August 30, 1788 (4:59); Benjamin Lincoln letter to George Washington, September 24, 1788 (4:69); James Madison letter to Edmund Randolph, October 28, 1788 (4:83); *Herald of Freedom*, December 1, 1788 (4:104); and Tobias Lear letter to Benjamin Lincoln, February 5, 1789 (4:167).

42. Benjamin Lincoln letter to George Washington, January 4, 1789, *DHFFE*, 4:129.

43. Theodore Sedgwick letter to Alexander Hamilton, November 2, 1788, *DHFFE*, 4:85.

44. Letter of Alexander Hamilton to Theodore Sedgwick, October 9, 1788, in *DHFFE*, 4:76–77.

45. The documents referred to are: Theodore Sedgwick letter to Alexander Hamilton, October 16, 1788, in *DHFFE*, 4:78; Theodore Sedgwick letter to Alexander Hamilton, November 2, 1788 (1:480); Alexander Hamilton letter to Theodore Sedgwick, November 9, 1788 (4:87); Alexander Hamilton letter to James Madison, November 23, 1788 (4:94–95).

46. See Benjamin Lincoln letter to George Washington, September 24, 1788, in *DHFFE*, 4:68–70; Henry Knox letter to George Washington, December 21, 1788 (4:116); George Washington letter to Benjamin Lincoln, October 26, 1788 (4:81–83); and George Washington letter to Henry Knox, January 1, 1789 (4:123).

47. Edward Carrington letter to James Madison, December 19, 1788, in *DHFFE*, 4:115; and Robert Smith letter to Tench Coxe, January 21, 1789 (4:145).

48. See *Federal Gazette*, January 6, 1789, in *DHFFE*, 4:131 (emphasis in original).

49. Letter from New York City Federal Republican Committee to Antifederalists in Other States, c. November 13, 1788, *DHFFE*, 4:91.

50. For the full text of the law, see *DHFFE*, 2:136–40.

51. This type of ballot would later be called the Australian ballot, and would not be widely adopted in the United States until the late 1880s and early 1890s. See Jerrold G. Rusk, "The Effect of the Australian Ballot Reform on Split Ticket Voting: 1876–1908," *American Political Science Review* 64 (December 1970): 1220–38.

52. See especially Philip E. Converse, "The Nature of Belief Systems in Mass Publics," in *Ideology and Discontent*, ed. David E. Apter (London, UK:

Collier–Macmillan, 1964), 206–61; and Michael X. Delli Carpini and Scott Keeter, *What Americans Know about Politics and Why It Matters* (New Haven, CT: Yale University Press, 1996).

53. *Maryland Journal*, December 26, 1788, in *DHFFE*, 2:161–62. The legislative caucus nominations are also discussed in Nathaniel Ramsay letter to Otho Holland Williams, December 29, 1788 (2:164); A Marylander, *Maryland Gazette*, December 30, 1788 (2:165); A.B., *Maryland Journal*, December 30, 1788 (2:168); and Aristides, *Maryland Gazette*, January 1, 1789 (2:178).

54. For listings of the Federalist and Antifederalist slates, see *Maryland Journal*, December 26, 1788, in *DHFFE*, 2:162; A Marylander, *Maryland Gazette*, December 30, 1788 (2:165); *Maryland Gazette*, December 30, 1788 (2:166–67); A.B., *Maryland Journal*, December 30, 1788 (2:168); "Antifederalist Ticket," c. January 1, 1789 (2:170–71); "Federalist Ticket," c. January 1, 1789 (2:171); and Aristides, *Maryland Gazette*, January 1, 1789 (2:179).

55. See A.B., *Maryland Journal*, December 30, 1788, in *DHFFE*, 2:168–69.

56. The two quotations are taken from, respectively, Henry Hollingsworth letter to William Tilghman, January 30, 1789, in *DHFFE*, 2:185; and Publius, *Maryland Journal*, Feburary 6, 1789 (2:215). For other discussions of local electioneering, see Richard Pindell letter to Otho Holland Williams, January 6, 1789 (2:186); "Communications Interesting to the Public," January 6, 1789 (2:190); William Matthews letter to William Tilghman, January 8, 1789 (2:194); and John Stull letter to Otho Holland Williams, January 9, 1789 (2:196–97).

57. For the full text of the law, see *DHFFE*, 1:299–302.

58. In Forrest McDonald's survey of state politics at the time of the Constitutional Convention, Pennsylvania is the only state he describes as having "well–organized political parties." All other states' politics were characterized by "factions" or (in one case) "many small political groups." See McDonald, *We the People: The Economic Origins of the Constitution* (New Brunswick, NJ: Transaction, 1992 [1958]), chap. 2.

59. See "Proceedings of a Cumberland County Meeting," July 3, 1788, in *DHFFE*, 1:239.

60. Both quotations are taken from "Cumberland County Circular Letter," *DHFFE*, 1:240.

61. From the moment the Harrisburg convention ended, there were numerous charges from the Federalists that while the convention was held with "the ostensible pretensions of procuring amendments," its real purpose was "to form a ticket for Representatives in Congress." See "Philadelphia County Meeting," *Pennsylvania Mercury*, October 14, 1788, in *DHFFE*, 1:314. For other examples, see Thomas Hartley letter to Tench Coxe, September 9, 1788 (1:266); "A Federal Centinel," *Pennsylvania Gazette*, September 10, 1788 (1:269); and Samuel Miles letter to Timothy Pickering, September 11, 1788 (1:270). Yet the official report on the convention is silent on this subject. See "Report of the Proceedings," *Pennsylvania Packet*, September 15, 1788, in *DHFFE*, 1:260–64. As noted in the text, the first public mention of the Harrisburg ticket was published in early November. See "A Friend to Liberty and Union to the Freemen of Pennsylvania," November 7, 1788 (1:332–35). Yet the existence of a Harrisburg ticket must have been more than just election propaganda. A letter from

William Shippen, Jr., to Thomas Lee Shippen, written on October 10–15, 1788, says that "the Anti ticket was formed at the Harrisburg Convention," and then names six of the eight men who were later declared to be on the ticket. See *DHFFE*, 1:312.

62. See "Proceedings of a Philadelphia Meeting," October 1, 1788, in *DHFFE*, 1:297.

63. The key document here is "To the German Inhabitants of the State of Pennsylvania," November 13, 1788, in *DHFFE*, 1:339–40.

64. All statistics in this paragraph are based on the votes reported in *DHFFE*, 1:378–79.

65. The slate is reported in "Harrisburg Ticket for Presidential Electors," *Independent Gazetteer*, November 24, 1788, in *DHFFE*, 1:358. The quotation is taken from Alexander Kennan and George Logue letter to John Nicholson, January 8, 1789 (1:382). The votes are given at 1:390–91.

66. See *DHFFE*, 2:81–92.

67. James Duncanson letter to James Maury, February 17, 1789, in *DHFFE*, 2:405.

68. Arthur Lee's declaration of candidacy appears in *DHFFE*, 2:352; his withdrawal is discussed in Henry Lee letter to James Madison, January 14, 1789 (2:394). The description of him as "violently" Antifederal is taken from Walter Jones letter to Robert Carter, c. January 1789 (2:351). On Henry Lee's withdrawal, see Henry Lee letter to George Washington, December 11, 1788; and George Washington letter to Henry Lee, December 12, 1788, both at 2:350. Other "withdrawals" yielded more equivocal results. Despite Isaac Avery's withdrawal from an eastern Virginia congressional race, he still received over 200 votes. Compare Avery's letter to John Cropper, January 30, 1789 (2:357), with the final results shown at 2:364.

69. Henry Lee letter to James Madison, December 8, 1789, in *DHFFE*, 2:381.

70. See George Washington letter to Henry Knox, January 1, 1789, in *DHFFE*, 2:386; and James Madison letter to George Washington, January 14, 1789 (2:394).

71. All available vote returns from the 1789 Virginia presidential election are reported in *DHFFE*, 2:306–08. The districts I classify as having a two–person, Federalist v. Antifederalist race are 3, 9, and 11. The two that include a larger number of major candidates are districts 7 and 8. The district numbers used here, it should be noted, were added by *DHFFE* editors for ease of reference. In actuality, the Virginia state legislature did not number either the congressional or the elector districts it created.

72. See, for example, Tobias Lear letter to Benjamin Lincoln, February 5, 1789, *DHFFE*, 2:400.

73. Two months before this, Hamilton had raised the issue of an inadvertent election, but only in a general way and without recommending any concrete steps to remedy the problem. See his letter to James Madison, November 23, 1788, in *The Papers of Alexander Hamilton*, ed. Harold C. Syrett, 27 vols. (New York: Columbia University Press, 1962), 5:235–37.

74. Alexander Hamilton letter to James Wilson, January 25, 1789, in *Papers of Alexander Hamilton*, 5:247–49 (emphasis in original).

75. See, for example, Cunliffe, "Elections of 1789 and 1792," 13–15; McCormick, *Presidential Game*, 33–35; Stanwood, *History*, 25–27; and David McCullough, *John Adams* (New York: Simon & Schuster, 2001), 393–94.

76. The list is: Christopher Gore letter to Theodore Sedgwick, August 17, 1788, in *DHFFE*, 4:53; Federalist, *Massachusetts Centinel*, August 20, 1788 (4:56); William Tilghman to Tench Coxe, January 2, 1789 (4:125); Henry Hollingsworth letter to Levi Hollingsworth, January 5, 1789 (2:186); Tench Coxe letter to Benjamin Rush, January 13, 1789 (4:140); William Smith letter to James Wilson, January 19, 1789 (4:143–44); Benjamin Rush letter to Tench Coxe, January 19, 1789 (4:144–45); and Wallace & Muir letter to Tench Coxe, January 25, 1789 (4:149–50).

77. On the electoral vote in Connecticut, see Alexander Hamilton letter to James Wilson, January 25, 1789, in *DHFFE*, 4:148; Jeremiah Wadsworth letter to Alexander Hamilton, c. February 5, 1789 (2:50); and John Trumbull letter to John Adams, April 17, 1790 (4:290). For the Pennsylvania vote, see Hamilton letter to Wilson (4:148); and Benjamin Rush letter to Tench Coxe, February 5, 1789 (1:401). For the Maryland vote, see William Tilghman letter to Tench Coxe, January 25, 1789 (2:230); and William Tilghman letter to Tench Coxe, February 9, 1789 (2:233); and Wallace & Muir letter to Tench Coxe, January 25, 1789 (4:149–50). For the New Jersey vote, see Hamilton letter to Wilson (4:148); and Trumbull letter to Adams (4:290).

78. In Delaware and Georgia, we have numerous contemporary observers predicting that Adams would sweep the electoral vote in both states—yet Adams won not a single vote in either place. We do not, however, have any conclusive evidence as to why this shortfall occurred. On the Delaware vote, see Alexander Hamilton vote to James Wilson, January 25, 1789, in *DHFFE*, 4:148. On the Georgia vote, see Jeremiah Wadsworth letter to Alexander Hamilton, c. February 5, 1789 (2:50); James Seagrove letter to Samuel Blachley Webb, January 2, 1789 (2:438); and Tench Coxe letter to John Adams, March 1, 1789 (4:186). In New Jersey, all of the sources cited in the preceding footnote indicate that Hamilton tried to have two or three votes withheld from Adams—but in the end, Adams received just one of six votes in that state. The other two–to–three votes may have been given to John Jay as further insurance against an inadvertent election—or simply because the electors thought Jay was the most qualified candidate.

79. These numbers are my own count, based primarily on the brief biographical sketches of the electors provided at the end of each of the state chapters in *DHFFE*, vols. 1–3.

80. For the full text of the announcement, see *Maryland Journal*, December 26, 1788, in *DHFFE*, 2:161–62.

81. Both quotations are from *Federal Gazette*, December 20, 1788, in *DHFFE*, 4:115.

82. See, among many others, A Marylander, *Maryland Gazette*, December 30, 1788, in *DHFFE*, 2:165; Abraham Shepherd letter to David Shepherd, November 15, 1788 (2:375); Henry Lee letter to James Madison, November 19, 1788 (2:377); A Mechanic, *Federal Gazette*, November 22, 1788 (1:356); A German, *Pennsylvania*

Packet, November 25, 1788 (1:362–63); and Federal Gazette, December 13, 1788, (4:112).

83. William Tilghman letter to Tench Coxe, January 2, 1789, in *DHFFE*, 4:125; and Alexander Hamilton letter to James Wilson, January 25, 1789 (4:148). The emphasis in both quotations is my own.

84. Note in particular that all of the electoral votes received by these last three candidates were cast by electors who did not live in the candidates' home states.

Appendix

By the Numbers: A Statistical Guide to the Presidential Nomination Process

Alan Silverleib and William G. Mayer

Statistics are the food of love. So said the great baseball writer Roger Angell, writing about his favorite sport. But for political scientists, campaign journalists, political consultants, and political junkies, the observation also applies to elections in general and the presidential nomination process in particular. The road to the White House is thickly marked by numbers: poll standings, fund-raising totals, announcement and withdrawal dates, voting results, and delegate accumulations. The purpose of this appendix is to present a lot of data about the presidential nomination process, with a bare minimum of explanation and commentary. While our principal focus is on contemporary nomination contests—roughly speaking, those that have taken place since 1972—in many cases we also provide data extending back to 1952, to make clear just what is and is not distinctive about the current system.

Table A.1. Announcement Dates for Major Presidential Candidates, 1952–2008

When does a presidential nomination campaign begin? The traditional way of marking this milestone is the date on which a presidential candidate formally announces his or her candidacy. To be sure, many (perhaps most) presidential aspirants have been planning their campaigns and maneuvering for support well before they make this announcement. Yet, up until rather recently, the announcement date was nonetheless a significant piece of information: a sign that any indecision had been finally resolved, that the campaign was now moving to a more active and public phase.

As the data in Table A.1 demonstrate, in the 1950s and 1960s presidential candidates generally did not announce their candidacies until the election year itself or the final months of the preceding year. Beginning in the early 1970s, however, and accelerating throughout the decade, a different pattern started to emerge: most presidential candidates entered the race within a few months after the preceding midterm election. (Indeed, some candidates didn't wait that long. Philip Crane announced his candidacy for the 1980 Republican nomination in August 1978.) Today, it is widely accepted that anyone who hopes to be elected president must devote almost two full years to the effort.

There is some reason, however, to think that the timing of a candidate's formal announcement has become progressively less meaningful. Over the last several election cycles, public declarations of candidacy have to a large extent degenerated into a media event: a way for a candidate to get a bit of additional television time or newspaper space even though he or she has already spent a considerable amount of time raising money and courting votes. In the 2000 election cycle, for example, Bill Bradley did not formally announce his candidacy until September 8, 1999, even though he had been campaigning full-time since early in the year. To further muddy the waters, many candidates now call press conferences to announce that they will announce their candidacy on some date in the future.

In recent years, then, a better indicator of when candidates begin their presidential campaigns is the date on which they file two forms with the Federal Election Commission (FEC). Since 1974, any person who raises or spends more than $5,000 in seeking nomination or election to the presidency, or authorizes someone else to raise or spend such money, must file a Statement of Candidacy with the FEC and a Statement of Organization for their principal campaign committee. (Most campaigns file both statements on the same day.) For all major-party candidates since 1974, Table A.1 therefore provides both pieces of information: the formal announcement date and the date of a candidate's earliest filing with the FEC.

A. Democrats

Year	*Candidate*	*Formal Announcement Date*	*Date of First Filing with the FEC*
1952	Estes Kefauver	January 23, 1952	
	Richard Russell	February 28, 1952	
	Robert Kerr	March 31, 1952	
	Averell Harriman	April 22, 1952	
	Alben Barkley	July 6, 1952	
	Adlai Stevenson	None	
1956	Adlai Stevenson	November 15, 1955	
	Estes Kefauver	December 16, 1955	
	Averell Harriman	June 9, 1956	
1960	Hubert Humphrey	December 30, 1959	
	John Kennedy	January 2, 1960	
	Stuart Symington	March 24, 1960	

A. Democrats *(continued)*

Year	*Candidate*	*Formal Announcement Date*	*Date of First Filing with the FEC*
1960	Lyndon Johnson	July 5, 1960	
1964	George Wallace	March 6, 1964	
	Lyndon Johnson	None	
1968	Eugene McCarthy	November 30, 1967	
	Robert Kennedy	March 16, 1968	
	Hubert Humphrey	April 27, 1968	
	George McGovern	August 10, 1968	
1972	George McGovern	January 18, 1971	
	Henry Jackson	November 19, 1971	
	Eugene McCarthy	December 17, 1971	
	John Lindsay	December 28, 1971	
	Edmund Muskie	January 4, 1972	
	Hubert Humphrey	January 10, 1972	
	George Wallace	January 13, 1972	
	Terry Sanford	March 8, 1972	
1976	Morris Udall	November 23, 1974	February 10, 1975
	Jimmy Carter	December 12, 1974	February 25, 1976
	Fred Harris	January 11, 1975	March 10, 1976
	Henry Jackson	February 6, 1975	June 17, 1974
	Sargent Shriver	September 20, 1975	July 15, 1975
	Birch Bayh	October 21, 1975	October 28, 1975
	George Wallace	November 12, 1975	November 14, 1975
	Jerry Brown	March 12, 1976	March 25, 1976
	Frank Church	March 18, 1976	February 25, 1976
1980	Edward Kennedy	November 7, 1979	October 29, 1979
	Jerry Brown	November 8, 1979	July 30, 1979
	Jimmy Carter	December 4, 1979	March 16, 1979
1984	Alan Cranston	February 2, 1983	November 19, 1982
	Gary Hart	February 17, 1983	January 10, 1983
	Walter Mondale	February 21, 1983	January 3, 1983
	Reubin Askew	February 23, 1983	October 13, 1981
	Ernest Hollings	April 18, 1983	January 18, 1983
	John Glenn	April 21, 1983	January 13, 1983
	George McGovern	September 13, 1983	September 21, 1983
	Jesse Jackson	November 3, 1983	November 9, 1983
1988	Richard Gephardt	February 23, 1987	February 24, 1987
	Bruce Babbitt	March 10, 1987	January 12, 1987
	Gary Hart	April 13, 1987	April 15, 1987
	Michael Dukakis	April 29, 1987	March 25, 1987
	Paul Simon	May 18, 1987	April 16, 1987
	Joseph Biden	June 9, 1987	April 3, 1987
	Al Gore	June 29, 1987	April 27, 1987

(continued)

A. Democrats *(continued)*

Year	*Candidate*	*Formal Announcement Date*	*Date of First Filing with the FEC*
1988	Jesse Jackson	October 10, 1987	September 22, 1987
1992	Paul Tsongas	April 30, 1991	March 9, 1991
	Douglas Wilder	September 13, 1991	March 27, 1991
	Tom Harkin	September 15, 1991	September 16, 1991
	Bob Kerrey	September 30, 1991	September 18, 1991
	Bill Clinton	October 3, 1991	August 16, 1991
	Jerry Brown	October 21, 1991	September 2, 1991

Year	*Candidate*	*Formal Announcement Date*	*Statement of Organization*	*Statement of Candidacy*
1996	Bill Clinton	None	October 14, 1994	April 14, 1995
2000	Al Gore	June 16, 1999	January 11, 1999	January 4, 1999
	Bill Bradley	September 8, 1999	December 4, 1998	January 12, 1999
2004	Al Sharpton	January 3, 2003	January 21, 2003	April 28, 2003
	Joseph Lieberman	January 13, 2003	January 13, 2003	January 13, 2003
	Richard Gephardt	February 19, 2003	January 7, 2003	January 6, 2003
	Bob Graham	May 6, 2003	February 27, 2003	February 27, 2003
	Howard Dean	June 23, 2003	May 31, 2002	May 31, 2002
	John Kerry	September 2, 2003	December 4, 2002	December 4, 2002
	Wesley Clark	September 16, 2003	October 2, 2003	October 2, 2003
	John Edwards	September 16, 2003	January 2, 2003	January 2, 2003
	Carol Moseley Braun	September 22, 2003	February 19, 2003	February 19, 2003
	Dennis Kucinich	October 13, 2003	February 21, 2003	February 19, 2003
2008	Mike Gravel	April 17, 2006	April 21, 2006	April 14, 2006
	Dennis Kucinich	December 11, 2006	December 19, 2006	December 29, 2006
	John Edwards	December 28, 2006	January 5, 2007	January 3, 2007
	Christopher Dodd	January 11, 2007	January 11, 2007	January 11, 2007
	Hillary Clinton	January 20, 2007	January 22, 2007	January 22, 2007
	Bill Richardson	January 21, 2007	January 22, 2007	January 22, 2007
	Joseph Biden	January 31, 2007	January 31, 2007	January 31, 2007
	Barack Obama	February 10, 2007	January 16, 2007	February 12, 2007

B. Republicans

Year	*Candidate*	*Formal Announcement Date*	*Date of First Filing with the FEC*
1952	Robert Taft	October 16, 1951	
	Earl Warren	November 14, 1951	
	Harold Stassen	December 27, 1951	
	Dwight Eisenhower	June 4, 1952	
1964	Nelson Rockefeller	November 7, 1963	
	Barry Goldwater	January 3, 1964	
	Margaret Chase Smith	January 27, 1964	
	William Scranton	June 12, 1964	
1968	George Romney	November 18, 1967	
	Richard Nixon	February 1, 1968	
	Nelson Rockefeller	April 30, 1968	
	Ronald Reagan	August 5, 1968	
1976	Gerald Ford	July 8, 1975	June 20, 1975
	Ronald Reagan	November 20, 1975	May 11, 1976
1980	Philip Crane	August 2, 1978	August 2, 1978
	John Connally	January 24, 1979	January 24, 1979
	George Bush	May 1, 1979	February 5, 1979
	Robert Dole	May 14, 1979	February 21, 1979
	John Anderson	June 8, 1979	May 29, 1979
	Howard Baker	November 1, 1979	January 31, 1979
	Ronald Reagan	November 13, 1979	May 18, 1979
1988	Pierre du Pont	September 16, 1986	June 3, 1986
	Alexander Haig	March 24, 1987	April 8, 1987
	Jack Kemp	April 6, 1987	April 6, 1987
1988	Pat Robertson	October 1, 1987	October 15, 1987
	George H. W. Bush	October 12, 1987	February 19, 1987
	Robert Dole	November 9, 1987	March 3, 1987
1992	Pat Buchanan	December 10, 1991	October 11, 1991
	George H. W. Bush	February 12, 1992	December 26, 1991

Year	*Candidate*	*Formal Announcement Date*	*Statement of Organization*	*Statement of Candidacy*
1996	Phil Gramm	February 24, 1995	November 14, 1994	November 14, 1994
	Lamar Alexander	February 28, 1995	January 18, 1995	January 18, 1995
	Pat Buchanan	March 20, 1995	February 16, 1995	April 13, 1995
	Arlen Specter	March 30, 1995	January 20, 1995	January 20, 1995
	Robert Dole	April 10, 1995	January 12, 1995	January 12, 1995

(continued)

B. Republicans (*continued*)

Year	*Candidate*	*Formal Announcement Date*	*Statement of Organization*	*Statement of Candidacy*
1996	Richard Lugar	April 19, 1995	March 3, 1995	March 3, 1995
	Pete Wilson	June 15, 1995	April 3, 1995	April 3, 1995
	Steve Forbes	September 22, 1995	September 22, 1995	September 22, 1995
	Robert Dornan	April 13, 1995	March 8, 1995	March 8, 1995
	Alan Keyes		May 26, 1995	May 26, 1995
2000	Robert Smith	February 18, 1999	January 4, 1999	January 4, 1999
	Pat Buchanan	March 2, 1999	March 2, 1999	March 1, 1999
	Lamar Alexander	March 9, 1999	January 11, 1999	January 11, 1999
	Steve Forbes	March 16, 1999	March 16, 1999	March 16, 1999
	Dan Quayle	April 14, 1999	February 3, 1999	January 28, 1999
	Gary Bauer	April 21, 1999	February 4, 1999	April 6, 1999
	George W. Bush	June 12, 1999	March 8, 1999	March 8, 1999
	Orrin Hatch	June 22, 1999	July 9, 1999	July 1, 1999
	Alan Keyes	September 20, 1999	June 17, 1999	August 20, 1999
	John McCain	September 27, 1999	January 7, 1999	December 30, 1998
	Elizabeth Dole	None	March 18, 1999	March 10, 1999
2008	Sam Brownback	January 20, 2007	December 4, 2006	December 19, 2006
	Duncan Hunter	January 25, 2007	January 12, 2007	January 23, 2007
	Mike Huckabee	January 28, 2007	January 29, 2007	January 29, 2007
	Mitt Romney	February 13, 2007	January 3, 2007	January 3, 2007
2008	Rudy Giuliani	February 14, 2007	November 20, 2006	February 5, 2007
	Ron Paul	March 12, 2007	March 12, 2007	March 12, 2007
	Tommy Thompson	April 1, 2007	December 13, 2006	January 11, 2007
	Tom Tancredo	April 2, 2007	January 22, 2007	April 13, 2007
	John McCain	April 25, 2007	November 16, 2006	November 16, 2006
	Fred Thompson	September 5, 2007	September 7, 2007	September 6, 2007
	Alan Keyes	September 17, 2007	September 13, 2007	September 14, 2007

Source: Formal announcement dates are generally taken from the New York Times and Facts on File. All data on FEC filing dates are based on the actual forms, available at www.fec.gov.

Table A.2. National Polls Standings during the Invisible Primary Period, 1980–2008

As nomination campaigns have grown longer, more attention has, not surprisingly, been focused on the period *before* the start of the primary and caucus season. Often referred to as the "invisible primary," it has often been argued—with and without evidence—that the candidates' success in using this period to define the major themes of their campaign, raise money, and set up an effective organization in states such as Iowa and New Hampshire has a major effect on how they will fare in the real primaries and, thus, on who finally wins the nomination. But how exactly does one measure a candidate's "success" during the invisible primary, when no actual delegates are being selected?

The most commonly used measure is the candidates' relative standing in polls of the national party electorate. For at least a year before the first caucus and primary, pollsters ask national samples of Democratic and Republican identifiers whom they would like to have their party nominate as its next presidential candidate. Table A.2 shows the Gallup Poll's results from four (approximate) time points during the invisible primary: early in the year preceding the election, in mid-summer, in the fall, and the final poll before the beginning of delegate selection. In most years, the candidate leading the polls at the end of the invisible primary went on to win the nomination—though that was conspicuously not the case in each of the last three contested nomination races.

Race and Candidate				
1980 Democrats	*Feb. 23–26 1979*	*July 13–16 1979*	*Sept. 28– Oct. 1, 1979*	*Jan. 4–7 1980*
Jimmy Carter	28	30	27	51
Edward Kennedy	60	66	59	37
1980 Republicans	*Feb. 2–5 1979*	*July 13–16 1979*	*Nov. 2–5 1979*	*Jan. 4–7 1980*
Ronald Reagan	43	41	41	41
John Connally	16	14	13	13
Howard Baker	9	16	18	14
George H.W. Bush	2	*	2	9
Robert Dole	3	6	3	*
John Anderson	3	3	*	4
Philip Crane	2	2	*	*
1984 Democrats	*March 11–14 1983*	*July 22–25 1983*	*Sept. 9–12 1983*	*Feb. 10–13 1984*
Walter Mondale	32	41	34	49
John Glenn	13	25	23	13

(continued)

Race and Candidate (*continued*)

1984 Democrats	*March 11–14 1983*	*July 22–25 1983*	*Sept. 9–12 1983*	*Feb. 10–13 1984*
Alan Cranston	3	7	5	3
Gary Hart	2	4	3	3
Reubin Askew	2	2	3	2
Ernest Hollings	1	2	1	1
George McGovern	4	--	8	5
Jesse Jackson	--	--	8	13

1988 Democrats	*April 10–13 1987*	*July 10–13 1987*	*Oct. 23–26 1987*	*Jan. 22–24 1988*
Gary Hart	46	--	--	23
Jesse Jackson	18	17	22	15
Michael Dukakis	4	13	14	16
Richard Gephardt	3	3	5	9
Bruce Babbitt	2	2	1	4
Al Gore	2	8	7	6
Paul Simon	--	7	8	9

1988 Republicans	*April 10–13 1987*	*July 10–13 1987*	*Oct. 23–26 1987*	*Jan. 22–24 1988*
George H.W. Bush	34	40	47	45
Robert Dole	18	18	22	30
Jack Kemp	9	10	4	5
Al Haig	7	7	4	2
Pat Robertson	4	5	7	8
Pierre du Pont	2	3	1	2

1992 Democrats	*August 23–25 1991*	*Oct. 31–Nov. 3 1991*	*Jan. 31–Feb. 2 1992*
Mario Cuomo	22	--	--
Jesse Jackson	18	--	--
Lloyd Bentsen	12	--	--
Bill Clinton	5	9	42
Douglas Wilder	3	12	--
Paul Tsongas	4	7	9
Jerry Brown	6	21	16
Tom Harkin	4	10	9
Bob Kerrey	--	10	10

1992 Republicans	*Dec. 5–8 1991*	*Jan. 31–Feb. 2 1992*
George Bush	86	84
David Duke	6	4
Pat Buchanan	5	11

Race and Candidate (*continued*)

1996 Republicans	*April 5–6 1995*	*July 7–9 1995*	*Sept. 22–24 1995*	*Jan. 5–7 1996*
Robert Dole	46	49	46	47
Phil Gramm	13	7	10	10
Pat Buchanan	8	6	9	7
Lamar Alexander	3	4	2	2
Richard Lugar	5	3	2	5
Steve Forbes	--	--	--	11

2000 Democrats	*April 13–14 1999*	*June 25–27 1999*	*Oct. 21–24 1999*	*Jan. 17–19 2000*
Al Gore	54	64	57	60
Bill Bradley	34	28	32	27

2000 Republicans	*Jan. 8–10 1999*	*June 25–27 1999*	*Oct. 21–24 1999*	*Jan. 17–19 2000*
George W. Bush	42	59	68	63
Elizabeth Dole	22	8	--	--
John McCain	8	5	11	19
Dan Quayle	6	6	--	--
Steve Forbes	5	6	8	6
Gary Bauer	2	2	1	2
Orrin Hatch	--	2	3	1

2004 Democrats	*Jan. 10–12 2003*	*July 25–27 2003*	*October 6–8 2003*	*January 9–11 2004*
Joseph Lieberman	19	20	13	8
John Kerry	16	16	12	9
Richard Gephardt	13	14	8	7
John Edwards	12	6	3	6
Bob Graham	7	5	--	--
Howard Dean	4	10	15	25
Al Sharpton	4	5	5	4
Carol Moseley Braun	--	6	4	5
Dennis Kucinich	--	2	2	2
Wesley Clark	--	--	20	19

2008 Democrats	*Feb. 9–11 2007*	*July 6–8 2007*	*Nov. 2–4 2007*	*Dec. 14–16 2007*
Hillary Clinton	40	37	43	45
Barack Obama	21	21	18	27
John Edwards	13	13	14	15
Al Gore	14	16	14	--
Joseph Biden	1	3	1	3
Bill Richardson	4	2	3	2

(continued)

Race and Candidate (*continued*)

2008 Democrats	*Feb. 9–11 2007*	*July 6–8 2007*	*Nov. 2–4 2007*	*Dec. 14–16 2007*
Christopher Dodd	1	*	1	--
Dennis Kucinich	*	2	1	2

2008 Republicans	*Feb. 9–11 2007*	*July 6–8 2007*	*Nov. 2–4 2007*	*Dec. 14–16 2007*
Rudy Giuliani	40	30	34	27
John McCain	24	16	18	14
Newt Gingrich	9	6	--	--
Mitt Romney	5	9	14	14
Mike Huckabee	2	2	6	16
Fred Thompson	--	20	17	14
Ron Paul	--	*	1	3

Source: All results are taken from the Gallup Poll
"--" indicates that candidate's name was not included in the list read to respondents.
"*" indicates that the candidate received less than one-half of 1 percent of the vote.

Table A.3. Effect of Iowa and New Hampshire on the Presidential Nomination Preferences of National Party Identifiers, 1980–2008

Not all primaries and caucuses are created equal. By almost every relevant measure—attention from the candidates and the media, campaign spending, and effect on the final outcome—the Iowa caucuses and the New Hampshire primary, traditionally the first two events that actually led to the selection of real convention delegates, matter far more than states that are much larger and have many more delegates at stake. A win or just a "better-than-expected" showing in one or both of these states can catapult a candidate from obscurity to front-runner in a remarkably short span of time. This process by which early primary results affect the vote in later primaries also has a name: it is called *momentum.*

Table A.3 shows one way to quantify *part* of Iowa and New Hampshire's impact: their effect on the national polls of party identifiers shown in the previous table. On the eve of the 2008 Iowa caucuses, for example, John McCain was the preferred presidential candidate of just 14 percent of the nation's Republicans, putting him well behind the front-running Rudy Giuliani. Less than two weeks later, after winning the New Hampshire primary, McCain saw his support in the national polls jump by 19 percentage points, vaulting him into first place.

Race and Candidate	*Last Poll before Iowa*	*Poll(s) between Iowa and New Hampshire*		*First Poll after New Hampshire*	*Total Change*
1980 Democrats[a]					
Carter	51	63	61	66	+15
Kennedy	37	29	32	27	–10
1980 Republicans[a]					
Reagan	41	32	47	55	+14
Baker	14	8	8	9	–5
Connally	13	11	8	3	–10
Bush	9	32	25	25	+16
1984 Democrats					
Mondale	43	57		31	–12
Glenn	16	7		7	–9
Jackson	12	8		7	–5
Hart	1	7		38	+37
1988 Democrats					
Hart	17	9		7	–10
Dukakis	13	16		22	+9
Jackson	13	12		14	+1
Gephardt	9	20		13	+4
1988 Republicans					
Bush	43	38		39	–4
Dole	24	32		30	+6
Robertson	6	10		7	+1
Kemp	4	5		5	v+1
1992 Democrats					
Clinton	42	na		41	–1
Brown	16	na		7	–9
Kerrey	10	na		6	–4
Tsongas	9	na		31	+22
1992 Republicans					
Bush	84	na		78	–6
Buchanan	11	na		20	+9
Duke	4	na		*	–4

(continued)

Race and Candidate	Last Poll before Iowa	Poll(s) between Iowa and New Hampshire	First Poll after New Hampshire	Total Change
1996 Republicans				
Dole	47	na	41	–6
Forbes	16	na	8	–8
Buchanan	7	na	27	+20
Alexander	3	na	14	+11
2000 Democrats				
Gore	60	67	65	+5
Bradley	27	21	24	–3
2000 Republicans				
Bush	63	65	56	–7
McCain	19	15	34	+15
Forbes	6	7	2	–4
2004 Democrats				
Dean	25	na	14	–11
Clark	19	na	9	–10
Kerry	9	na	49	+40
Lieberman	8	na	5	–3
Edwards	6	na	13	+7
2008 Democrats				
Clinton	45	33	45	0
Obama	27	33	33	+6
Edwards	15	20	13	–2
2008 Republicans				
Giuliani	27	20	13	–14
Huckabee	16	25	19	+3
McCain	14	19	33	+19
Thompson	14	12	9	–5
Romney	14	9	11	–3

[a] In 1980, there were 36 days between Iowa and New Hamsphire. From 1984 through 2004, there were 8 days between the two events. In 2008, the two events were separated by just 5 days.

Table A.4. Withdrawal Dates for Major Presidential Candidates, 1952–2008

If contemporary nomination campaigns begin early, for most candidates they also end quite early. And this, too, is a distinctive feature of the post-1972 nomination process. In the 1950s and 1960s, candidates who got into the race generally stayed in the race—at least to the end of the primary season, usually all the way to the convention. In 1976, however, presidential races began to march to a different rhythm. As shown in Table A.4, candidates were withdrawing from the race just days after the first delegates were selected. For many contemporary candidates, Iowa and New Hampshire weren't just the first inning; they were the entire ball game.

A. Democratic Candidates

Year	*Candidate*	*Withdrawal Date*	*Number of Days after the Date of the First Primary*[a]
1952	Alben Barkley	July 21	132
	Averell Harriman	July 25	136
	Estes Kefauver	None	137
	Richard Russell	None	137
	Robert Kerr	None	137
1956	Estes Kefauver	July 31	140
	Averell Harriman	None	156
1960	Hubert Humphrey	May 10	63
	Lyndon Johnson	None	127
	Stuart Symington	None	127
1964	George Wallace	July 19	131
1968	Lyndon Johnson	March 31	19
	Eugene McCarthy	None	169
	George McGovern	None	169
1972	John Lindsay	April 4	28
	Edmund Muskie	April 27	51
	Henry Jackson	May 2	56
	Hubert Humphrey	July 11	126
	Eugene McCarthy	July 12	127
	George Wallace	None	127
	Terry Sanford	None	127
	Shirley Chisholm	None	127
1976	Birch Bayh	March 4	9
	Milton Shapp	March 12	17
	Sargent Shriver	March 16	21
	Fred Harris	April 8	44
	Henry Jackson	May 1	67

(continued)

A. Democratic Candidates (*continued*)

Year	*Candidate*	*Withdrawal Date*	*Number of Days after the Date of the First Primary*[a]
1976	George Wallace	June 9	106
	Morris Udall	June 14	111
	Frank Church	June 14	111
	Jerry Brown	None	141
1980	Jerry Brown	April 1	35
	Edward Kennedy	August 11	167
1984	Alan Cranston	February 29	1
	Reubin Askew	March 1	2
	Ernest Hollings	March 1	2
	George McGovern	March 14	15
	John Glenn	March 16	17
	Gary Hart	None	141
	Jesse Jackson	None	141
1988	Bruce Babbitt	February 18	2
	Gary Hart	March 11	24
	Richard Gephardt	March 28	41
	Paul Simon	April 7	51
	Al Gore	April 22	65
	Jesse Jackson	None	155
1992	Bob Kerrey	March 5	16
	Tom Harkin	March 9	20
	Paul Tsongas	March 19	30
	Jerry Brown	None	148
2000	Bill Bradley	March 9	37
2004	Richard Gephardt	January 20	–7
	Joe Lieberman	February 3	7
	Wesley Clark	February 10	14
	Howard Dean	February 18	22
	John Edwards	March 3	36
	Al Sharpton	March 15	48
	Dennis Kucinich	July 22	177
2008	Joseph Biden	January 3	–5
	Christopher Dodd	January 3	–5
	Bill Richardson	January 10	2
	Dennis Kucinich	January 24	16
	John Edwards	January 30	22
	Mike Gravel	March 26	78
	Hillary Clinton	June 7	151

(continued)

B. Republican Candidates

Year	*Candidate*	*Withdrawal Date*	*Number fo Days after the Date of the First Primary*[a]
1952	Robert Taft	None	122
	Earl Warren	None	122
	Harold Stassen	None	122
1964	Nelson Rockefeller	June 15	97
	Margaret C. Smith	None	127
	William Scranton	None	127
1968	Ronald Reagan	None	149
	Nelson Rockefeller	None	149
1976	Ronald Reagan	None	177
1980	Howard Baker	March 5	8
	John Connally	March 9	12
	Robert Dole	March 15	18
	Philip Crane	April 17	51
	John Anderson	April 24	58
	George Bush	May 26	90
1988	Alexander Haig	February 12	–4
	Pierre du Pont	February 18	2
	Jack Kemp	March 10	23
	Robert Dole	March 29	42
	Pat Robertson	April 6	50
1992	Patrick Buchanan	August 17	181
1996	Phil Gramm	February 14	–6
	Lamar Alexander	March 6	15
	Richard Lugar	March 6	15
	Steve Forbes	March 14	23
	Patrick Buchanan	None	176
2000	Orrin Hatch	January 26	–6
	Gary Bauer	February 4	3
	Steve Forbes	February 10	9
	John McCain	March 9	37
	Alan Keyes	July 25	175
2008	Duncan Hunter	January 19	11
	Fred Thompson	January 22	14
	Rudy Giuliani	January 30	22
	Mitt Romney	February 7	30
	Mike Huckabee	March 4	56
	Alan Keyes	April 15	98
	Ron Paul	June 12	156

Note: Table does not include candidates who dropped out before the start of the delegate selection season.

[a]For candidates who did not withdraw, figure is the number of days between the first primary and the party's final presidential roll call vote.

Table A.5. Dates on Which Presidential Candidates in Contested Nomination Races Clinched Their Party's Nomination, 1972–2008

In the 1950s and 1960s, national conventions still were an important component of the presidential nomination process. Though most of the nominees-to-be came into the convention with a clear lead over their rivals, it was generally at the convention that the final deals were struck and the last, crucial delegate votes were added to the winning coalition. In the early years of the post-reform nomination process, as shown in Table A.5, one candidate usually clinched the nomination by winning a majority of the delegates available in the primaries and caucuses, but this milestone was not reached until late May or early June, after the primary season had been completed. But as the delegate selection calendar became more *front-loaded*—as more and more states sought to schedule their primaries and caucuses as soon after Iowa and New Hampshire as was feasible—it soon became possible, even likely, that one candidate would clinch the nomination by the middle of March. Of the last five contested nomination races, only the Obama-Clinton battle of 2008 lasted until June.

Year	*Date When Eventual Nominee Clinched His Party's Nomination*	*Opening Day of the National Convention*
Democratic Party		
1972	July 11	July 10
1976	June 24	July 12
1980	June 3	August 11
1984	June 6	July 16
1988	June 7	July 18
1992	June 2	July 13
2000	March 14	August 14
2004	March 12	July 26
2008	June 3	August 25
Republican Party		
1976	August 16	August 16
1980	May 24	July 14
1988	April 26	August 15
1992	May 5	August 17
1996	March 26	August 12
2000	March 14	July 31
2008	March 4	September 1

Note: Date shown is the day on which the eventual nominee won enough pledged delegates to guarantee a first-ballot convention victory.

Source: 1976 and 2004 Democratic dates based on unpublished data from the Associated Press. All other dates are based on contemporary reports in the *New York Times* and *Congressional Quarterly Weekly Report*.

Table A.6. Number of Presidential Primaries That Were Used to Select or Bind Delegates, 1952–2008

One way that the contemporary presidential nomination process differs from those that went before it is a huge increase in the number of presidential primaries. Though everyone agrees on this point, it is surprisingly difficult to get an accurate count on the number of meaningful presidential primaries. In constructing Table A.6, our criterion has been to count only those primaries that were actually used to select or bind national convention delegates. That means, on the one hand, that we exclude primaries that were purely advisory: that had no effect on delegate selection. On the other hand, we do count primaries—they were quite common in the so-called mixed system that existed between 1912 and 1968—that elected delegates but did not include a presidential preference vote. (Such primaries are never mentioned in many standard reference sources on presidential elections.) We also count only *state* primaries: i.e., we exclude presidential primaries held in such places as Puerto Rico and American Samoa.

Year	*Number of Democratic Primaries*	*Number of Republican Primaries*
1952	18	14
1956	20	19
1960	18	16
1964	18	17
1968	17	16
1972	23	23
1976	29	28
1980	30	33
1984	24	28
1988	33	34
1992	35	38
1996	34	41
2000	37	42
2004	35	30
2008	38	38

Source: Compiled by the authors after a detailed review of state delegate selection procedures.
Note: Table includes all state primaries that were to select or bind national convention delegates. That is, it includes some states that selected delegates by primary even though they did not hold a presidential preference poll; but excludes (a) purely advisory primaries; and (b) primaries held in territories.

Table A.7. FEC Contribution and Spending Limits for the Presidential Nomination Process, 1976–2012

The rules and regularities that govern the raising and spending of money in presidential nomination campaigns are amply discussed in Chapter 3 of this book. This table simply reports two important features of federal law: the individual contribution limits (the maximum amount of money one person can contribute to a presidential candidate during the nomination campaign); and the spending limits (the maximum amount of money that a candidate who accepts federal matching funds can spend during the prenomination phase of a presidential campaign). As will be noted, the contribution limit was not indexed to inflation until the passage of the Bipartisan Campaign Reform Act in 2002; the spending limits, by contrast, have always been adjusted every four years to reflect changes in the cost of living.

Year	*Individual Contribution Limit*	*Spending Limit*[a]	*Fund-Raising Allowance*[a]	*Total*[a]
1976	$1,000	10.9	2.2	13.1
1980	$1,000	14.7	2.9	17.7
1984	$1,000	20.2	4.0	24.2
1988	$1,000	23.1	4.6	27.7
1992	$1,000	27.6	5.5	33.1
1996	$1,000	30.9	6.2	37.1
2000	$1,000	33.8	6.8	40.5
2004	$2,000	37.3	7.5	44.8
2008	$2,300	42.0	8.4	50.5
2012 (est.)[b]	$2,500	44.2	8.8	53.1

[a]In millions of dollars. Note that these limits apply only to candidates who accept federal matching funds.
[b]Spending limits for 2012 are an FEC estimate of what limits would apply "if the election were held in 2011."
Source: Federal Election Commission.

Table A.8. Superdelegates at the Democratic National Convention, 1984–2012

As many voters learned for the first time in 2008, there is a class of delegates in the Democratic Party who are *not* selected by ordinary voters in primaries and caucuses. Since 1984, about one-sixth of the votes at Democratic National Conventions have been cast by various kinds of party and elected officials who become delegates ex-officio—i.e., by virtue of the offices they hold. Known as "unpledged party leaders and elected officials" in the Democratic rules, these automatic delegates are more popularly known as superdelegates. For those interested in this phenomenon, Table A.8 provides information on the number of superdelegates in every Democratic convention since 1984 and a preliminary estimate of their presence at the 2012 convention.

Year	*Number of Superdelegates*	*Total Number of Delegates*	*Superdelegates as a Percentage of All Delegates*
1984	568	3,933	14.4
1988	645	4,162	15.5
1992	772	4,288	18.0
1996	777	4,298	18.1
2000	802	4,399	18.5
2004	802	4,322	18.6
2008	853	4,419	19.3
2012 (est.)	721	5,077	14.2

Source: Based on delegate allocation data provided by the Democratic National Committee. 2012 figures are as of December 15, 2010, and may change somewhat before the opening of the national convention.

Table A.9. Factors Affecting the Vote in the 2008 Democratic Primaries

Superdelegates notwithstanding, modern-day presidential nominations are won and lost in the primaries. Why one candidate succeeds with the voters and others are less successful is, of course, a complicated question. While this table does not provide a full answer, it does show some of the major factors that influenced (or were thought to influence) the vote in the 2008 Democratic primaries. After each major primary in 2008, the National Election Pool conducted an exit poll of voters leaving a random sample of precincts. To construct Table A.9, we have taken the results from 34 separate exit polls and weighted them by turnout. The result shows how various demographic and political groups voted in the primaries as a whole, treating each state as, in effect, one component of a national election survey.

Percentage of total primary vote		Clinton	Obama	(N of states for which data are available)
	GENDER			
43	Men	43	52	(34)
57	Women	52	45	(34)
	AGE			
15	18–29	37	60	(33)
25	30–44	42	55	(33)
33	45–59	50	47	(33)
27	60 and older	58	38	(33)
	RACE			
65	White	56	40	(34)
19	African-American	14	85	(25)
12	Latino	64	34	(10)
2	Asian	na	na	
2	Other	na	na	
	EDUCATION			
25	High school graduate or less	56	40	(34)
29	Some college	49	48	(34)
24	College graduate	43	53	(34)
21	Postgraduate education	44	54	(34)
	UNION MEMBER IN HOUSEHOLD			
30	Yes	51	45	(26)
70	No	48	49	(26)
	PARTY IDENTIFICATION			
75	Democrat	51	47	(34)
20	Independent	40	54	(34)
5	Republican	na	na	(34)
	IDEOLOGY			
46	Liberal	47	51	(34)
40	Moderate	50	47	(34)
14	Conservative	48	45	(31)

Source: Compiled by the authors based on data from the National Election Pool exit polls conducted after thirty-four Democratic primaries between January 8 and June 3, 2008. Data are not available in some states either because the question was not asked in those states' exit polls or because the number of respondents in that group was too small to permit reliable estimation.

Table A.10. Factors Affecting the Vote in the 2008 Republican Primaries

This table provides similar data on the 2008 Republican primaries, except that it uses data only from those primaries held up through March 4. On that day, John McCain clinched the Republican nomination and his last major opponent, Mike Huckabee, withdrew from the race. Primaries held after that date were essentially uncontested and obviously do not explain why McCain won the nomination.

Percentage of total primary vote		*Huckabee*	*McCain*	*Paul*	*Romney*	*(N of states for which data are available)*
	GENDER					
53	Men	21	43	6	25	(24)
47	Women	24	41	3	25	(24)
	AGE					
11	18–29	30	34	v9	22	(23)
22	30–44	26	39	5	24	(23)
33	45–59	23	42	4	25	(23)
34	60 and older	17	47	3	27	(23)
	EDUCATION					
19	High school graduate or less	25	44	4	20	(24)
32	Some college	23	40	5	25	(24)
29	College graduate	21	41	5	28	(24)
20	Postgraduate education	20	44	4	26	(24)
	CHURCH ATTENDANCE					
54	Weekly	27	33	3	30	(14)
35	Occasionally	8	47	4	33	(14)
10	Never	6	44	9	30	(14)
	EVER SERVED IN U.S. MILITARY?					
22	Yes	18	47	5	25	(23)
78	No	23	41	4	25	(23)

(continued)

Percentage of total primary vote		Huckabee	McCain	Paul	Romney	(N of states for which data are available)
	PARTY IDENTIFICATION					
76	Republican	23	42	3	26	(24)
20	Independent	19	43	11	21	(24)
3	Democrat	na	na	na	na	(24)
	IDEOLOGY					
10	Liberal	13	55	7	16	(19)
27	Moderate	13	53	6	20	(19)
63	Conservative	25	33	4	32	(19)
	MORE IMPORTANT IN DETERMINING VOTE					
54	Issues	23	30	7	35	(19)
44	Personal qualities	14	49	2	28	(19)

Source: Compiled by the authors based on data from the National Election Pool exit polls conducted after the first twenty-four Republican primaries, January 8 - March 4, 2008. McCain clinched the Republican nomination on the night of March 4. Data are not available in some states either because the question was not ask in those states' exit polls or because the number of respondents in some subgroups was too small to permit reliable estimation.

Table A.11 A Few Relevant Facts about the National Conventions

National nominating conventions, once one of the great spectacles in all of American politics, have now become mere formalities, that simply ratify a result already reached in the primaries and caucuses. Still, conventions are a part of the process, and though they do not actually make nominations in any meaningful sense, they do serve a number of other functions: writing the platform, helping to unify the parties, and giving the presidential and vice presidential candidates the opportunity to address a national television audience. Table A.11 provides three pieces of information about the national conventions since 1952: their location, dates, and the number of delegates in attendance.

Year	*Location*	*Dates*	*Number of Delegates*
DEMOCRATS			
1952	Chicago	July 21–26	1230
1956	Chicago	August 13–17	1372
1960	Los Angeles	July 11–15	1521
1964	Atlantic City	August 24–27	2316
1968	Chicago	August 26–29	2622
1972	Miami Beach	July 10–13	3016
1976	New York	July 12–15	3008
1980	New York	August 11–14	3331
1984	San Francisco	July 16–19	3933
1988	Atlanta	July 18–21	4161
1992	New York	July 13–16	4288
1996	Chicago	August 26–29	4289
2000	Los Angeles	August 14–17	4339
2004	Boston	July 26–29	4322
2008	Denver	August 25–28	4419
2012	Charlotte, NC	September 3–6	TBD
REPUBLICANS			
1952	Chicago	July 7–11	1206
1956	San Francisco	August 20–23	1323
1960	Chicago	July 25–28	1331
1964	San Francisco	July 13–16	1308
1968	Miami Beach	August 5–8	1333
1972	Miami Beach	August 21–23	1348
1976	Kansas City, MO	August 16–19	2259
1980	Detroit	July 14–17	1994
1984	Dallas	August 20–23	2235
1988	New Orleans	August 15–18	2277
1992	Houston	August 17–20	2210
1996	San Diego	August 12–15	1990
2000	Philadelphia	July 31–August 3	2066
2004	New York	August 30–September 2	2509
2008	St. Paul, MN	September 1–4	2380
2012	Tampa	August 27–30	TBD

"TBD": Final size of the 2012 conventions is still to be determined

Index

abortion issues, 67–68; Tea Party and, 75
ADA. *See* Americans for Democratic Action
Adams, Charles Francis, 61
Adams, John, 170–71, 172, 174–75, 183, 197n38, 201n78; electoral votes, 186–89
Adkins, Randall E., 2; forecast model by, 7; momentum model, 8
advertising, 128; broadcast, 40; Facebook, 122; Internet, 38, 122
Albright, Madeleine, 98
American Crossroads, 51
American Exceptionalism, 76
American Liberty Alliance, 71
American National Election Studies project, 115, *116*, *117*, *118*, *119*
American Policy Summit, 85
Americans for Democratic Action (ADA), 65
American Solutions for Winning, 71
Angell, Roger, 203
anticommunists, 64
Antifederalists, 172–73, 176, 190–92; Adams, J., and, 186; electioneering efforts, 179; in Maryland, 178–80; in Pennsylvania, 180–83; vice presidency and, 173, 177; in Virginia, 183–85
anti-Vietnam war movement, 64–65
AOL, 122
Armey, Richard, 71
Articles of Confederation Congress, 165
attack campaign, 104–5, 123; Defense Department to counter, 105
attendant complications, 124–29
Australian ballot, 198n51

Bachmann, Michelle, 84
Bailey, Doug, 109
bailout bill, 69–70
Baldwin, Abraham, 163
Bassik, Michael, 128
BCRA. *See* Bipartisan Campaign Reform Act of 2002
Beck, Glenn, 70, 78
Beeman, Richard R., 196n29
Bentsen, Lloyd, 102
Biden, Joseph, 138, 155n17; fund-raising, 29
Bill of Rights, 172
Bipartisan Campaign Reform Act of 2002 (BCRA), 15, 25, 220
Black Congressional Caucus, 77
Bradley, Bill, 144–45, 148–49, 204

Breitbart, Andrew, 77
bridge period, 25–26, 50
broadband, 31
broadcast advertising, 40
Brountas, Paul, 102
Brown, Scott, 79
Bryan, William Jennings, 62
Buchanan, Pat, 139; news coverage and tone, 146
Buckley, William F., 64, 86
bundlers, 43–45
Bush, George H. W., 102, 126; news coverage and tone, 146
Bush, George W., 39, 69–70; closed primaries, 14; fund-raising, 23, 24, 52n2; Internet and, 30; matching funds denial, 26; news coverage and tone, 142, 146, 149
bus tours, 104

campaign, 15–17; communication activities and citizen participation, 115; first presidential, 169; fund-raising, 2008, 32–34; Internet-savvy, 114; management, 124, 127–28; mistakes in, 105; nomination forecasting and, 15–17; preprimary, 4–5; resources, 128; staff, 18; staff building, 98; strategic elements, 18. *See also* discourse, presidential campaign; nomination campaigns; *specific candidates*
candidates: announcement dates for major, 1952–2008, *204–208*, 211; answers, 124–29; Dukakis, M., experience, 93–106; establishment-backed, 139; family of, 94–95; health of, 94; individual donor sources for 2008, *44*; news coverage fairness in amount and tone of, 139–46; nomination clinched by, 1972–2008, 218, *218*; in 1788–1789 elections, 167–70, *168*, 193; Tea Party-supported, 79; viability, 141; withdrawal dates for major, *215–17*. *See also* Democratic candidates; Republican candidates; vice presidential candidates, 1788–1789; *specific candidates and political parties*
candidate field: nature and size of, 16–17; 2008, 29
Cannon, Lou, 59
Carender, Keli, 70
Carrington, Edward, 176
Carter, Jimmy, 13
cash reserves, 2
categories, densification of, 123–24
caucuses, 12, 17–18, 77, 84; schedule of, 2008, 28; state rules, 14. *See also* Iowa caucuses
"Chief Magistrate of the United States" (Hamilton), 162
Christian Coalition, 67
Christian right. *See* Religious Right
citizen participation, 128; campaign communication activities and, 115; Internet and, 115; news consumption and, 114; questions, 124–29; Tea Party and, 72
Citizens United v. Federal Election Commission, 50
Clark, Wesley, 144
Cleveland, Grover, 62
Clinton, Bill, 13, 103, 126, 139; bundlers and, 45; Internet and, 30; news coverage and tone, 144; TV question-and-answer sessions, 104
Clinton, George, 172, 176–77, 183, 186, 190, 192
Clinton, Hillary, 155n19; broadcast advertising, 40; campaign fund-raising, 2008, 29, 32; early fund-raising, 35; Internet fund-raising, 39, 40–41; large donors and, 43; matching funds denial, 27; news coverage and tone, 141, 143, 148–49; nomination race, 2008, 15; Obama's race against, 34, 40, 137, 218; in polls, 2008, 2; primary vote, 2008, 8

closed primaries, 14
coalitions, 108
coding systems, 134
Cohen, Marty, 2; forecasting model, 7
Commission on Presidential Debates, 126
Committee of Eleven, 164
communications: activities and citizen participation, 115; balanced, 120; contact techniques, 122; costs, 57n82; democratic, 130; election, 50–51; electioneering, 57n82; forms of, 114–15; infrastructure, 32. *See also* discourse, presidential campaign; *specific technologies for communication*
competitive elections, 28–29
Concerned Democrats, 65
Congress, 51, 75–76, 105; financial crisis, 2008, 69–70; response to financial abuses in 1972 election, 25; 1788–1789, 159, 161, 165, 172, 173, 182, 184; Tea Party and, 77–80, 83–84
Connally, John, 53n10
Conservatives, 63–64
Constitution: Article II, Section I, 159–60, 161–65, 170, 186; Article VII, 165; presidential selection process and, 160–61. *See also* Framers of the Constitution
Constitutional Convention, 159, 162, 163
contact techniques, 122
content management, 107
conventions: nomination, 225, *225*; state rules at, 14
corporation, 50–51; fund-raising, 51, 57n82
Corrigan, Jack, 101
Courser, Zachary, 85
Coxe, Tench, 188
Crane, Philip, 211
cross-listing, 62
Crossroads GPS, 51
Crotty, William J., 66
cultural traditionalists, 64
Cuomo, Mario, 8

Dean, Howard, 138, 151, 152, 158n64; fund-raising, 24, 46; Internet and, 30; matching funds denial, 26; news coverage and tone, 142, 144
debate, town hall meeting style, 126
Defense Department, 105
Delaware electors, 1788–1789, 183, 201n78
delegate selection and primaries, 218, *218*
Democratic Party: debate, 126; early fund-raising and, 34–35; matching funds denials, 26; money and, 45–46; spending, 50; 2008, 28
Democratic candidates: announcement dates for major, 1952–2008, 203, *204–8*; primary season news coverage for, 142–45, *143*; withdrawal dates for major, 215, *215–17*
Democratic Federation, 63
Democratic National Committee, 48
Democratic National Conventions, 221; superdelegates at, 1984–2010, *221*
Democratic nomination: race, *3*; rules, 66, 69; 2008, 29
Democratic primaries: cash reserves and, 7; factors affecting vote in, 2008, 221, *222*, *224*; poll standings and, 7
demographic characteristics, of voters, 11
densification, 107; of categories, 123–24; enhancement of, 110; five dimensions of discourse, 110–24; of places, 121–22; prolongation and, 123; of remarks and messages, 115, 120–21; of time, 122–23; of voices, 114–15
Digital Campaign Director, 129
digitally stored information, 123

discourse, presidential campaign, 120–21; judging quality of, 129–31; progression of, 108–10
discourse densification: campaign management and, 124, 127–28; five dimensions of, 110–24
discourse moments, 121
Dissenting Democrats, 65
Dodd, Chris, 138, 155n17
Dole, Robert, 26; news coverage and tone, 146
Dornan, Robert, 53n10, 156n43; news coverage and tone, 146
Dowdle, Andrew J., 2; forecast model by, 7; momentum model, 8
dual-vote system, 164–65, 186, 192–93
Dukakis, Andrea, 96
Dukakis, John, 95
Dukakis, Kara, 95–96
Dukakis, Kitty, 95, 100
Dukakis, Michael S., 154n6; experience of running for president, 93–106
Dump Johnson effort, 65
Duncanson, James, 184, 185

economic conservatives, 64
economic forecasts, 2
economic indicators, 10–11
Edwards, John: fund-raising, 27, 29; news coverage and tone, 141, 143, 144, 148–49
Eisenhower, Dwight, 125
"Eisenhower Answers America," 125
elected officials, endorsements by, 7
election, presidential, 1788–1789, 159–94, *168*, *188*
Election Day, 16
electioneering, 27; communications, 57n82; Federalist and Antifederalist, 179; finance, 28, 50; group, 52
election forecasting, 2–4; for general elections, 16–17
election ordinance, 1788–1789, 166
electoral college, 1788–1789, 159
electoral constituencies, 108
electoral vote, 1789, 186–89, *188*
electors, 1788–1789, 177–85; decision-making process, 161–62, 189–91; in Delaware, 183; in Maryland, 178–80, 190; out of state, 202n84; in Pennsylvania, 180–83, 190; selection process of, 161, 165–66, *166–67*, 189; state legislatures to choose, 195n20; in Virginia, 183–85
elite endorsements, 2, 7, 139
e-mail, 36
Estrich, Susan, 100, 101
evangelicals, 67

Facebook, 31, 36, 109, 111; advertisements, 122
face-to-face "retail politics," 138
Falwell, Jerry, 67
Farmer, Bob, 101
Farmers' Alliances, 61
FEC. *See* Federal Election Commission
FECA. *See* Federal Election Campaign Act
federal courts, 160
Federal Election Campaign Act (FECA), 25
Federal Election Commission (FEC), 25, 52n1; contribution and spending limits for nomination process, 1976–2012, 220, *220*; filing with, 204
Federal Gazette, 190
Federalists, 172–73, 190–92; Adams, J., and, 186; correspondence, 169–70, 176; in Delaware, 183; electioneering efforts, 179; in Maryland, 178–80; in Pennsylvania, 180–83; vice presidency and, 177; in Virginia, 183–85
Federalist 68, 162
Feingold, Russ, BCRA and, 15
feminist movement, 68
fightthesmears.com, 123
financial crisis, 2008, 69–70
First Federal Elections project, 167–68, 193

Forbes, Malcolm "Steve," 53n10, 150–51
Ford, Gerald, 64
forecast models, 1, 2; by Adkins and Dowdle, 7; Mayer's, 20n13; predictive accuracy, 8–9; by Steger and Cohen, 7. *See also specific forecast models*
Fowler, Mayhill, 127, 131
Framers of the Constitution, 159; expectations, 161–65, 189–93
Franklin, Benjamin, 198n40
FreedomWorks, 78, 85
free media, 139
Free Soil movement, 60–61
Free Soil Party, 61
Frum, David, 81
fund-raising: allowance for nomination process, 1976–2012, *220*; campaign, 2008, 32–34; changing environment of, 24–32; corporation, 51, 57n82; early, 34–36; escalation, 15; grassroots, 38; Internet and, 16, 30, 36–42; labor union, 51, 57n82; national poll results and, *3*; nomination forecasting and, 2, *3*, 4, 24; nomination receipts and expenditures, 2008, *33*; nonprofit advocacy groups, 51; PAC, 51; political context, 27–29; prenomination, 52n1; primaries and, 7; public funding and, 25–27; Section 527 committee, 51; small donor, 39, 52; strength, 23; total, 2, *4*, 24; in 2012, 45–52; volunteer, 38; Web 2.0 and, 29–32. *See also* large donor fund-raising; Obama campaign fund-raising; individual donor fund-raising
fund-raising efforts: by Biden, 29; by Bush, G. W., 23, 24, 52n2; by Clinton, H., 29, 32, 35, 39, 40–41; by Dean, H., 24, 46; by Edwards, J., 27, 29; by Giuliani, 34, 46; by Huckabee, 46; by Kerry, 23, 24, 33–34, 52n2; by McCain, 32, 41–42, 46, 49; by Romney, 32, 36, 46
furlough program, 104–5
fusion tickets, 62

Game Change (Halperin & Heilemann), 110
gay marriage, Tea Party and, 75
Genachowski, Julius, 37
general election forecasts, 16–17
Georgia electors, 1788–1789, 201n78
Gephardt, Dick, 100
German Antifederalist ticket, 182–83
German Federalist ticket, 182–83
Germond, Jack, 96
Gerry, Elbridge, 164
Get-Out-The-Vote (GOTV), 16
Giffords, Gabrielle, 77, 90n67
Gingrich, Newt, 71, 84–85
Giuliani, Rudolph, 29, 36; fund-raising, 34, 46; news coverage and tone, 141, 146; in 2008 polls, 2
Gold Standard, 62
Goldwater, Barry M., 64
Goodwyn, Lawrence, 61
Google, 41, 109, 120, 124, 128
GOP. *See* Republican Party
Gore, Al, 101, 103, 148–49; matching funds, 26; news coverage and tone, 142
GOTV. *See* Get-Out-The-Vote
Gramm, Phil, 156n43
grassroots fund-raising, 38
grassroots organizing, 98
Great Recession, 69
Green, John, 47
Greenback movement, 61
Greenberger, Peter, 41
group electioneering, 52
gun rights, Tea Party and, 75

Halperin, Mark, 110
Hamilton, Alexander, 162, 175, 186–87, 188, 192, 197n39, 200n73

Hancock, John, 169, 174–75, 186, 192, 197n32
Hannity, Sean, 70
Harrisburg convention, 182–83, 199n61
Harvard University's Institute of Politics, 108
health care, 76; government takeover of, 70; reform protests, 78
Heilemann, John, 110
Henry, Patrick, 169–70, 177, 183, 196n29
Hillary: The Movie, 50
Hindman, Matthew, 115
Hofstadter, Richard, 195n12
horse-race coverage, 137–38, *138*, 154n13, 155n20
Horton, Willie, 104–5
The Hotline, 109
House of Representatives, 80; races, 81–82; 1788–1789, 159, 161, 163, 173, 179–84
Houstoun, William, 162
Huckabee, Mike, 13, 84–85, 226; fund-raising, 46; news coverage and tone, 141, 145–46, 150
Huffington Post, 127
Hughes, Chris, 37
Humphrey, Hubert, 65

illegal immigration, Tea Party and, 75
independent expenditure, 57n82; groups, 51
indexing terminology, 123, 128
individual donor fund-raising, 35, 57n82; limit for nomination process, 1976–2012, 220, *220*; source of, 2008, *44*
intercoder reliability, 134
interest groups, 2012, 50
Internet: advertising, 38, 122; applications, 31; campaign savvy with, 114; citizen participation and, 115; debate access and, 126; focused approach, 152; fund-raising and, 16, 30, 36–42; *Hotline* on, 109; news consumption on, 111, *112*; nomination campaigns use of, 15–16; political activities on, 114; services, 109; Tea Party and, 71
invisible primary, 4–5, 7, 214–15; national polls standings during, 1980–2008, *209–212*; poll results and fund-raising at end of, *3*
Iowa, 157n45, 212; Dukakis, M., in, 100; importance of, 151; momentum forecasts and, 12; nomination preferences of party identifiers and effects of, 1980–2008, *213–14*
Iowa caucuses, 8; impact, 212; as kingmaker, 13; losses, 13
pre-Iowa forecasting models, 8
Iran-Contra scandal, 94
issue coverage, 137–38

Jackson, Jesse, 101
Jay, John, 174, 192, 201n78
Johnson, Lyndon, 12–13, 64, 65
Johnson, Ron, 80

Kaplan, Marty, 100
Kennedy, Edward, 79, 139
Kennedy, John F., 108
Kennedy, Robert, 65
Kerry, John, 138, 156n38; fund-raising, 23, 24, 33–34, 52n2; Internet and, 30; matching funds denial, 26; news coverage and tone, 144; vote share, 2004, 13
Kingsbury, Diana, 47
Knox, Henry, 174, 175–76
Kremer, Amy, 84

labor union fund-raising, 51, 57n82
Lancaster ticket, 182–83
"Large C" constitutional concerns, 76
large donor fund-raising, 52; in 2008, 42–45
Lee, Arthur, 185, 200n68
Lee, Henry, 185
Lee, James, 90n67

Lincoln, Benjamin, 175–76
"The Living Room Candidate," 125
Loughner, Jared, 90n67
Lowenstein, Allard, 65
Lugar, Richard, 156n43

Madison, James, 162, 163, 164, 166, 175, 176, 184
Magleby, David, 25
Main, Jackson Turner, 195n12
The Making of the President 1960 (White, T.), 108
Malkin, Michelle, 70
"The Man in the Arena," 125–26
Mann, Horace, 99
"man on the street" format, 124–25
Martin, Jenny Beth, 83
Maryland electors, 1788–1789, 178–83, 190; voting results, *181*
Maryland Journal, 179
Mason, George, 163, 164
Massachusetts Miracle, 93
mass media, 133, 151. *See also specific media*
mass partisan support, 7
matching funds program, 15, 25, 220; forgoing, 26–27; recipients, 53n17. *See also* public funding program
Mayer, Henry, 196n29
Mayer, William G., 1–2, 6–7, 25; forecast model, 20n13
McCain, John, 29, 34, 134, 155n19, 212, 223; BCRA and, 15; bundlers and, 45; campaign fund-raising, 2008, 32; fund-raising, 46, 49; Internet fund-raising, 41–42; large donors and, 43; news coverage and tone, 141, 145–46, 149, 150; open primaries, 14; in 2008 polls, 2; vote share, 2008, 13
McCarthy, Eugene, 12–13, 65–66
McCormick, Richard, 195n20
McGovern, George, 13, 66
McKinley, William, 62, 63
McNeal, Ramona S., 115
Meckler, Mark, 84
message: development, 107, 125. *See also* remarks and messages, densification of
momentum, 8, 215; effects of, 13–14; forecasts, 12; nature of, 12
momentum model: Adkins and Dowdle, 8; 1980–2008, *9*
money primary, 139
Moral Majority, 67
Mossberger, Karen, 115
MSN, 122
My.BarackObama.com (MyBo), 37–38, 48
MySpace, 31, 36, 111

national conventions, 225, *225*, *227*
national poll results, fund-raising at end of invisible primary and, *3*
National Progressive Republican League, 63
National Tea Party Coalition, 71
New Deal liberalism, 63–64
New Democratic Coalition, 66
New Hampshire, 157n45, 217; importance of, 151; momentum forecasts and, 12; nomination preferences of party identifiers and effects of, 1980–2008, 212, *213–14, 216–17*
New Hampshire primary, 8, 138; impact, 215; as kingmaker, 13
New Jersey electors, 1788–1789, 201n78
New Left radicals, 65
New Politics, 64–67
news consumption, 111, *112*, 134; frequency, *113*; political participation and, 114
news coverage, 155n20; accelerators, 142; compensatory, 144–45; content, 134; fairness in amount and tone of candidates, 139–46, *147*, 148–50; international, 136, 154n9; issue coverage *versus* horse-race coverage,

137–38, *138*; key problems with mainstream, 133–34; nomination campaigns phases and, 134–35. *See also* preseason news coverage; primary season news coverage
newspaper, *112*
New York City Federal Republican Committee, 177
Nixon, Richard, 64, 66–67, 108, 125–26
nominations, 101; clinched by candidate, 1972–2008, 218, *218*; conventions, 226, *226*; Framers expectations for, 162–64, 191–92; by natural consensus, 163; 1980, 11–12; political movement and, 60–69; power in, 18; preferences of party identifiers and Iowa and New Hampshire, 1980–2008, 212, *213–14*; prior to 1972, 5; receipts and expenditures, 2008, *33*; running for, 106; in 1788–1789, 190–91; 2008, 27–29. *See also* Democratic nomination; Republican nominations
nomination campaigns, 212; Internet and, 15–16; lessons for, 149–50; news content and phases of, 134–35; start of, 211; uncertainty and, 17
nomination forecasting, 1–2, 4–9; campaigning and, 15–17; challenges of, 10; fund-raising and, 2, *3*, 4, 24; nominating structure and process and challenges of, 12–15; predicted order of finish of eventual nominee and, *6*; preprimary, 12; value of, 17–18; voter choice and, 10–12
nomination process: FEC contribution and spending limits for, 1976–2012, 220, *220*; statistical guide to, 203–25; structure and, 12–15; TV coverage of, 133–52
nomination races: possible predictors of, 2, *3*, 4; 2008, 15; 2012, 8, 86. *See also* open nomination races
non-front-runners, 150–52
nonparty political organizations, 49–52; 2012, 50. *See also specific organizations*
nonprofit advocacy groups, 49; fund-raising, 51
Noonan, Peggy, 82

Obama, Barack, 69, 139, 151, 152, 155n19; broadcast advertising, 40; bundlers and, 45; campaign, 2012, 48; citizenship questioning, 76–77; Clinton, H., race against, 34, 40, 137, 218; financial crisis and, 70; large donors and, 43; news coverage and tone, 141, 142–43, 148–49; nomination race, 2008, 15; Tea Party and, 75–77; in 2008 polls, 2; vote share, 2008, 13
Obama campaign, 2008, 8, 16, 55n39, 121–22, 150; "man on the street" format and, 126–27; Plouffe's review of, 130
Obama campaign fund-raising, 23, 29, 32, 42–45, 49; early, 35; Internet, 36–40; model, 47–48
open nomination races, 20n13; momentum model and, *9*; predicted order of finish of eventual nominee in, *6*
open primaries, 14
opinion polls, 5
opposition researchers, 127
Organizing for America, 48
Our Country Deserves Better, 71
outside money, 121
over-and under-predictions, 8

PAC. *See* political action committee
Palin, Sarah, 83–85
Paul, Ron, 42
Paulson, Henry, 69
Pelosi, Nancy, 71
Pennsylvania electors, 1788–1789, 180–83, 190

People's Party. *See* Populist Party
Perot, Ross, 126
phone apps, 16
places, densification of, 121–22
"The Pledge," 81
Plouffe, David, 130
pocketbook voting, 10
political action committee (PAC), 25, 49, 50–51, 85; fund-raising, 51
political movements, 59–60, 82; nominations in history and, 60–69; in recent history, 68–69. *See also specific movements*
political participation: Internet and, 115; news consumption and, 114
political parties, 164, 191–92, 195n12, 226; endorsements by, 7; identification, 10; 1790s, 197nn33–34, 199n58
political violence, Tea Party and, 77
poll standings, national, *3*, *4*; during invisible primary, 1980–2008, *209–212*
poll standings, preprimary, 7
popular vote, 10
Populist movement, 61–62
Populist Party, 61–62
prenomination: fund-raising, 52n1; spending by organized groups, 50
preprimary campaign, 4–5; poll standings, 7. *See also* invisible primary
preprimary forecasting models, 10
preprimary nomination forecasts, 12
preseason news coverage, 134–35; amount of, *135*, 135–37; military action and, 136; tone of, *140*, 141
presidential contenders, 1788-1789, 167–70
presidential selection process: Constitution and, 160–61; original, 163–64
primaries, 12, 17–18, 63; closed, 14; fund-raising and, 7; open, 14; schedule of, 2008, 28; state rules, 14; subsequent, 12; used to bind delegates, 1952–2008, 219, *219*, *222*. *See also* Democratic primaries; New Hampshire primary; Republican primaries
primary season news coverage, *136*; amount of, 135–37; for Democratic candidates, 142–45, *143*; for Republican candidates, *145*, 145–46; tone changes during, 146–49, *147*
primary vote, 8, 12; cash reserves and, 2; predictors, 7; shares forecasting model, *4*. *See also* Democratic primaries; Republican primaries
private financing, 24, 49
pro-choice, 68. *See also* abortion issues
Progressive movement, 62–63
public funding program, 23, 53n10, 55n39; collapse of, 26–27; demise of, 25–27. *See also* matching funds program
pyramid-style network, 16

racism, Tea Party and, 77, 91n70
Rae, Nicol, 64
Rainbow Coalition, 68–69
rank-and-file membership, 7
Rasmussen, Scott, 72, 76
Reagan, Ronald, 67; nomination, 1980, 11–12
Religious Right, 67–68
re-marketing, 122
remarks and messages, densification of, 115, 120–21
Republican Party, 64; debate, 126; early fund-raising and, 34–35; money and, 46; Religious Right and, 67; Tea Party and, 72–73, 80
Republican candidates: announcement dates for major, 1952–2008, *207–208*; primary season news coverage for, *145*, 145–46; withdrawal dates for major, *217*

Republican National Committee, 73
Republican nominations: 2008, *3*, 29; race, *3*; 2012, 8, 86, 158n59
Republican primaries: cash reserves and, 7; factors affecting vote in, 2008, *223–24*; poll standings and, 7; Tea Party and, 83–85
Republican progressives, 63
Robertson, Pat, 67
Robinson, Michael J., 139, 141
Romney, Mitt, 29, 84–85; early fund-raising, 36; fund-raising, 32, 46; large donors and, 43; news coverage and tone, 141, 145–46, 148–49; on Wikipedia, 123–24
Roosevelt, Theodore, 63
Rospars, Joe, 37
running mate, 102–3
Russo, Sal, 71
Ryan, Paul, 84

Santelli, Rick, 70, 71–73
Sasso, John, 100, 101
Schoen, Douglas, 72, 76
SDS. *See* Students for a Democratic Society
Secret Service, 103
Section 527 committees, 49; fund-raising, 51
Sedgwick, Theodore, 175
Sheehan, Margaret A., 139, 141
Sherman, Roger, 163
Shippen, William, Jr., 200n61
Simon, Paul, 100, 101
"small c" constitutional concerns, 76
small donor fund-raising, 39, 52
Smart Girl Politics, 71
smart mobile devices, 110
social networks: engagement with elections, 111, 114; news consumption on, 111; political participation and, 115. *See also specific social networks*
sociotropic voting, 10
South Carolina, 151
SpeechNow.org v. Federal Election Commission, 51
spending limits, 26; for nomination process, 1976–2012, 220, *220*
Spirou, Chris, 97
Stantelli, Rick, 59
state legislatures, electors chosen by, 195n20
Statement of Candidacy, FEC, 204
Statement of Organization, FEC, 204
Stavis, Ben, 66
Steele, Michael, 73
Steger, Wayne P., 2; forecasting model, 7
Steinhauser, Brendan, 86
Students for a Democratic Society (SDS), 65
Sununu, John, 99
superdelegates, at Democratic National Conventions, 1984–2010, 221, *221*
Super Duper Tuesday, 157n44
Super Tuesday, 28, 101, 154n6
Surowiecki, James, 130

Taft, William Howard, 63
TARP. *See* Troubled Assets Relief Program
Tax Day protests, 70, 74, 84
Taxpayer March, 78
Taylor, Maurice, 53n10
Taylor, Zachary, 61
Tea Party: abortion issues and, 75; actions, 77–82; approval ratings, 75; call for modern, 59; Congress and, 77–80, 83–84; decentralization, 85; elections, 2010, 79–82; gay marriage and, 75; gun rights and, 75; House races, 81; illegal immigration and, 75; Internet and, 71; leadership, 81–82; members of, 71–73; movement, 69–70; Obama and, 75–77; participation levels,

72; political violence and, 77; polls, 89n44, 89n48; principles and priorities, 73–77, 89n49, 91n70; protests, 70, 78; racism and, 77, 91n70; Republican Party and, 72–73, 80; Republican primaries and, 83–85; Senate races, 80; supported candidates, 79; supporter, 72–73; in 2012, 82–86. *See also* Tax Day protests
Tea Party Caucus, 84
Tea Party Declaration of Independence, 73
Tea Party Express, 71, 73, 84
Tea Party Nation, 71
Tea Party Patriots, 71, 73, 78, 83, 84, 85
technology, 110–11
telecommunication, 121
televangelist, 67
television (TV), 125; advertising, 40; local, 111, *112*; news consumption, 111, *112*, 134; nomination process coverage, 133–52; question-and-answer sessions, 104; reality programming, 126–27
Thompson, Fred, 141
Tilghman, William, 192
time, densification of, 122–23
Tolbert, Caroline J., 115
Top Conservatives on Twitter, 71
transparency, 129–30
Troubled Assets Relief Program (TARP), 69
Truman, Harry, 12–13
Tsongas, Paul, 144
TV. *See* television
Twitter, 111, 122

uncertainty, 17
unemployment, 1970s, 93
unit rule, 66

Van Buren, Martin, 61
vice presidential candidates, 1788–1789, 170–77, 190–91, 197n38; Antifederalists and, 173, 177; Federalists and, 177; mentions, *171*, 193
viral candidates, 16
Virginia electors, 1788–1789, 183–85
Virginia General Assembly, 184
voices, densification of, 114–15
volunteer fund-raisers, 38
voter: choice, 10–12; demographic characteristics of, 11; resonating with, 18; wasting vote, 13–14

Washington, George, 163, 168–69, 173, 176, 183, 185, 186–87, 190, 197n39
Web 2.0, 29–32. *See also* Internet
Whig Party, 61
White, Theodore H., 108, 109
Wikipedia, 123–24
Williams, Mark, 77
Williamson, Hugh, 164
Wilson, James, 163, 186–87, 188
Wilson, Woodrow, 63
withdrawal dates, for major candidate, *218–20*
Wright, Jeremiah, 127
Wurzelbacher, Joe, 127, 131

Yahoo, 122
YouTube, 31, 36, 126

Zwick, Spencer, 34

About the Contributors

Randall E. Adkins is the Ralph Wardle Diamond Professor of Arts and Sciences and chair of the Department of Political Science at the University of Nebraska at Omaha. He is the editor of *The Evolution of Political Parties, Campaigns, and Elections*, the co-editor of *Cases in Congressional Campaigns*, and is the author of numerous articles and book chapters on the presidency and campaigns and elections. Adkins is also a former American Political Science Association Congressional Fellow where he worked for the Hon. David E. Price (NC-4).

Jonathan Bernstein writes A Plain Blog About Politics and also writes for *The New Republic, Salon,* and other publications. His academic research has focused on parties, elections, and democracy.

Andrew E. Busch is professor of government at Claremont McKenna College. He is the author or coauthor of ten books on American government and politics, including *Epic Journey* and *Reagan's Victory: The Presidential Election of 1980 and the Rise of the Right*. He has also published several articles and book chapters on American elections and the presidency.

Michael Cornfield, a political scientist, is the author of *Politics Moves Online* and coeditor of *The Civic Web: Online Politics and Democratic Values*. His essay "The Net and the Nomination," co-written with Jonah Seiger, appeared in *The Making of the Presidential Candidates 2004*. Cornfield teaches at The George Washington University Graduate School of Political Management and blogs at duckrabbitpolitics.

Anthony Corrado is professor of government at Colby College and nonresident senior fellow at the Brookings Institution. He also serves as chair of the board of trustees of the Campaign Finance Institute, a nonpartisan research organization located in Washington, DC. He is the author or coauthor of numerous books and articles on national elections and campaign finance, including *Financing the 2008 Election*, *The New Campaign Finance Sourcebook*, and *Paying for Presidents*.

Andrew J. Dowdle is associate professor of political science at the University of Arkansas. He is the editor of *The American Review of Politics* and was the William Jefferson Clinton History Project Coordinator for the David and Barbara Pryor Center for Arkansas Oral and Visual History. His research interests include the presidential nomination system, campaign finance, and African military budgetary politics.

Michael S. Dukakis is a Distinguished Professor at Northeastern University as well as a Visiting Professor at UCLA. He began his political career as an elected town meeting member for the town of Brookline, Massachusetts, followed by four terms as a state representative. He served Massachusetts as governor from 1975 to 1979 and from 1983 to 1991 and was the Democratic Party's nominee for president in 1988. Governor Dukakis has a wife, Kitty, and three children, John, Andrea, and Kara, along with eight grandchildren.

Stephen J. Farnsworth teaches courses in political communication and journalism at George Mason University, where he is associate professor of communication. He is the author or coauthor of four books and numerous articles on media, politics, and public opinion and is also a former daily newspaper journalist.

S. Robert Lichter is professor of communication at George Mason University, where he directs the Center for Media and Public Affairs and the Statistical Assessment Services (STATS). He is the author or coauthor of twelve books and numerous articles and monographs on the media and politics.

William G. Mayer is professor of political science at Northeastern University. He is the author or coauthor of nine previous books, including *The Changing American Mind* and *The Front-Loading Problem in Presidential Nominations*. His major research interests include public opinion, voting behavior, political parties, and media and politics.

Alan J. Silverleib is a CNN Washington news desk editor, responsible for the network's online national political and policy coverage. He has also served as CNN's political researcher, helping to oversee election night exit poll analysis and coordinate the network's campaign debates. Previously, he was the International Republican Institute's Resident Program Director for Political Party Development and Public Opinion in Baghdad, Iraq.

Wayne P. Steger is professor of political science at DePaul University. He has published numerous articles, chapters, and essays on campaigns, elections, and the American presidency, in such journals as *Political Research Quarterly, American Politics Research*, and *Presidential Studies Quarterly*. He is a former editor of the *Journal of Political Marketing* and co-edited *Campaigns and Political Marketing*. His current research focuses on presidential nominations, party politics, and economic policy.

CPSIA information can be obtained at www.ICGtesting.com
Printed in the USA
BVOW011503021211

277349BV00002B/4/P